FOURTH EDITION

WORLD LINK 2

DEVELOPING ENGLISH FLUENCY

JOHN HUGHES

NANCY DOUGLAS

JAMES R. MORGAN

D1604406

NATIONAL GEOGRAPHIC
LEARNING

Australia · Brazil · Canada · Mexico · Singapore · United Kingdom · United States

National Geographic Learning,
a Cengage Company

World Link Level 2: Developing English Fluency,
Fourth Edition

Publisher: Sherrise Roehr

Executive Editor: Sarah Kenney

Development Editor: Katie Davis

Director of Global Marketing: Ian Martin

Heads of Regional Marketing:

   Charlotte Ellis (Europe, Middle East and Africa)

   Irina Pereyra (Latin America)

Senior Product Marketing Manager:

   Caitlin Thomas

Content Project Manager: Beth Houston

Media Researcher: Stephanie Eenigenburg

Cover/Text Design: Lisa Trager

Art Director: Brenda Carmichael

Operations Support: Hayley Chwazik-Gee,

   Avi Mednick, Katie Lee

Manufacturing Planner: Mary Beth Hennebury

Composition: MPS North America LLC

For permission to use material from this text or product,
submit all requests online at **cengage.com/permissions**
Further permissions questions can be emailed to
permissionrequest@cengage.com

Student's Book
ISBN: 978-0-357-50217-4
Student's Book + My World Link Online:
ISBN: 978-0-357-50218-1

National Geographic Learning
200 Pier 4 Boulevard
Boston, MA 02210
USA

Locate your local office at **international.cengage.com/region**

Visit National Geographic Learning online at **ELTNGL.com**
Visit our corporate website at **www.cengage.com**

Printed in Mexico
Print Number: 01 Print Year: 2021

Acknowledgments

Thank you to the educators who provided invaluable feedback throughout the development of the *World Link* series:

Asia

Michael Jake Arcilla, Aii Language Center, Phnom Penh; Fintan Brennan, Meisei University, Tokyo; Tyler Burden, Meisei University, Tokyo; Catherine Cheetham, Tokai University, Tokyo; Will Fan, Xiamen Wanda, Xiamen; Mark Firth, Oberlin University, Machida; Hiroshi Fukuda, Jumonji University, Niiza; Thomas Goetz, Hokusei Gakuen University, Sapporo; Helen Hanae, Reitaku University, Kashiwa; Louis Liu, Meten English, Shenzen; Shaun McLewin, Hanseo University, Seosan; Raymond Monk Jr., Meten English, Dalian; Donald Patterson, Seirei Christopher University, Hamamatsu City; Mongkol Sodachan, Rangsit University, Pathum Thani; Robert Wright, Meten English, Chengdu; Elvira Wu, Meten English, Quanzhou; I-Cheng Wu, Southern Taiwan University of Science and Technology, Tainan City; Xie Yu, SFLEP, Shanghai; Vince Zhang, Thinktown, Hangzhou; Vivi Zhang, Xiamen Wanda, Xiamen

Latin America

Anthony Acevedo, ICPNA, Lima; Jorge Aguilar, Centro de Estudios de Idiomas UAS, Culiacan; Lidia Stella Aja, Centro Cultural Colombo Americano, Cali; Ana Laura Alferez, Instituto Domingo Savio, Mexico City; Lúcia Rodrigues Alves, Seven, Sao Paulo; Alessandra Atarcsay, WOWL Education, Rio de Janeiro; Isabella Campos Alvim, IBEU Copacabana, Rio de Janeiro; Ana Berg, Ana Berg EFL School, Rio de Janeiro; Raul Billini, Santo Domingo; Isabela Villas Boas, Casa Thomas Jefferson, Brasilia; Lourdes Camarillo, Escuela Bancaria Comercial, Mexico City; Cinthia Castañeda, Centro de Idiomas, Coatzacoalcos; Enrique Chapuz, Universidad Veracruzana, Coatzacoalcos; Giseh Cuesta, MESCyT, Mexico City; Carlos Fernández, ICPNA, Lima; Vania Furtado, IBEU Copacabana, Rio de Janeiro; Mariana Garcia, BUAP, Puebla; Jeanette Bravo Garonce, IPA Idiomas, Brasilia; Luiz Henrique Bravo Garonce, IPA Idiomas, Brasilia; Fily Hernandez, Universidad Veracruzana, Coatzacoalcos; Manuel Hidalgo Iglesias, Escuela Bancaria Comercial, Mexico City; Dafna Ilian, ESIME, Azcapotzalco; Rubén Jacome, Universidad Veracruzana, Coatzacoalcos; Beatriz Jorge, Alumni, Sao Paulo; Gledis Libert, ICDA, Santo Domingo; Rocio Liceaga, International House, Mexico City; Elizabeth Palacios, ICPNA, Lima; Emeli Borges Pereira Luz, UNICAMPI, Sao Paulo; Patricia McKay, CELLEP, Sao Paulo; Victor Hugo Medina, Cultura Inglesa Minas Gerais, Belo Horizonte; Maria Helena Meyes, ACBEU, Salvador; Isaias Pacheco, Universidad Veracruzana, Coatzacoalcos; Miguel Rodriguez, BUAP, Puebla; Nelly Romero, ICPNA, Lima; Yesenia Ruvalcaba, Universidad de Guadalajara, Guadalajara; Eva Sanchez, BUAP, Puebla; Marina Sánchez, Instituto Domingo Savio, Mexico City; Thais Scharfenberg, Centro Europeu, Curitiba; Pilar Sotelo, ICPNA, Lima; Rubén Uceta, Centro Cultural Domínico Americano, Santiago De Los Caballeros; Italia Vergara, American English Overseas Center, Panama City; Maria Victoria Guinle Vivacqua, UNICAMP, Sao Paulo

United States and Canada

Bobbi Plante, Manitoba Institute of Trades and Technology, Winnipeg; Richard McDorman, Language On Schools, Miami, FL; Luba Nesteroba, Bilingual Education Institute, Houston, TX; Tracey Partin, Valencia College, Orlando, FL

SCOPE AND SEQUENCE

UNIT	LESSON	WARM-UP VIDEO	VOCABULARY	LISTENING	GRAMMAR
1 MY LIFE P. 2	**LESSON A** People p. 4 **LESSON B** Lessons Learned p. 9	Shabana Basij-Rasikh: The Fearless Educator p. 2	**People I know** p. 4 (*classmate, coworker, friend*) **Classes and lessons** p. 9 (*get good grades, prepare for exams, take classes*)	Conversations about people's relationships p. 5 Interview with a student about her school p. 12	The simple present vs. the present continuous p. 7 Review of the simple past p. 13
2 LET'S EAT! P. 16	**LESSON A** Foods We Like p. 18 **LESSON B** Eating Well p. 23	Holy Mole! p. 16	**Describing food** p. 18 (*delicious, spicy, sweet*) **Healthy habits** p. 23 (*diet, health benefits, lifestyle*)	Conversation about regional dishes p. 19 Talk about dinner times in different cultures p. 26	The comparative form of adjectives p. 21 The superlative form of adjectives p. 27
3 MYSTERIES P. 30	**LESSON A** You're in Luck! p. 32 **LESSON B** Unsolved Mysteries p. 37	The Luckiest Unlucky Man to Ever Live p. 30	**Lucky or unlucky?** p. 32 (*by chance, good / bad luck, on purpose*) **Solving mysteries** p. 37 (*explanation, investigate, proof*)	Talk about making your own luck p. 33 News report on changes in human behavior during a full moon p. 40	Stative verbs p. 35 Modals of present possibility p. 41

REAL WORLD LINK 1 Create a TV Quiz Show p. 44

UNIT	LESSON	WARM-UP VIDEO	VOCABULARY	LISTENING	GRAMMAR
4 TRENDS P. 46	**LESSON A** How We Shop p. 48 **LESSON B** Fashion on Demand p. 53	The Future of the American Mall p. 46	**Describing trends** p. 48 (*about, exactly, increase*) **Fashion** p. 53 (*inexpensive, style, unique*)	Talk about online shopping trends p. 49 Conversation about an online clothing service p. 56	Quantity expressions p. 51 Advice with *could, should, ought to,* and *had better* p. 57
5 MY NEIGHBORHOOD P. 60	**LESSON A** Chores and Errands p. 62 **LESSON B** Getting Around p. 67	A Whirlwind Look at Shanghai p. 61	**Doing chores and running errands** p. 62 (*do laundry, make dinner, sweep*) **Getting around** p. 67 (*cyclists, get around, sidewalks*)	Conversations about appointments p. 63 Podcast about a popular neighborhood p. 70	Requests with modal verbs and *mind* p. 65 Subject relative clauses with *that* p. 71
6 GOALS P. 74	**LESSON A** Starting Out p. 76 **LESSON B** After Graduation p. 81	What Should I Do After High School? p. 75	**Applying to college** p. 76 (*apply, consider, decide*) **Life after graduation** p. 81 (*do an internship, opportunity, someday*)	Podcast about an unusual school p. 77 Conversation about future plans p. 84	Plans and decisions with *be going to* and *will* p. 79 Predictions with *be going to* and *will* p. 85

REAL WORLD LINK 2 Design a Survey p. 88

PRONUNCIATION	SPEAKING	READING	WRITING	ACTIVE ENGLISH	ACADEMIC SKILL	GLOBAL VOICES
Question stress p. 5	Introducing a person to someone else and responding to introductions p. 6	Try, Try Again! p. 10	Write about something you learned to do p. 14	Ask questions to get to know your classmates p. 8 Talk about past school experiences p. 14	Summarize p. 11	English in Your Life p. 15
Sentence stress p. 19	Making and responding to suggestions p. 20	The Best Foods to Eat p. 24	Write a restaurant review p. 28	Make a radio ad for a new restaurant p. 22 Create a restaurant menu and compare places to eat p. 28	Word webs p. 18	Alex Sigrist: How to Make an Omelet p. 29
Dropped syllables p. 33	Saying something is likely or not likely p. 34	Mysterious Artwork p. 38	Write about an unsolved mystery p. 42	Play a game of chance and guess information about group members p. 36 Identify and present possible theories and explanations for mysteries p. 42	Using synonyms p. 37 Predicting information p. 39	Nora Shawki: Mysteries from the Past p. 43
Unstressed *of* p. 51	Polite / direct disagreement p. 50	The Facts about Fast Fashion p. 54	Fill out a style profile p. 58	Discuss shopping experiences p. 52 Give advice as a personal shopper p. 58	Scanning p. 55 Infer meaning from context p. 56	Amanda Cosco: The Trend of Rental Fashion p. 59
Reduced forms of *could you* and *would you* p. 63	Making appointments p. 64	Flying to Work p. 68	Write about a neighborhood p. 72	Create your own service and role-play making appointments p. 66 Play a game to describe a neighborhood p. 72	Listening for words connected to a topic p. 70	Welcome to Lima! p. 73
Reduced forms of *going to* and *will* p. 79	Responding to bad news and offering to help p. 78	Life's Essential Questions p. 82	Write a personal profile p. 86	Interview classmates about future plans p. 80 Talk about personal profiles and ask a partner for personal information p. 86	Retelling p. 83	Getting Started with Your Goals p. 87

SCOPE AND SEQUENCE

UNIT	LESSON	WARM-UP VIDEO	VOCABULARY	LISTENING	GRAMMAR
CELEBRATIONS P. 90 **7**	**LESSON A** Parties p. 92 **LESSON B** Festivals and Holidays p. 97	Celebrating the World's Favorite Sport p. 90	**Hosting a party** p. 92 (*celebrate, guests, invite*) **Festivals and events** p. 97 (*gather, participate, take place*)	Talks about coming of age celebrations p. 93 News report about a race p. 100	Agreeing with other people's statements: *so, too, neither,* and *either* p. 95 Time clauses with *before, after, when* p. 101
ONCE UPON A TIME P. 104 **8**	**LESSON A** What's the Story About? p. 106 **LESSON B** Modern Fairy Tales p. 111	Snack Attack p. 105	**Discussing stories** p. 106 (*based on, characters, fiction*) **Modern fairy tales** p. 111 (*brave, discover, incredible*)	Conversation about writing a story with crowdsourcing p. 107 Story about Thunder and Lightning p. 114	The past continuous: statements / questions p. 109 Adverbs of manner p. 115
WORK P. 118 **9**	**LESSON A** Skills and Qualities p. 120 **LESSON B** Dream Jobs p. 125	Volcanology: Life in the Field p. 118	**Qualities needed for work** p. 120 (*adventurous, punctual, responsible*) **Describing a job** p. 125 (*demanding, rewarding, well paid*)	Talks about different jobs p. 121 Interview with a storyboard artist p. 128	The present perfect p. 123 The simple past and the present perfect p. 129

REAL WORLD LINK 3 Give an Elevator Pitch p. 132

UNIT	LESSON	WARM-UP VIDEO	VOCABULARY	LISTENING	GRAMMAR
STAY IN TOUCH P. 134 **10**	**LESSON A** On a Call p. 136 **LESSON B** Always Connected p. 141	The Google before Google p. 134	**Using the phone** p. 136 (*check your phone, get a text, make a call*) **Phone etiquette** p. 141 (*allow, ignore, rude*)	Phone call and video call conversations p. 137 Conversations about phone etiquette p. 144	Asking for permission p. 139 Verb + infinitive vs. verb + gerund p. 145
TECHNOLOGY P. 148 **11**	**LESSON A** Then and Now p. 150 **LESSON B** Making Life Better p. 155	Kids React to Old Computers p. 148	**Describing devices** p. 150 (*affordable, durable, rechargeable*) **Using appliances and devices** p. 155 (*log in, plug in, scroll down*)	Lecture about bad technology predictions p. 151 Interview about new technology to help blind people p. 158	*Used to* p. 153 Comparisons with *as ... as* p. 159
TRAVEL P. 162 **12**	**LESSON A** Before You Go p. 164 **LESSON B** Adventures in Traveling p. 169	The Airport That Never Sleeps p. 162	**Preparing for travel** p. 164 (*apply for a visa, book tickets, get travel insurance*) **Travel plans** p. 169 (*boarding, delayed, depart*)	Conversation about an upcoming trip p. 165 Interview with Andrés Ruzo about travel experiences p. 172	Modal verbs of necessity p. 167 Question form review p. 173

REAL WORLD LINK 4 Make a Travel Ad p. 176

PRONUNCIATION	SPEAKING	READING	WRITING	ACTIVE ENGLISH	ACADEMIC SKILL	GLOBAL VOICES
Reduced *want to* p. 94	Inviting someone to do something; accepting or refusing an invitation p. 94	Get Ready to Get Messy p. 98	Write about a holiday or festival p. 102	Plan a party, and make and respond to invitations p. 96 Invent an unusual holiday p. 102	Make connections p. 93	Celebrating the New Year p. 103
Pausing p. 114	Telling a story; showing interest and finding out what happened p. 108	The Cinderella Story p. 112	Write a modern fairy tale p. 116	Tell stories with classmates and guess if they are true p. 110 Find the differences between two fairy tale images p. 116	Using parts of words to guess meaning p. 107	How to Tell an Impactful Story p. 117
Reduced *for* in time expressions p. 123	Interviewing for a job p. 122	Asher Jay: Creative Conservationist p. 126	Write a formal email p. 130	Discuss job requirements and role-play a job interview p. 124 Read a job ad and choose the best email response p. 130	Word forms p. 120	Corey Arnold: Two Jobs, Two Passions p. 131
Stress with clarification p. 137	Using the phone p. 138	Have Smartphones Changed Our Lives for Better or for Worse? p. 142	Write informal messages p. 146	Role-play a customer service phone call p. 140 Read and discuss informal messages p. 146	Collocations p. 143	Talking Tech p. 147
used to / use to p. 153	Offering a counterargument p. 152	How Smart Is Your Home? p. 156	Write about a robot p. 160	Describe how your life has changed in the past five years p. 154 Design a robot that solves a problem p. 160	Taking notes p. 151 Discourse markers p. 157	Amber Case: Calm Technology p. 161
Reduced *have to* and *has to* p. 165	Saying you've forgotten something p. 166	Going Solo Is the Way to Go! p. 170	Write a customer satisfaction survey p. 174	Decide as a group what to pack for a trip p. 168 Discuss travel-related customer surveys p. 174	Closed and open questions p. 174	Travel Experiences p. 175

1

MY LIFE

LOOK AT THE PHOTO. ANSWER THE QUESTIONS.

1. What are the people doing?
2. Does the activity look fun to you? Why or why not?

WARM-UP VIDEO

A Watch a video about a day in the life of Shabana Basij-Rasikh and her students in Afghanistan. Number the actions (1–5) in the order you see them.

_____ a. The teacher writes on the board.

__1__ b. Shabana arrives at the school.

_____ c. A girl learns to ride a bicycle.

_____ d. The girls describe their future plans.

_____ e. The girls have a lesson in their classroom.

B Read the sentences and then watch the video again. Write the missing words.

1. When Shabana was young, there were no _____ for girls.

2. _____ percent of women in Afghanistan have a college degree.

3. Shabana needed to _____ an educator.

4. SOLA is the _____ girls' boarding school in Afghanistan.

5. At SOLA, they create a _____ space for girls.

6. The girls come to SOLA to _____ to become future leaders.

7. When you educate a girl, you educate her _____, her community, her society, and the world.

C Imagine you are making a similar video about a day in your life. What five actions do you want to show in the video? Tell a partner.

People talk and laugh at the Bottletree Cafe in Alabama, US.

GOALS

Lesson A

/ Make introductions

/ Ask questions about other people's lives

Lesson B

/ Talk about classes and lessons

/ Describe something you learned to do

VOCABULARY

A Mario is describing people in his life. Complete the sentences with the words in blue.

classmate coworker / colleague friend girlfriend neighbor

1. "My name's Mario, and this is Jason. He's my best _____.
   We met when we were in elementary school, and we often **spend** our
   free **time together**."

2. "Lei is my _____ at City College. We have two classes
   together. We sometimes say hello, but I **don't know her very well**."

3. "I'm working part time in an office these days, and Julia is my
   _____ there. She's in a different department, but
   sometimes we **work together**."

4. "David is my _____. We live on the same street."

5. "I met Sally at City College last year. She's my _____.
   We **got along well** right away, and now we**'re going out**."

WORD BANK

We're $\left\{\begin{matrix} good \\ close \\ best \\ old \end{matrix}\right\}$ friends.

They're my next-door neighbors.

B Work in pairs. Answer the questions.

1. Do you know everyone in your English class? Who don't you know very well?

2. Which people in your life do you get along well with? Do you spend your free time together?

C Look at the words in blue and think of people in your life. On a piece of paper, write *People I Know* at the top of the page. List five people and write a sentence or two about each one.

D Tell a partner about the people in your life.

❝ Sergio is my friend. We met in class last year.

An elementary school in Shenzhen, China. Elementary school is usually for ages 5–11.

LISTENING

A **PRONUNCIATION: Question stress** Listen. Notice how the answer to the question is different depending on the stressed word. Then listen again and repeat. 🎧2

1. **A:** Is he your <u>boyfriend</u>?
   B: No, we're just friends.

2. **A:** Is <u>your</u> boyfriend?
   B: No, he's going out with Maria.

3. **A:** Is <u>he</u> your boyfriend?
   B: No, <u>he</u> is.

B **PRONUNCIATION: Question stress** Say the three sentences and responses. Then listen for the stressed word in each sentence. Choose the best answer. 🎧3

1. Are you a student at City College?
   a. No, I work there.
   b. No, I go to Essex College.

2. Are you her classmate?
   a. No, my brother is.
   b. No, I'm her coworker.

3. I think his best friend lives next door, right?
   a. No, I think it's his colleague.
   b. No, I think he lives down the street.

C **Listen for gist.** Listen to the conversations. Write the number of the conversation (1, 2, or 3) that goes with each photo. 🎧4

D **Listen for details.** Read the sentences about each conversation. Then listen again and circle the correct answers. 🎧4

1. a. They **are** / **aren't** dating now.
   b. They **are** / **aren't** friends now.

2. a. They **are** / **aren't** friends.
   b. They **know** / **don't know** each other well.

3. a. They **know** / **don't know** each other.
   b. They **are** / **aren't** classmates now.

E Work in pairs. Write a conversation between two people similar to the conversations from **C** and **D**. Try to use all the expressions in the box. Then perform your conversation for another pair.

Do you know . . .?	Is he / she your . . .?	Nice to meet you.	We're friends.
Excuse me, are you . . .?	Is this your first day?	We met . . .	

When you first meet someone, do you always shake hands? If not, what do you do instead?

SPEAKING

A Listen to the conversations. Which one is more informal? In each conversation, who is meeting for the first time? 🎧5

Conversation 1

Maria: Hi, Junko.

Junko: Hi, Maria. It's good to see you again! How are you?

Maria: Fine. How about you?

Junko: Pretty good.

Maria: Oh, and this is my friend Ricardo. We both go to City University.

Junko: Hey, Ricardo. Nice to meet you.

Ricardo: Yeah, you, too.

Conversation 2

Mr. Otani: Morning, Miriam.

Miriam: Good morning, Mr. Otani. Oh, Mr. Otani, I'd like you to meet Andre Garcia. He started working here yesterday. Andre, Mr. Otani is our VP of Sales.

Mr. Otani: Nice to meet you, Andre.

Andre: It's very nice to meet you, too, Mr. Otani.

B Read and practice the conversations in pairs.

C Work in groups of three. Follow the steps below.

   1. **Student A:** Choose a famous person to be. Write down your identity on a piece of paper and give it to Student B.

   2. **Student B:** Read the identity of Student A. Then introduce Student A to Student C formally. Use the Speaking Strategy to help you.

   3. **Student C:** Respond to the introduction.

   4. Switch roles and repeat steps 1–3.

SPEAKING STRATEGY 🎧6

	Introducing a person to someone else	Responding to introductions
formal	Mr. Otani, **I'd like to introduce you to** Andre. Mr. Otani, **I'd like you to meet** Andre.	It's (very) nice to meet you. (It's) nice / good to meet you, too.
informal	Junko, **this is** Ricardo. Junko, **meet** Ricardo. Junko, **Ricardo**.	Nice / Good to meet you. You, too.

Asking for someone's name again
I'm sorry, I'm terrible with names.
I'm sorry, I've forgotten your name.

D Now introduce the "famous friends" you met in **C** to your other classmates. Use a formal or informal style.

    ❝ Ana, I'd like you to meet Leonardo DiCaprio.

    It's nice to meet you, Leo. ❞

GRAMMAR

A   Read the Unit 1, Lesson A Grammar Reference in the appendix. Complete the exercises. Then do the exercises below.

THE SIMPLE PRESENT VS. THE PRESENT CONTINUOUS	
I <u>always</u> **take** a shower in the morning. She**'s taking** a shower <u>right now</u>. Can she call you back?	Use the simple present to talk about habits, schedules, and facts. Use the present continuous to talk about actions happening right now.
I **live** in Tokyo. <u>At the moment</u>, I**'m living** in Tokyo.	The present continuous can show that a situation is more temporary.
Do you **study** English? What **are** you **studying** <u>this term</u>?	Use the present continuous to talk about actions happening in the extended present (nowadays).
With the simple present, we often use adverbs of frequency, such as *always*, *sometimes*, and *never*. With the present continuous, we often use time expressions such as *at the moment*, *right now*, and *currently*.	

B   Read the sentences below. Circle the simple present verbs and underline the present continuous verbs. Then match each sentence to its use on the right.

_____ 1. Sophia is my classmate.

_____ 2. She's living at home at the moment.

_____ 3. She always arrives at school at 8:00.

_____ 4. She's taking a science class this term.

_____ 5. We're studying for a test now.

a. describing a routine

b. stating a truth or fact

c. happening right now

d. happening in the extended present

e. suggesting a temporary situation

C   Complete the questions in the simple present or the present continuous. Use the verbs in the box.

do	eat	have	~~study~~	take	talk

1. **A:** Why ___are you studying___ English now?

   B: I need it for work.

2. **A:** _____ two classes this term?

   B: Yes, I am. Two business classes.

3. **A:** When _____ breakfast?

   B: Around 7:00, usually.

4. **A:** How many brothers and sisters _____?

   B: Four brothers and one sister.

5. **A:** What _____ on the weekends?

   B: I relax and hang out with friends.

6. **A:** Who _____ to right now?

   B: Alex.

D   Now take turns asking and answering the questions in **C** with a partner.

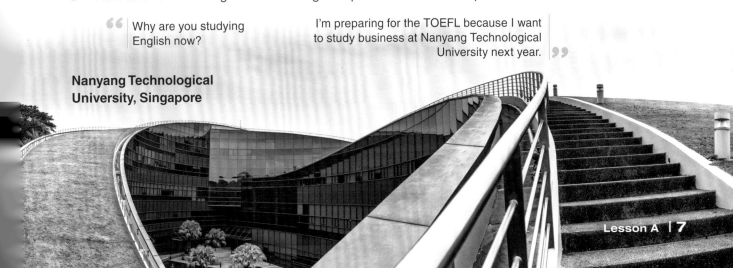

Why are you studying English now?

I'm preparing for the TOEFL because I want to study business at Nanyang Technological University next year.

Nanyang Technological University, Singapore

Bruce Pascal collects toy cars. He has over 3,500 of them!

ACTIVE ENGLISH Try it out!

A Take a piece of paper and cut it into five strips. On each strip, write a sentence about one of the following items.

- one of your daily routines
- a general fact about you
- an unusual fact about you
- an activity you are doing these days
- why you are studying English at the moment

      " I always get up at 5 am.

      I collect toy cars. "

      " I'm learning to play the guitar these days.

B Give your sentences to your teacher. He or she will mix up the sentences and give you five new ones. Prepare a question for each sentence.

For example:

Sentence: I always get up at 5 am.

Your question: Do you always get up at 5 am?

C Stand up and talk to your classmates. Ask your questions from **B** to find out who wrote each sentence.

      " Do you collect toy cars?

      No, I don't. I collect sneakers. "

      Yes, I do! I have around 200. "

D Introduce one of your classmates to the class and tell an interesting fact you learned about him or her.

1A GOALS   Now I can . . .

Make introductions _____

Ask questions about other people's lives _____

1. Yes, I can.
2. Mostly, yes.
3. Not yet.

VOCABULARY

A Read the text about the Last Bell ceremony. Where and when is it? Why do students celebrate it?

In May, students around the world are **taking** their last **classes** and **preparing for** their final **exams**, hoping to **get** good **grades** for college or a new job. Music and sports **lessons** also end before summer break. When classes finish in countries such as Russia and Ukraine, everyone **meets** at the Last Bell ceremony on May 25th. After, students celebrate with friends— it's their last chance to **have fun** together before they take their exams and either **pass** or **fail**!

B Complete the sentences with the blue words from **A**. Then check your answers with a partner.

1. I can't go out tonight. I'm _____ for my final _____ next week.

2. If I study hard, I know I can _____ the test!

3. This term, I'm _____ two computer science _____ at City University.

4. Our English class _____ on Tuesdays and Thursdays.

5. My piano _____ aren't long. They're only 30 minutes.

6. I had to retake my math class. I don't want to _____ it again!

7. Tyler never studies, so he always _____ bad _____.

8. After our exams, let's go out and _____ some _____!

WORD BANK
have free time / fun
meet friends
a class **meets**
take classes, exams, (music / tennis) lessons
take a(n) exam / test / class

C Ask and answer the questions with a partner.

1. What classes are you taking now? When do they meet?

2. Are you taking any music or sports lessons?

3. How are you doing in your classes? Are you getting good grades?

4. How do you have fun? Do you meet friends after class?

Students play in a fountain after the Last Bell ceremony in Kiev, Ukraine.

TRY, TRY
AGAIN!

At some point in our lives, we all fail at something. Maybe we don't pass an important exam or get good grades. Failure isn't easy, but when things are hard, try not to give up. You can still find success—as these two personal stories show.

1. BLACK is a successful Japanese entertainer,[1] but as a teenager his life was very different. In school, he was quiet and shy, and other boys bullied[2] him. People often said to him, "Play a sport!" but BLACK wasn't good at sports. Then one day, BLACK bought a yo-yo and his

life changed. At first, he couldn't do any tricks, but he didn't give up. He watched videos and worked hard for four years. At age eighteen, he entered the World Yo-Yo Contest[3] and won. He was a world champion.[4] Now he performs all over the world.

2. Lindsey Stirling is an American musician. She mixes classical violin with dance music and hip-hop. As a child, her parents didn't have a lot of money, so Lindsey could only take lessons part time. Despite this, she practiced a lot, and in high school she started writing her own music.

In the Cirque du Soleil show *Kurios*, BLACK does tricks with two yo-yos at once.

Then at age twenty-three, Lindsey was on a popular TV talent show. She did well, but she didn't win. However, she kept trying, and in time, she made an album and won an important music award. Today, she has a very popular channel online. 🎧7

[1]An **entertainer** is someone like an actor, musician, dancer, or singer.
[2]If someone **bullies** you, they try to hurt you or make you afraid.
[3]A **contest** is an event that people try to win.
[4]The winner of the contest is the **champion**.

A The title of the reading is part of a longer expression: *If at first you don't succeed, try, try again.* What do you think it means? Is it good advice?

> **WORD BANK**
> **Opposites**
> fail (v) ⟷ succeed (v)
> failure (n) ⟷ success (n) successful (adj)
> give up (quit) (v) ⟷ keep trying (v)

B **Read for the main idea.** Read the first paragraph of the text. Choose the main idea.

  a. Sometimes it's best to give up.

  b. When you fail, don't give up.

  c. Some successful people give up.

C Work in pairs. Read about your person and answer the questions.

  Student A: Read about BLACK. (Part 1)

  Student B: Read about Lindsey Stirling. (Part 2)

  1. What is the person's job?

  2. What difficult things happened to the person?

  3. What finally happened? Was he or she successful?

D **Summarize.** Ask your partner the questions in **C** about his or her person. Write down the answers. Then read about the other person and check your partner's answers. If you are unsure, see the answers on page 211.

> **ACADEMIC SKILL**
> **Summarize**
> After you read a text, try to summarize the most important information. Look for the main idea in each paragraph and use the key words.

E Think about a time you failed at something. Take some notes to answer the questions.

  1. What did you fail at?

  2. Did you give up or try again?

  3. What did you learn from it?

F In pairs, ask and answer the questions in **E**.

The Himalayan Mountains near the
village of Phortse in Nepal

LISTENING

A Look at the photo. What activity do you think people come to this place to learn?

B Listen to an interview. Where is the interviewer speaking from? Who does he interview? 🎧 8

C **Listen for key words.** Listen again and take notes about the school and its classes. 🎧 8

1. **Name of school:** Khumbu Climbing Center, Phortse, Nepal _____
2. **Type of students (age):** _____
3. **Year the school started:** _____
4. **Number of students:** _____
5. **Types of classes:** _____
6. **Are there tests?** _____
7. **Length of typical day:** _____

D **Think critically.** Work in pairs and choose a job or occupation (climber, teacher, musician, etc.). Then follow the steps.

1. Imagine you have a school for people who want to learn this job. Make a list of the types of classes you need to have—for example, language learning or business management.

2. Present your list of classes to another pair, but do not say the job. Can they guess what the job is?

GRAMMAR

A Read the Unit 1, Lesson B Grammar Reference in the appendix. Complete the exercises. Then do the exercises below.

REVIEW OF THE SIMPLE PAST		
	Yes / No questions	Answers
With *be*	**Were** you in class today?	Yes, I **was**. / No, I **wasn't**.
With other verbs	**Did** you **pass** the test?	Yes, I **did**. / No, I **didn't**.
	Wh- questions	Answers
With *be*	Where **were** you today?	(I **was**) in class.
With other verbs	When **did** you **start** classes?	(I **started**) last week.

B Complete the text with the simple past form of the verbs in parentheses. Then take turns reading it aloud with a partner.

Apple cofounder Steve Jobs (1. not graduate) _____ from college. Jobs (2. be) _____ a smart guy, but his school (3. be) _____ expensive, and he (4. not have) _____ enough money to finish. So he (5. leave) _____ college, and he (6. take) _____ a calligraphy class instead.

    When his parents (7. hear) _____ this, they (8. be) _____ worried. "Why calligraphy?" (9. ask) _____ his parents. "What can you do with that?" Jobs (10. not be) _____ sure. The class (11. not help) _____ him get a job, but years later, it (12. help) _____ him in another way. Jobs (13. use) _____ ideas from his calligraphy class to create Apple's famous computer fonts.

C Read the text about Steve Jobs again. Write down three *Yes / No* and three *Wh-* questions in the simple past about the information in the text.

D In pairs, take turns asking and answering your questions about Jobs.

  ❝ Did Steve Jobs graduate from college?   No, he didn't. ❞   ❝ Why not?

E Think of a famous person from the past. Your partner from **D** asks you five simple past questions and tries to guess the person. Then switch roles and repeat.

The Old English alphabet in calligraphy

ACTIVE ENGLISH Try it out!

A Read the questions below. Then add one simple past *Yes / No* question and one simple past *Wh-* question.

In middle school or high school, . . .

1. were you a good or bad student?
2. did you play any sports?
3. what was your favorite class?
4. which subject couldn't you do very well?
5. _____ ?
6. _____ ?

B Think about your answers to the questions in **A** and make notes.

C Get into groups of three and follow the steps.

1. One student begins and chooses a question from **A**.

Speaker: Answer the question. Talk for a minute without stopping.

Listeners: Listen to the speaker and give one point if you answer *yes* to both questions:

- Did the speaker talk for one minute without stopping a lot?
- Could you understand the speaker clearly?

2. Repeat step 1 with a different speaker until each speaker has gone five times. The student with the most points is the winner!

> 66 I was a good student in high school. I got good grades and . . .

D Turn to the Unit 1 Writing appendix and read the paragraph. Then answer the questions.

1. What couldn't the person do?
2. Why was this a problem?
3. How did the person learn?
4. Was the person successful?

E **WRITING** Think about something you couldn't do but learned to do. Answer the questions in **D** for you. Then use your ideas and write your own paragraph. Remember to use simple past verbs.

F Exchange paragraphs with a partner. Read your partner's writing and answer the questions in **D**. Did your partner use the simple past correctly?

USEFUL EXPRESSIONS
When I was . . ., I couldn't . . .
Usually, this wasn't a problem, but . . .
Finally, I decided to . . .
At first, I was very nervous . . .
By the end, I was . . .

1B GOALS Now I can . . .

Talk about classes and lessons _____

Describe something I learned to do _____

1. Yes, I can.
2. Mostly, yes.
3. Not yet.

GLOBAL VOICES

A You are going to watch a video with students talking about learning English. Watch the first part of the video and complete the table with the missing numbers.

	Daniele	Francielen	Chiyuki	Jaqueline
Number of classes per week			Classes: Private lessons:	
Number of classmates				

B Watch part two of the video and circle the correct word or phrase to complete each sentence.

1. Daniele **is** / **isn't** living in the US at the moment.

2. She **is** / **isn't** preparing for an English exam right now.

3. Francielen is a nutritionist in **Brazil** / **the US**.

4. As a mental health counselor, Chiyuki will need English to speak with **clients** / **students**.

5. Jaqueline wants to study for **a master's degree** / **an English test**.

C Watch the third part of the video and match the speaker to the difficulty they have.

_____ 1. Daniele   a. Understanding accents and abbreviations

_____ 2. Francielen   b. Pronouncing *l* and *r* sounds

_____ 3. Chiyuki   c. Remembering grammar rules

D Work in pairs and take turns interviewing each other with the questions below. You can also video or audio record your answers on your phone.

1. How many classes do you have a week?

2. Who do you study with?

3. How many students are in your class?

4. Why are you learning English?

5. Why is English important for you?

6. Are you preparing for any English exams at the moment?

7. What do you think is difficult about learning English?

This is a word cloud showing the words students said in the video. The larger the word, the more times you can hear it in the video.

2
LET'S EAT!

LOOK AT THE PHOTO. ANSWER THE QUESTIONS.

1. What foods can you see in the photo?
2. Are these foods healthy? Why or why not?
3. What are your three favorite foods? Why do you like them?

WARM-UP VIDEO

A Do you know which countries have these national dishes? Does your country have a national dish?

curry   kimchi   mole   pasta   sushi

B Watch a video about mole. Number the parts of the video (1–4) in the correct order.

_____ a. Grandma's story

_____ b. The family has lunch together.

_____ c. mole ingredients and recipe

_____ d. the women who run the business

C Watch the video again and answer the questions.

1. How many pounds of mole do they make each day?
2. What ingredients are in mole?
3. Why do you need strong arms to make mole?
4. How long does the recipe take?
5. Who checks the quality of the mole?
6. Where do they sell and deliver to?
7. Why is 2 pm the most important part of the day?

D Is food from your country important to you? Why or why not? How important is it for people and families to eat meals together in your country?

A family eats a traditional Turkish breakfast.

GOALS

Lesson A
/ Describe and suggest food
/ Compare places to eat

Lesson B
/ Describe a healthy diet and lifestyle
/ Recommend a place to eat

VOCABULARY

A Look at the photo of *kulfi* below. What do you think it is made with?

B Read the text and check your guess from **A**. Would you like to try this food? Why or why not?

> Kulfi is a **delicious**, **frozen** dessert or snack. It's made with milk and sugar, so it's very **sweet**. This **tasty** treat is popular in countries such as India and Malaysia, and in the Middle East. You can add different fruits and nuts. In some countries, kulfi is **spicy**, too.

C Complete the word web with the words in blue from the text.

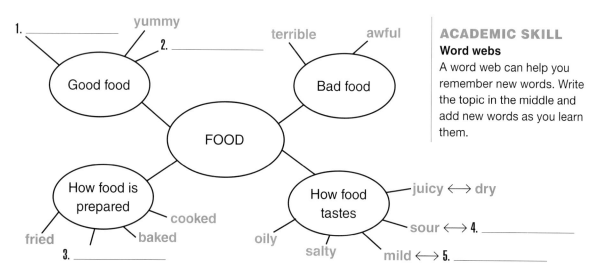

ACADEMIC SKILL

Word webs

A word web can help you remember new words. Write the topic in the middle and add new words as you learn them.

D Think of a popular snack or street food in your country. Write the information.

Name of the food: _____

Taste: _____

How the food is prepared: _____

Now tell a partner about the food using your notes.

❝ Banh mi sandwiches are a popular street food in Vietnam. They are very tasty! My favorite kind has grilled chicken, cucumbers, and carrots.

Kulfi is often served on a stick.

Shrimp and grits can be eaten for breakfast, lunch, or dinner.

LISTENING

A **Make predictions.** Look at the bowl of food. Which part of the world do you think it comes from? What do you think the food tastes like?

B Listen to the conversation and check (✓) the food that Marta ordered at a southern restaurant in the state of Georgia, US. 🎧9

☐ fried chicken   ☐ lemon pie   ☐ salad

☐ fried green tomatoes   ☐ Mississippi mud pie   ☐ steak and fries

☐ grits   ☐ tomato soup

C **Listen for details.** Listen again and write the missing words. Which food didn't Marta like? 🎧9

1. Southern cooking is _____tasty_____!

2. The food was _____.

3. The chicken tasted _____.

4. Grits have a _____ flavor.

5. The fried green tomatoes were a little _____, but they went _____ with the chicken and grits.

6. The pie was too _____ for Marta.

WORD BANK

Too + adjective is a negative description. If someone says, "The food is too sweet," then they don't like it.

D **PRONUNCIATION: Sentence stress** Listen to the sentences and underline the stressed words. Then listen again and repeat. 🎧10

1. The cooking was tasty!

2. The food was delicious.

3. The chicken was dry.

4. The grits were too salty.

5. The tomatoes were sour.

6. The tomato soup was too hot.

E Tell a partner about a meal you ate recently (at home, in a restaurant, at school, etc.). Describe each dish using the correct sentence stress.

" I had dinner last night in a restaurant. The soup was cold!

The French fries were too salty! "

SPEAKING

A Listen to the conversation. Then answer the questions. 🎧11

Pedro: So, Jill, where do you want to go to dinner tonight?

Jill: I don't know. Why don't we go to the pizza place on the corner?

Pedro: Pizza again? I don't really feel like it.

Jill: OK, how about Thai food instead?

Pedro: Fine with me. Where do you want to go?

Jill: Well, Thai House is near here. And there's another place—The Thai Cafe—but it's downtown.

Pedro: Thai House is closer. Let's go there.

Jill: Sounds good!

1. What are Pedro and Jill going to eat for dinner?

2. How do Pedro and Jill make and respond to suggestions? Underline the words.

Bird's eye peppers, often used in Thai food, are very spicy.

B Practice the conversation with a partner.

C Study the Speaking Strategy. Then complete the conversations below with a partner.

1. **A:** _____ stop at that cafe for coffee.

   B: Good _____!

2. **A:** What time do you want to meet in the morning?

   B: _____ meet at 7:00?

   A: That's a little early. _____ meeting at 8:00 instead?

   B: That's _____ with me. See you then.

3. **A:** What do you want to do today?

   B: _____ going to the beach?

   A: I don't _____ to. _____ see a movie instead.

   B: OK, _____ good.

SPEAKING STRATEGY 🎧12

Making suggestions			Responding to suggestions
Statements			Good / Great idea!
Let's	have	Thai food.	(That) sounds good (to me).
Questions			(That's) fine with me.
Why don't we	have	Thai food?	I don't really want to.
How about	having		I don't really feel like it.
When rejecting a suggestion, it's common to give an explanation: *I don't really feel like it. I'm too tired.*			

D Get into groups of three and follow the steps.

1. On your own, think of two good restaurants.

2. Suggest one of the restaurants to your partners. They can accept or refuse. If a person refuses, he or she should say why and suggest something else.

3. Switch roles and repeat steps 1 and 2 until each student has made a suggestion.

❝ Why don't we go to Parr's Steakhouse for lunch?

That's a great idea! ❞

❝ I don't really feel like steak. How about having Indian food instead?

GRAMMAR

A Read the Unit 2, Lesson A Grammar Reference in the appendix. Complete the exercises. Then do the exercises below.

THE COMPARATIVE FORM OF ADJECTIVES			
One syllable	Two syllables	Three or more syllables	Irregular forms
old → older nice → nicer big → bigger	quiet → quieter spicy → spicier famous → more famous	comfortable → more comfortable	good → better bad → worse
Note: The comparative form of *well* (an adverb) is *better*.			

B Read about two places to eat and complete the sentences. Choose an adjective and write it in the comparative form.

Tony's Family Restaurant	Le Jules Verne Restaurant
• Space for 50 people	• Space for 120 people
• Typical meal for two costs $60	• Typical meal for two costs $500
• Serves food in fifteen minutes	• Serves food in about one hour
• Metal tables and plastic chairs	• Wooden tables and comfortable chairs
• Customer reviews: ☆☆☆	• Customer reviews: ☆☆☆☆

1. Tony's Family Restaurant (small / big) _____is smaller than_____ Le Jules Verne Restaurant.
2. Le Jules Verne Restaurant (cheap / expensive) _____ Tony's.
3. The service at Tony's (slow / fast) _____ at Le Jules Verne.
4. Le Jules Verne (comfortable / uncomfortable) _____ Tony's.
5. Customers think Le Jules Verne (good / bad) _____ Tony's.

C In pairs, choose a topic below and give your partner two topic words. Then your partner will compare them. Switch roles until you have done all the topics.

animals	famous people	sports
countries	food	transportation

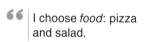 I choose *food*: pizza and salad.

 Salad is healthier than pizza.

Le Jules Verne Restaurant is located on the second floor of the Eiffel Tower in Paris, France.

The hamburgers at the 66 Diner
in New Mexico, US are famous.

ACTIVE ENGLISH Try it out!

A Work in groups. Imagine you are going out to eat together, and you need to choose a restaurant. Discuss the list and decide as a group which items are more or less important.

- price
- location
- quality of food
- comfortable tables and chairs
- fast service
- cleanliness
- friendly service
- type of food

" I think the location is more important than the type of food. I don't want to travel a long way.

B JoJo's Burger Restaurant closed six months ago, but it is reopening. Listen to the radio advertisement and answer the questions. 🎧13

1. What is different about the restaurant now?

2. What is the same?

C In pairs, imagine you are going to open a new restaurant. Discuss and write the information.

1. The name of your restaurant and its location: _____

2. The type of restaurant: _____

3. A description of a special dish on the menu: _____

4. The type of customer and price: _____

5. What makes your restaurant better than others? _____

D Write a 30-second radio ad for your new restaurant and practice reading it aloud with your partner.

E Present your ad to the class. Whose ad was the best? Whose restaurant would you go to? Why?

" Come to our new Chinese restaurant. It's bigger and better than all the rest!

2A GOALS Now I can . . .

Describe and suggest food _____

Compare places to eat _____

1. Yes, I can.
2. Mostly, yes.
3. Not yet.

2B EATING WELL

VOCABULARY

A You are going to read about the healthiest countries in the world. What types of food do you think they eat? Tell the class. Then read and find out.

Experts studied the **diets** and **lifestyles** of 163 nations to find the healthiest countries in the world.

- Spain was number one! The Spanish diet has **plenty** of olive oil and fresh vegetables. Also, Spanish people eat less fast food than any other European country.

- Japan was also in the top ten with the oldest population in the world. The Japanese know that eating more fresh fish than red meat can bring **health benefits** and **prevent** illnesses.

- Australians, at number seven, love being outdoors, and their healthy diet **increases** energy for sports and exercise. In recent years, Australians also **reduced** unhealthy **habits**, like smoking.

B Match the words in **blue** from **A** to the definitions.

1. usual food you eat: _____ diet _____
2. a lot: _____
3. the way you live: _____
4. do something less: _____
5. something you often do: _____

6. stop something from happening: _____
7. make more of something: _____
8. something that helps your body: _____

C Choose the answers that are true for you. Circle **T** for *true* or **F** for *false*.

1. I need to eat less fast food.	T	F
2. I eat plenty of fruits and vegetables.	T	F
3. I get plenty of exercise and have an outdoor lifestyle.	T	F
4. I have one or two bad habits, like eating too much candy.	T	F

D Tell a partner about your answers in **C**. Do you have a healthy diet and lifestyle? Why or why not?

> " I have a healthy diet and lifestyle. I get plenty of exercise, and I eat . . .

La Boqueria Market in Barcelona, Spain sells many different fruits and vegetables.

THE BEST
FOODS
TO EAT

There are many different types of chicken soup around the world. This one has chicken, corn, and asparagus.

In their book *What to Eat When*, Dr. Michael Roizen and Dr. Michael Crupain describe the benefits of eating certain foods in different situations.

When you're going on a first date

Feeling nervous? Eat a sandwich with turkey and avocado. Unlike sugar, these two foods give you energy slowly, so you feel calm.

When you don't feel well

It's the world's oldest advice, but it's true. When you have a cold, eat plenty of chicken soup. Because it's warm and salty, the soup is good for your throat. It helps you breathe easier, too.

Are headaches your problem? If yes, eat more spinach. Spinach can reduce pain and prevent headaches. It's also high in B vitamins, so make it part of your normal diet.

When you have a job interview

On the morning of the interview, eat a good breakfast. It's the most important meal of the day! A hot cereal, like oatmeal, is good because it gives you a lot of energy quickly and improves attention. Also, coffee or tea can help you think better. Have one or two cups forty-five minutes before the interview.

When you're *hangry*

It's late afternoon, and you're in a bad mood because you're hungry. In other words, you're *hangry!*[1] What do you eat? Some people like to eat something sweet, but eating a snack like nuts or something high in protein[2] is much better. Protein reduces hunger more quickly, and it's healthier than sweets. 🎧14

[1] **Hangry** *(informal, slang) is a combination of the words* hungry *and* angry.
[2] **Protein** *is found in foods like meat, nuts, beans, and eggs.*

A **Read for the gist.** Look quickly at the title, photo, and first paragraph. What is the main goal of the article?

   a. to explain why a healthy diet is good for you

   b. to compare the benefits of different types of food

   c. to give advice about the best foods for different times

   d. to describe how to cook different foods

B Read the article. What is the best food or drink for the people below?

   1. "We're meeting at eight. Is my hair OK? Will she like this shirt?"

   2. "It's been a terrible day! I missed breakfast, and I'm so angry with my boss!"

   3. "I think I need to see the doctor. My headaches are getting worse."

   4. "I'm so stressed. I really need to get this job today."

C **Take notes.** Read the article again and take notes in your notebook on why these types of food are good for you.

   1. turkey and avocado *Gives energy slowly. Helps you feel calm.*

   2. chicken soup

   3. spinach

   4. hot cereal, like oatmeal

   5. coffee or tea

   6. nuts

D Work in groups. What do you think are the best foods to eat in these situations? Why?

   1. in the morning for breakfast

   2. the night before an important test or exam

   3. when you feel hungry between meals

   4. when you go for a long walk in the countryside

   5. at a special occasion, like a birthday party or wedding

LISTENING

A Write down the times you normally eat breakfast, lunch, and dinner. Then compare your times with a partner. Are the times similar or very different? Why?

B **Listen for time.** Listen to a talk about eating in different cultures. Take notes about the dinner times in these cultures and countries. 🎧15

1. In (northern) Norway _____
2. In China _____
3. In the US _____
4. In Mexico, France, and Brazil _____
5. In Spain _____

C Listen again. Circle **T** for *true* or **F** for *false*. 🎧15

1. When you visit another country, it's good to know something about meal times there.   **T**   **F**

2. Eight-thirty pm is one of the most common times to eat dinner around the world.   **T**   **F**

3. Dinner is usually the biggest and longest meal in countries like Mexico and France.   **T**   **F**

4. In Brazil, people often eat dinner while traveling from work to home.   **T**   **F**

5. If you are invited for dinner in Spain, the speaker suggests you have something to eat earlier in the evening.   **T**   **F**

D Work in pairs and discuss the questions about your country and culture.

1. Do people eat meals at different times in different parts of your country?
2. How often do you get takeout or eat on the go?
3. Is it important for families to eat together? Why or why not?

E In pairs, imagine a person from another country is visiting your home for dinner. What do you tell them about the time, the food, and any other cultural differences?

People eat dinner at a restaurant in Chongqing, China.

A diver cleans the windows of Under, an underwater restaurant in Lindesnes, Norway.

GRAMMAR

A Read the Unit 2, Lesson B Grammar Reference in the appendix. Complete the exercises. Then do the exercises below.

THE SUPERLATIVE FORM OF ADJECTIVES			
One syllable	Two syllables	Three or more syllables	Irregular forms
old → **the** old**est** large → **the** larg**est** big → **the** big**gest**	quiet → **the** quiet**est** spicy → **the** spic**iest** famous → **the most** famous	comfortable → **the most** comfortable important → **the most** important relaxing → **the most** relaxing	good → **the best** bad → **the worst**

B Complete the restaurant profile with the superlative form of the adjectives in parentheses.

Are you looking for an interesting place to have a meal? One of (1. unusual) _____ places in the world is Under, a restaurant in Norway where you eat underwater! Under is actually (2. large) _____ underwater restaurant in the world, and many say it is (3. cool) _____. It's not (4. cheap) _____ restaurant, but it's (5. good) _____ way to see the local sea life. The food is good, too. "I had (6. delicious) _____ meal of my life," says one visitor to the restaurant. His girlfriend agrees. "It was (7. strange) _____ but (8. interesting) _____ dining experience I ever had!"

C Answer the questions with a partner.

1. Why is the restaurant in **B** unusual?

2. Why do people like it?

3. Does it sound interesting to you? Why or why not?

D Work with a partner. Use the adjectives in the box to talk about restaurants and cafes you know.

bad	cheap	noisy
boring	cool	romantic

❝ El Taco Loco is the noisiest cafe in this area.

ACTIVE ENGLISH Try it out!

A With a partner, create a menu for a new restaurant or coffee shop. Divide the menu into sections (appetizers, main dishes, desserts, drinks). Include the name of the restaurant and the prices.

B Post your menu for the class to see. Then walk around and learn about your classmates' restaurants. Answer the questions below.

1. Which restaurant or coffee shop is the cheapest? _____

2. Which is the most expensive? _____

3. Which is the healthiest? _____

4. Which is the most unusual? _____

5. Which do you think is the best? Why? _____

C Join another pair and compare your answers from **B**. Do you all agree on the best place?

D Read the restaurant review and take notes about the information below. Then ask and answer questions about the restaurant with a partner.

Amazon Sun

Amazon Sun is the best Brazilian restaurant in this city. The food is delicious, the service is friendly, and the prices are moderate. One of the tastiest dishes on the menu is the *feijoada completa*—a traditional dish of meat, beans, and Brazilian spices. It's excellent! I recommend you try it!

> " Is it an expensive restaurant?
>
> No, the prices are moderate. "

Restaurant name: _____

Type of food: _____

Prices: _____

Service: _____

Best dish: _____

E **WRITING** Choose a restaurant you like and take notes about it using the items in **D**. Then use your notes to write your own restaurant review.

F Exchange your writing with a partner. Read his or her review.

1. Are there any mistakes? If yes, circle them.

2. Take notes about your partner's restaurant using the items in **D**.

3. Give the review back to your partner. Do you want to try his or her restaurant? Why or why not?

2B GOALS   Now I can . . .

Describe a healthy diet and lifestyle _____

Recommend a place to eat _____

1. Yes, I can.

2. Mostly, yes.

3. Not yet.

GLOBAL VOICES

A   Do you ever make an omelet? Check (✓) the ingredients you might use.

☐ cheese ☐ meat ☐ mushrooms ☐ onions ☐ salt and pepper

☐ eggs ☐ milk ☐ oil ☐ peppers ☐ other: _____

B   Watch a video of a cooking demonstration. Which ingredients in **A** does he use?

C   Complete the sentences. Then watch the video again to check your answers.

add	break	chop	flip	grate	heat	pour	put in

1. First of all, I'll _____ the eggs in this bowl and stir them together.
2. I'll _____ the onions, the mushrooms, and the peppers.
3. And I need to _____ the cheese.
4. I'm going to _____ up this saucepan and _____ a bit of oil.
5. Next, I _____ my onions and peppers and let them cook for a minute or so.
6. Finally, I _____ in the egg mixture and cook it on a lower heat.
7. Some people _____ their omelets over, but I like to fold mine, like this.

D   In pairs, prepare your own cooking demonstration by following the steps.

1. Choose a dish to present. Write down the instructions for cooking the dish using some of the verbs in **C**.
2. Practice your presentation. You can use real ingredients or act it out.
3. When you are ready, join another pair and give your cooking demonstration.

USEFUL EXPRESSIONS

Today, we'd like to show you one of the best dishes . . .
Let's start with the ingredients. We have . . .
We think the dish is tastier with some . . .
First of all, / Next, / After that, / Then, . . .
And finally, it's ready to eat!

A potato, onion, and cheese omelet with vegetables on the side

MYSTERIES

3

LOOK AT THE PHOTO. ANSWER THE QUESTIONS.

1. What do you think is creating the mysterious light in the photo? Guess.

2. Read the caption. Can you explain this mystery?

3. What other mysteries do you know about? Can science explain them?

WARM-UP VIDEO

A Watch a video about Frane Selak, "the luckiest unlucky man to ever live." Number the events in the correct order.

_____ His car went off a mountain road.

_____ He was in a plane crash.

_____ He was in a bus crash.

__1__ He was in a train accident.

_____ His car burst into flames.

_____ A bus hit him.

_____ His car burst into flames—again.

B Watch again. Match the events in **A** (1–7) to the reasons why Frane was lucky (a–g).

_____ a. A door blew off, and Frane landed in a haystack.

__1__ b. Frane only broke his arm.

_____ c. Frane jumped free before the car exploded.

_____ d. Four people were killed, but not Frane.

_____ e. Frane survived.

_____ f. Frane jumped out and landed in a tree.

_____ g. Frane survived, but with less hair.

C In pairs, close your books and retell the story of Frane Selak. Try to remember each unlucky event and why he was lucky in 2003.

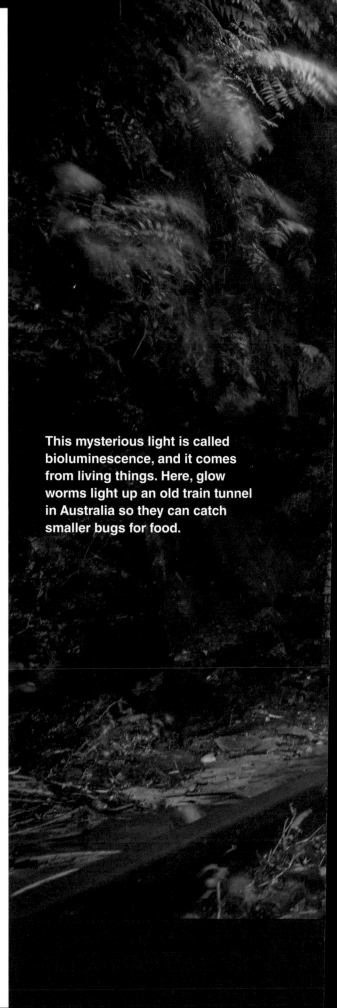

This mysterious light is called bioluminescence, and it comes from living things. Here, glow worms light up an old train tunnel in Australia so they can catch smaller bugs for food.

GOALS

Lesson A

/ Say how likely something is

/ Talk about states and feelings

Lesson B

/ Say if something is possible or impossible

/ Explain a mystery

VOCABULARY

A Read about things people do for good luck. Which do people do in your country? Do they do any others?

Lucky or Unlucky?

- In some countries, if you see a black cat **by chance**, it's unlucky. But in other countries, it can **bring good luck**.

- Eight is the luckiest number in China. People prefer to have eight in their telephone number, and people often live on the eighth floor **on purpose**.

- Placing your wallet or purse on the ground in many countries means you're **more likely to** have bad luck with money.

- Saying the phrases *Knock on wood* or *Touch wood* in a number of English-speaking countries helps to **avoid bad luck** (but only if you actually knock on or touch real wood at the same time).

- In the lottery, eleven is the most popular number. More people **take a chance** on this number than any other—they think it might **increase** their **chances** of winning!

Many people throw coins in the Trevi Fountain in Rome, Italy to bring good luck and help them return to the city someday.

B Complete the questions with words in blue from the text.

1. Do you think you are a lucky person or are you often _____? Why?

2. Do you ever wear a lucky color or carry a lucky object to _____ good luck?

3. Are you more _____ to choose a lucky number on _____?

4. Some people _____ more chances on certain days. Do you have a lucky day?

5. Do you do anything to _____ bad luck?

C Ask and answer the questions in **B** with a partner.

WORD BANK
lucky ⟷ unlucky
(bring) good luck ⟷ (avoid) bad luck
on purpose ⟷ by chance
likely ⟷ unlikely
more likely ⟷ less likely
take a chance (risk)
increase your chances (opportunities)

" Do you do anything to avoid bad luck?

Yes, in Italy we say *Touch iron*, not *Touch wood*, to avoid bad luck. "

LISTENING

A **PRONUNCIATION: Dropped syllables** Say the words. Look up any that you don't know. Then listen and repeat. 🎧16

1. interesting   2. generally   3. everywhere   4. finally

B Read the sentences. Which one do you agree with more? Tell a partner.

1. Some people are just lucky in life.
2. You can learn to be lucky in life.

C **Listen for gist.** You will hear the beginning of a talk about psychology professor Richard Wiseman and his research on luck. Listen. Which statement in **B** (1 or 2) does he believe? Circle it. 🎧17

D **Make predictions.** Read the sentences. Do they describe lucky people or unlucky people? Guess. Write **L** for *lucky people* or **U** for *unlucky people*. Write **B** if it is true for *both* types of people. Then listen and check your answers. 🎧18

1. _____ They spend more time alone.
2. _____ They don't like surprises.
3. _____ They have a lot of friends.
4. _____ They make decisions.
5. _____ They listen to their own feelings.
6. _____ They have bad experiences.
7. _____ They try to find the good in a bad situation.

WORD BANK
intuition a feeling that causes someone to act in some way without understanding why

on the other hand a phrase used to introduce an opposite (or contrasting) idea

E Answer the questions with a partner.

1. Was your answer in **B** the same as Professor Wiseman's? Do you agree with him now? Why or why not?
2. Look at the statements in **D**. Which ones are true for you?

In some Asian countries, these cats are believed to bring good luck to their owners.

SPEAKING

A Nico and Sandra are talking about a news article. Listen and answer the questions. 🎧19

Sandra: Anything interesting in today's news?

Nico: Yeah, I'm reading about a woman in New York City. She just won $25,000.

Sandra: That's a lot of money. Did she win the lottery?

Nico: No, she guessed the correct number of candies in a jar.

Sandra: Really? How many were there?

Nico: 7,954.

Sandra: Wow. That was a lucky guess!

Nico: I know. I doubt that I could do that!

Sandra: So, what's she going to do with the money?

Nico: I don't know. Perhaps she'll go on a vacation or use it for school.

1. What did a woman in New York City do?

2. What is she going to do now?

B Practice the conversation with a partner.

C On the lines below, write two things about yourself that are true. Write one thing that is a lie.

_____

_____

_____

D Get into groups of three or four people. Follow the steps below.

1. One person tells the group his or her sentences from **C**.

2. The others . . .

- ask the speaker questions to find out which sentence is a lie.

- use the Speaking Strategy to discuss their ideas.

- guess which sentence is a lie. If you guess correctly, you get a point.

3. Switch roles and repeat steps 1 and 2. The person with the most points at the end wins.

SPEAKING STRATEGY 🎧20

Saying something is likely	
I bet (that)	Marco plays the drums.
Marco probably	plays the drums.
Maybe / Perhaps	Marco plays the drums.
Saying something is *not* likely	
I doubt (that)	Marco plays the drums.

You can use *Are you sure?* to ask if a person is certain about something.

" I bet Marco plays the drums. I saw him with a pair of drumsticks one time.

Are you sure they were his drumsticks? Maybe they belong to someone else. "

GRAMMAR

A Read the sentences and write the verbs in bold in the grammar chart in **B**. What verb form is used in all of the sentences?

*If you **see** a black cat, it's unlucky.*

*Unlucky people don't **like** surprises.*

*Do you **believe** you are a lucky person?*

*He **wants** to teach you how to be luckier in life.*

*Do you **own** a lucky object?*

B Read the Unit 3, Lesson A Grammar Reference in the appendix. Complete the exercises. Then do the exercises below.

STATIVE VERBS				
Thinking verbs	**Having verbs**	**Feeling verbs**	**Sensing verbs**	**Other verbs**
think	have	love	**4.** _____	need
know	**2.** _____	**3.** _____	taste	seem
1. _____	belong	hate	feel	**5.** _____
Stative verbs describe states, thoughts, and feelings, not actions. We normally use these verbs in the simple present, not the present continuous.				

C Complete the story with the verbs in the box. Write them in the simple present or the present continuous. There is one extra verb.

| have   have   know   live   not believe   not own   ~~seem~~   think   work |

For most people, winning the lottery (1.) _____seems_____ like the greatest luck. Unfortunately for the winners, it can be the opposite. Ian Walters won a million dollars five years ago. "Suddenly, you (2.) _____ a lot of money, and you (3.) _____ it will last forever," he explains. "But after a while, you (4.) _____ so much fun that you don't notice how much you're spending on new clothes and expensive vacations! And then, one day, it's all gone! At the moment, I (5.) _____ with my sister, and I (6.) _____ in a cafe. I (7.) _____ a car because I can't afford it." But Ian also says, "It's not so bad, though. Now, I (8.) _____ that money can buy you happiness. Family and friends are more important."

D Answer the questions with a partner.

1. *Winning the lottery seems like the greatest luck.* Do you think this is true? Why or why not?

2. Do you think that money is for spending or for saving? Why?

3. Do you believe that money can buy happiness? Why or why not? If yes, how much money?

According to a UK study, the most popular thing for lottery winners to buy was a new house.

ACTIVE ENGLISH Try it out!

A Work in groups of four. Read the instructions and play the game.

TAKE A CHANCE! A game of luck

1. Each group needs one coin and a game piece for each player. All players put their game pieces on START. Follow the instructions to see which player goes first.

2. Toss the coin at the start of each turn. For heads, move two squares; for tails, move one square. When you arrive on a square, read and follow the instructions.

3. On **TAKE A CHANCE!** squares, speak to another player and use language for describing how likely / unlikely something is; for example, *I bet that . . ., . . . probably . . ., Maybe / Perhaps . . ., I doubt that . . .* If you don't use this language, you cannot move forward!

Tips for Playing Online

• Keep track of everyone's place on your own board by using a piece of paper with each player's name.

• On each **TAKE A CHANCE!** square, choose a player to guess information about, but remember: you cannot choose the same person as another classmate.

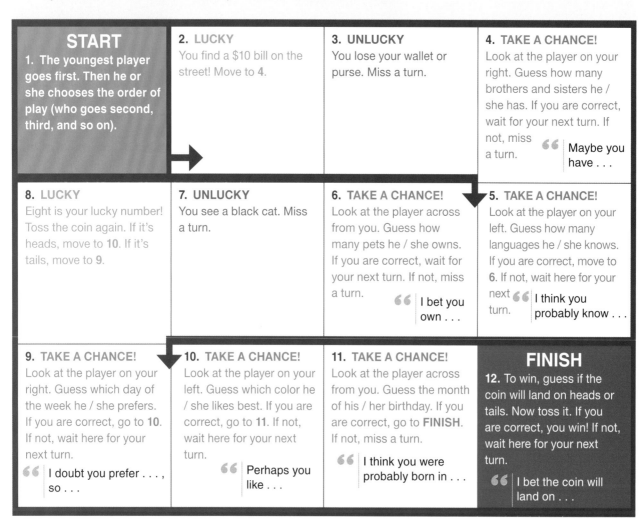

| START 1. The youngest player goes first. Then he or she chooses the order of play (who goes second, third, and so on). | 2. LUCKY You find a $10 bill on the street! Move to **4**. | 3. UNLUCKY You lose your wallet or purse. Miss a turn. | 4. TAKE A CHANCE! Look at the player on your right. Guess how many brothers and sisters he / she has. If you are correct, wait for your next turn. If not, miss a turn. 66 Maybe you have . . . |

| 8. LUCKY Eight is your lucky number! Toss the coin again. If it's heads, move to **10**. If it's tails, move to **9**. | 7. UNLUCKY You see a black cat. Miss a turn. | 6. TAKE A CHANCE! Look at the player across from you. Guess how many pets he / she owns. If you are correct, wait for your next turn. If not, miss a turn. 66 I bet you own . . . | 5. TAKE A CHANCE! Look at the player on your left. Guess how many languages he / she knows. If you are correct, move to **6**. If not, wait here for your next turn. 66 I think you probably know . . . |

| 9. TAKE A CHANCE! Look at the player on your right. Guess which day of the week he / she prefers. If you are correct, go to **10**. If not, wait here for your next turn. 66 I doubt you prefer . . ., so . . . | 10. TAKE A CHANCE! Look at the player on your left. Guess which color he / she likes best. If you are correct, go to **11**. If not, wait here for your next turn. 66 Perhaps you like . . . | 11. TAKE A CHANCE! Look at the player across from you. Guess the month of his / her birthday. If you are correct, go to **FINISH**. If not, miss a turn. 66 I think you were probably born in . . . | FINISH 12. To win, guess if the coin will land on heads or tails. Now toss it. If you are correct, you win! If not, wait here for your next turn. 66 I bet the coin will land on . . . |

3A GOALS Now I can . . .

Say how likely something is ___

Talk about states and feelings ___

1. Yes, I can.

2. Mostly, yes.

3. Not yet.

VOCABULARY

A Look at the photo below and the title of the text: *Why Do We Dream?* Think of an answer with a partner and tell the class. Then read the text.

> **Why Do We Dream?**
>
> Everyone dreams, but scientists can't **figure out** why. Here are two different **explanations**.
>
> "Our team is **investigating** the connection between dreams and our health. Dreams could help with stress. After we sleep and dream, we feel better."
>
> "We have a different **theory**. We believe that dreams might be images in our minds. The brain 'cleans out' unused information when we dream."
>
> Both ideas **make sense**, but for now there's no **proof** for either one. The only way to **solve** this mystery is to **do** more **research** and collect **data**.

B Match the words in blue with the synonyms below. Some words have the same synonym. Use a dictionary to help.

Synonyms	Words or phrases			
find out, study (v)	1.	figure out	3.	
	2.		4.	
a guess, an idea	5.		6.	
be understandable	7.			
facts, evidence	8.		9.	

ACADEMIC SKILL

Using synonyms

A synonym is a word or phrase that has the same or almost the same meaning as another word or phrase. When you learn more difficult words, match them with easier synonyms that you already know. Also, check the meanings of the new words in your dictionary.

C Complete each question with a word in blue. Then ask and answer the questions with a partner.

1. What are the two t_____ about dreams?

2. Do scientists have p_____ for either idea?

3. In your opinion, which e_____ makes more
   s_____?

WORD BANK

have / need / there's
(no) **proof**
have a **theory**

In some Native American cultures, dream catchers were traditionally believed to protect children from bad dreams and give them good dreams.

MYSTERIOUS
ARTWORK

The Nazca Desert in Peru is home to one of the most unusual sites in the world. We talked with Dr. Gabriel Reyes about the Nazca Lines and why they are one of history's greatest mysteries.

Interviewer: So, Dr. Reyes, tell us:

1. ▭

Dr. Reyes: On the ground in the Peruvian desert are hundreds of line drawings of different animals, humans, insects, and other symbols. These drawings, known as the Nazca Lines, are very large. Some are over 365 meters (1,200 feet) long. You can only see them clearly from a high place, like a plane or the mountains nearby.

Interviewer: 2. ▭

Dr. Reyes: For years, some people thought visitors from another planet drew them—maybe because it's easiest to see the lines from a high place. But, in fact, the Nazca people created the images. They lived in the area from 200 BC to the seventh century AD and probably made the drawings over 1,500 years ago.

Interviewer: 1,500 years ago?

3. ▭

Dr. Reyes: They probably used simple tools. We believe a team worked together and made the drawings in the desert ground. They didn't need airplanes or modern tools.

Interviewer: 4. ▭

Dr. Reyes: Good question. We can't be sure, but we have different theories. The images

The Nazca Desert in southern Peru

...may be religious symbols. The lines could also be a large map; perhaps the Nazca people used the lines to find water in the desert. Or maybe the lines were a type of calendar. Scientists are still investigating.

Interviewer: 5. ▮▮▮▮▮▮▮▮▮▮▮

Dr. Reyes: We are continuing to study maps of the area and to use photographs taken from planes, but nowadays new technology is helping us, too. We now have drones[1] that can fly much closer and take better photos of the lines. We're also using photographs from satellites,[2] so we're finding new information every day. ⌕21⌕

[1]**Drones** *are flying machines controlled by someone on the ground.*
[2]**Satellites** *are machines that are sent into space to move around the Earth.*

A   Predict information. Look at the title and photo and try to answer the questions below. Then read the interview and check your answers.

1. What do you think the drawing in the photo is?

2. Who do you think made it?

ACADEMIC SKILL

Predicting information
You can predict information about an article using the title or photos. This can help you understand the text better as you read it.

B   Read for main ideas. Read the interview again and match the questions below to the correct spaces (1–5). There is one extra question.

a. How did they make the lines?

b. What was the purpose of the lines?

c. How are you doing this research?

d. What exactly are the Nazca Lines?

e. Can anyone visit the Nazca Lines?

f. Who made the ground drawings?

C   The statements below are wrong. Change them so that they are correct. Underline the sentences in the interview that helped you make your changes.

1. The lines are small; you can only see them by looking closely at the ground.

2. North Americans probably created the lines in the year 1500.

3. People probably made the lines without simple tools.

4. The Nazca Lines definitely were a calendar, say scientists.

D   Look at the five questions in **B**. Take turns asking and answering them with a partner. When you answer a question, use your own words. Try not to look back at the article.

LISTENING

A **Make predictions.** Look at the photo below. What do some people think about a full moon?

WORD BANK
If something **affects** you, it causes you to change in some way.

behavior the way you act

B **Listen for main ideas.** Listen to the news report. Then read the sentences and circle **T** for *true* or **F** for *false*. 🎧22

1. City officials plan to put more police on the streets when there's a full moon. **T** **F**

2. City officials say there are more car accidents and people hurt in fights on these nights. **T** **F**

3. The woman and the man agree about whether the moon changes people's behavior. **T** **F**

C **Listen for details.** Read the questions and answers. Then listen again and check (✓) *Yes* or *No*, and complete the chart. 🎧22

	Does the moon affect our behavior?	What's the person's theory?
1. the woman	☐ Yes ☐ No	The moon affects the _____. Maybe it affects _____, too.
2. the man	☐ Yes ☐ No	On full moon nights, there's more _____, so more people _____.

D Answer the questions with a partner.

1. What do you think? Can the moon change our behavior?

2. Can you think of any other explanations for the higher crime and accident rates?

A full moon over the Acropolis in Athens, Greece

GRAMMAR

A Read the Unit 3, Lesson B Grammar Reference in the appendix. Complete the exercises. Then do the exercises below.

MODALS OF PRESENT POSSIBILITY			
Subject	**Modal**	**Main verb**	
Dreams	**may / might / could**	help	with stress.
Scientists	**can't**	be	sure.

Questions and short answers		
With *be*	Are dreams images in our minds?	They **may / might / could** be. No, they **can't** be.
With other verbs	Do dreams help with stress?	They **may / might / could**. No, they **can't**.

B Complete the conversations with a modal and a verb, if needed. Sometimes, more than one answer is possible. Then ask and answer the questions with a partner.

1. **A:** Does life exist on other planets?

   B: It _____. There are billions of planets.
   We _____ be the only intelligent life.

WORD BANK
pesticide a chemical used
to kill insects

2. **A:** Worldwide, millions of bees are dying. Scientists can't figure out why. What's happening?

   B: Pesticides _____ be killing the bees. But it _____
   be climate change, too.

3. **A:** Are ghosts real?

   B: Well, they _____. A lot of people see them.

   C: No, they _____. There's no scientific proof for them.

C Read each situation. Write two possible explanations for each one in your notebook.

1. Your friend isn't answering her phone.

2. You received a mysterious package in the mail.

3. The teacher isn't here today.

4. You can see a strange blue light in the night sky.

D Work with a partner. Follow the steps below.

1. **Student A:** Tell your partner one situation from **C**. Use *I* and *my*.

2. **Student B:** Give a possible reason, using one of your sentences from **C**.

3. **Student A:** Answer with *can't* or a different possibility.

4. **Student B:** Agree or give another possibility.

5. Switch roles and repeat steps 1–4 for the other situations in **C**.

“ My friend isn't
answering her phone.

Her phone
might be off. ”

“ It can't be. She called
me a minute ago.

Oh, then she
may be . . . ”

Could the Yonaguni Monument near Japan be an ancient underwater city or just some interesting rocks? What do you think?

ACTIVE ENGLISH Try it out!

A Look at the photo. Then turn to the Unit 3 Writing appendix and read about two mysteries. Underline the theories and explanations in each text.

B In pairs, think of one more explanation for each mystery. Then join another pair and present your new theories. Discuss your ideas and try to agree.

❝ The Marfa Lights might be lights from drones.

No, they can't be because . . . ❞

C Complete this paragraph with phrases from the Useful Expressions.

Many scientists (1.) _____ _____ life might exist on other planets. There are more than 100 billion other planets in the universe and many are similar to Earth. (2.) _____ _____, scientists recently found that there may be billions of similar planets. (3.) _____ _____ also shows that many of these planets might have water. (4.) _____ _____ that there could be life on some of them.

USEFUL EXPRESSIONS

Giving an opinion
Many scientists believe that . . .
Some people think that . . .
Experts say . . .

Stating facts and evidence
In fact, . . .
The evidence also shows that . . .
Research tells us . . .

Possibility
It might / could / may . . .
Scientists can't be sure that . . .

Conclusion
It's likely that . . .
Maybe one day we will solve . . .
We need to do more research.

D **WRITING** Choose another mystery from the list below or your own idea. Research the mystery and write a paragraph to provide a possible explanation. Use the Useful Expressions.

- Are ghosts real?
- Is the Loch Ness Monster real?
- How did the dinosaurs die out?
- Your own idea: _____

E Exchange paragraphs with a partner. Which Useful Expressions did your partner use? What theories or explanations does the paragraph describe?

3B **GOALS** Now I can . . .

Say if something is possible or impossible _____

Explain a mystery _____

1. Yes, I can.
2. Mostly, yes.
3. Not yet.

GLOBAL VOICES

A Watch a video about National Geographic Explorer Nora Shawki and number the items (1–6) in the order you see them.

   1   a. statues of the pharaohs

_____ b. the Egyptian pyramids

_____ c. a statue of Queen Cleopatra

_____ d. an archaeologist excavating in the sand

_____ e. a skeleton and a blue stone

_____ f. Nora on a site with her team looking for artifacts

B Watch the video again. Read the sentences and circle **T** for *true* or **F** for *false*.

1. King Tut and Queen Cleopatra lived more than 2,000 years ago. **T F**

2. Nora Shawki is most interested in famous people like the Egyptian pharaohs. **T F**

3. Nora usually digs for artifacts on her own. **T F**

4. Most of her work is done inside a lab where she does research. **T F**

5. She prefers working outside, digging for ancient things in the dirt. **T F**

6. One of the coolest things she ever found was a skeleton with a necklace made of gold. **T F**

7. Nora believes if we know more about history, we can learn more about who we are today. **T F**

8. Nora thinks everyone should follow their passion in life. **T F**

C Answer the questions for yourself. Then work in groups and share your answers.

1. Do you ever wonder about history? Which part of history are you most interested in? Why?

2. What is the oldest object in your house? Where did it come from?

3. Do you think it is important to know about history? Why or why not?

4. Do you agree with Nora that everyone must follow their passion? Why or why not?

5. What is your passion in life? How can you follow it?

Nora Shawki studies the mysteries of the past as an archaeologist in the Nile Delta of Egypt.

A diver explores a shipwreck in the Bermuda Triangle.

Who will be the next lucky winner in this quiz?
The harder the question, the more money you win!

PEOPLE

$100

1. What word beginning with the letter *n* means the person who lives next door to you?

$250

4. Percival R. Lugue has one of the biggest toy collections in the world with 14,500 toys. Where did he get them?

  a. In cereal boxes

  b. With fast food meals

  c. From toy stores

$500

7. The unluckiest driving student came from South Korea. How many times did she fail her test?

  a. 59 times

  b. 590 times

  c. 959 times

FOOD

$100

2. What word beginning with the letter *v* is something you should eat plenty of to be healthy?

$250

5. Which country has the national dish of *momos* served with a spicy sauce?

  a. Nepal

  b. Scotland

  c. Vietnam

$500

8. Josué Montero Durán holds the world record for eating the most hot dogs in three minutes. How many did he eat?

  a. nine

  b. nineteen

  c. ninety

PLACES

$100

3. What word beginning with the letter *d* is a very dry place?

$250

6. The Bermuda Triangle is a mysterious place where planes and ships disappear. Where is it?

  a. The North Atlantic Ocean

  b. The South Pacific Ocean

  c. The Black Sea

$500

9. The largest cooking lesson in the world was in China. How many students were there?

  a. 634

  b. 6,334

  c. 63,340

UNITS 1–3

A In pairs, guess the answers to the nine quiz questions. Then check your answers at the bottom of the page and find out how much money you won!

"The answer to question five might be Scotland.

I don't think that's likely because the food in Scotland isn't very spicy! It could be . . ."

B Answer the questions as a class.

1. Who won the most money in **A**?
2. Which question was the easiest for everyone?
3. Which question was the hardest? Did anyone answer it correctly?

WORD BANK
On TV quiz shows, the **host** asks the questions and the **contestants** answer them.

C In groups, think of some quiz shows on TV and answer the questions about them.

1. What is the name of the TV quiz show?
2. What are the rules?
3. What kinds of questions does the host ask?
4. How many contestants are there?
5. How do you score points?
6. What prizes do the winners receive?

D Work in the same group and follow the steps below.

1. Plan your own TV quiz show and decide . . .

- the name of the show and the rules.
- the types of questions the host needs to ask.
- the number of contestants.
- how contestants score points and what prizes they win.

2. Go online to research and prepare around ten quiz questions. Use the topics of people, food, and places.

E **You Choose** With your group, choose an option and follow the steps. Use the Useful Expressions.

Option 1: Organize the class like a TV quiz show. The people in your group are the hosts and ask the questions. The other groups are the contestants.

Option 2: Write out your quiz questions and then exchange with another group. Take turns answering quiz questions and giving the correct answers.

Option 3: Make a slideshow or video with the questions to show the class. Have your classmates guess the answers as contestants. At the end, go over the correct answers.

USEFUL EXPRESSIONS
The host
Here's your first question. What . . .?
For one hundred dollars, who . . .?
Your time is almost up.
Is that your final answer?
That is correct! Well done!
I'm sorry, but that is the wrong answer.
The contestants
It could be . . .
We think it might be . . .
We agree that . . .
Our answer is . . .

F Compare the different quiz shows. Which team prepared the hardest questions? Which quiz show was the most fun?

1. neighbor 2. vegetable / vegetables 3. desert 4. b 5. a 6. a 7. c 8. a 9. b

4

TRENDS

LOOK AT THE PHOTO. ANSWER THE QUESTIONS.

1. Would you like to go shopping in a place like this? Why or why not?

2. A trend is a change in which something is becoming more common or popular. What shopping or fashion trends do you know about?

WARM-UP VIDEO

A Watch a TV news report about a new type of shopping mall with entertainment. Check (✓) the types of entertainment you see.

☐ movie theater   ☐ ice skating rink

☐ roller coasters   ☐ football game

☐ indoor wave pool   ☐ ski slope

B Watch the video again. Read the statements and circle **T** for *true* or **F** for *false*.

1. The name of the new mall is   **T**   **F**
   American Dream.

2. Don Ghermezian owns the mall   **T**   **F**
   by himself.

3. Don likes to call the mall "an   **T**   **F**
   experiential center."

4. This is Don's family's first   **T**   **F**
   shopping mall.

5. In American Dream, there's about   **T**   **F**
   75% retail and 25% entertainment.

6. Nowadays, Don thinks it's a struggle*   **T**   **F**
   to make money from retail.

*A **struggle** is a difficulty, something needing effort.

C Discuss the questions in pairs.

1. Are malls or shopping centers popular in your town or city? Why or why not?

2. Do you think a shopping mall like American Dream would be popular in your country? Why or why not?

The West Edmonton Mall in Canada has two hotels, an indoor water park, an aquarium, and a mini golf course in addition to its over eight hundred stores.

GOALS

Lesson A
/ Interpret numbers and talk about trends
/ Disagree politely

Lesson B
/ Describe different personal styles
/ Give advice

VOCABULARY

A Look at the first Word Bank. Answer the questions.

1. Which words do you know?

2. Which words are new? Look them up in your dictionary.

B What do the bar graphs show? Tell a partner.

1 **ONLINE SHOPPING WORLDWIDE**

2020   2.05

2015   1.46

Number of online shoppers (in billions)

2 **US ONLINE GROCERY SHOPPING**

2020   52%

2018   23.1%

Percentage of people who bought groceries online

WORD BANK
about / approximately
almost / nearly
exactly
much ⌉
a lot ⌋ → more / less
increase ⟷ decrease
trend

WORD BANK
1,000 = one thousand
1,000,000 = one million
2,000,000,000 = two billion
(not *two billions*)
1.46 million = one point
four six million

WORD BANK
Groceries are food
items that you buy at a
supermarket.

C Look at the graphs in **B**. Then circle the correct words below.

1. a. In 2015, there were **almost** / **exactly** 1.5 billion online shoppers.

   b. In 2020, there were **nearly** / **approximately** 2 billion.

   c. This shows **an increase** / **a decrease** in online shopping.

   d. This may be because online shopping is **much more** / **much less** convenient.

2. a. In 2018, **about** / **exactly** twenty-three percent of people bought groceries online in the US.

   b. In 2020, it **decreased** / **increased** to **about** / **exactly** fifty-two percent.

   c. Buying groceries online is becoming **a lot less** / **a lot more** popular.

D Discuss the questions in pairs.

1. Describe the two online shopping trends from the graphs.

2. Are these trends the same or different in your country? What about in your own life?

❝ As you can see from the chart, . . . is increasing. In 2015, . . .

LISTENING

A Would you buy these things online? Why or why not? Tell a partner.

a computer   a T-shirt   a bag of chips

B **Listen for details.** What things are people buying online? Listen and check (✓) the ones you hear. 🎧23

☐ books   ☐ electronics   ☐ groceries

☐ clothing   ☐ furniture   ☐ makeup

C **Listen for numbers.** Read the questions. Then listen again and write a number or word. 🎧23

1. How much did the average person spend shopping   about _____
   online in China?

2. How about in Great Britain?   approximately _____

3. What do some people not like to buy online?   _____

D Read the sentences below. Then listen and match 1–3 with a–d. One answer is extra. 🎧24

1. Shoppers want fresh food. _____   a. They like the experience of shopping.

2. Shoppers want to choose their own food. _____   b. They want to see the food to make sure.

3. Shoppers want to leave their homes. _____   c. They don't want to pay a lot of money.

                                                  d. They don't want a stranger to do it.

E Which items in **D** are true for you?

Workers in Ganyu, China pack boxes on Singles Day (November 11), the world's biggest online shopping event.

SPEAKING

A Jessica and Maria are roommates. Listen to their conversation. Then answer the questions in pairs. 🎧25

Jessica: Hey, Maria. We need to do something about the TV.

Maria: Yeah. It's not working well. We need to get a new one.

Jessica: I have an idea. My brother is getting a new TV next month. Maybe we can have his old one.

Maria: That's not a bad idea, but I think we need one right now.

Jessica: Yeah, you're right.

Maria: Actually, we saw a nice TV at the mall last week. It was really cheap.

Jessica: I'm not sure about that. I think it was about $1,000. That's too expensive.

Maria: How about buying a new one online? Some of the websites have good deals.

Jessica: I know what you mean, but I want to go to a store. I want to see and test the TV first.

Maria: OK. Let's go to the mall and find a TV we like. Then we can buy it online.

Jessica: Good idea!

1. What are Jessica and Maria talking about? What are their ideas?

2. Which idea do you think is the best one?

B Practice the conversation with a partner.

C Work with a new partner. Imagine you are roommates. Follow the steps below.

1. You need to buy something for your apartment. Choose one of these items:

   a desk   a sofa   bookshelves   other: _____

2. Create a new conversation similar to the one in **A**. Include at least two expressions from the Speaking Strategy.

D Get together with another pair and perform your conversation for them. Then listen to their conversation. Which expressions for disagreement did you hear? Who do you agree with and why?

E Find a new pair, switch roles, and do **D** again.

SPEAKING STRATEGY 🎧26

Polite disagreement

I know what you're saying, but . . .
I see / know what you mean, but . . .
I'm not sure about that.
That's not a bad idea, but . . .

More direct disagreement

I'm afraid I disagree.
Sorry, but I disagree.
I totally / completely disagree.
You can use more direct expressions with people you know well (friends, family etc.).

GRAMMAR

A Read the Unit 4, Lesson A Grammar Reference in the appendix. Complete the exercises. Then do the exercises below.

QUANTITY EXPRESSIONS				
Quantity	*of*	Noun phrase	Verb	
All Most A lot Half Some None	of	my friends them	like	online shopping.

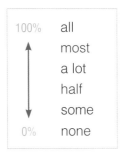

B **PRONUNCIATION: Unstressed *of*** Read the sentences below. Then listen and repeat. 27

1. All of my friends shop online.

2. Most of them use their phones.

3. Some of them use laptops.

C What do you like about online shopping? Rank these items 1–6 (1 = like the most). Share your answers with a partner.

_____ the convenience _____ the pop-up ads _____ the speed

_____ the customer service _____ the prices _____ the variety of items

D Read the infographic. In pairs, make sentences with quantity expressions using the words in parentheses.

WHAT DO YOU LIKE ABOUT ONLINE SHOPPING?

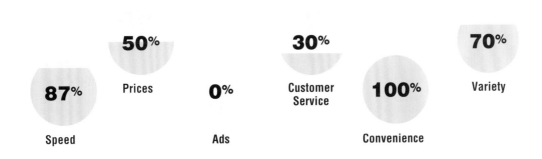

1. (all / people) *All of the people like the convenience of online shopping.*

2. (most / shoppers) _____

3. (a lot / them) _____

4. (half / them) _____

5. (some / people) _____

6. (none / them) _____

E How do the survey results compare with your ideas from **C**? Discuss with a partner.

 66 | Only half of the shoppers like the prices, but it's my favorite thing about online shopping.

ACTIVE ENGLISH Try it out!

An indoor rock climbing wall at Funan Mall in Singapore

A Read and guess the missing words. Then listen and check your answers. 🎧28

1. The number of online shoppers is _____.

2. People like online shopping because it's a _____ more convenient.

3. They also like the _____ of online products.

4. People don't buy _____ online, though.

5. Many people still buy their _____ in local stores.

6. Also, they like to _____ and test items first.

B Read. Then complete the steps with a partner.

Today's shoppers are looking for more than just an online bargain. There's a new trend: shoppers want to go to the mall, but most of them don't want to buy things. They want to have experiences.

1. Below are some examples of "shopping experiences." Check (✓) the ones that sound interesting to you.

☐ taking a yoga class   ☐ having dinner while watching a movie

☐ taking a cooking class   ☐ playing games at an arcade

☐ indoor rock climbing   ☐ posing for a photo shoot

2. Add three experiences to the list above.

C Join another pair. Follow the steps below.

1. You want to open a new store at a mall in your city. Your store will not sell things. It will offer an experience.

2. As a group, share your ideas from **B** and choose the best experience for your new store. Use the Useful Expressions to help you decide.

   ❝ A lot of people in the city do yoga. Let's open a yoga studio.

   I'm not sure about that. Most of our customers are teenagers. They don't do yoga. ❞

USEFUL EXPRESSIONS
Choosing an experience
Who are our customers?
What's popular now?

D Present your store to the class.

   ❝ A couple of us wanted to open a yoga studio. But in the end, all of us decided to . . .

WORD BANK
a couple of two

4A GOALS Now I can . . .

Interpret numbers and talk about trends _____

Disagree politely _____

1. Yes I can.
2. Mostly, yes.
3. Not yet.

VOCABULARY

A The woman in the photo is an *influencer*. Look up this word in your dictionary. What do influencers do? Do you follow any of them?

B Read about influencers. Look up words in blue you don't know. Answer the questions in pairs.

1. How many people follow influencers?
2. Why do people follow influencers?

C Circle the best words to complete 1–6 about the woman in the photo. Then explain your answers to a partner.

1. The woman's clothes are **casual / stylish / unique**.

2. Her shoes look **comfortable / unique / inexpensive**. Sales of these shoes might **increase / decrease** now.

3. The dress is probably **expensive / inexpensive**.

4. In my opinion, the clothes **look great on / don't suit** her.

5. **I / My friend / My sister** would **look good / look terrible** in her clothes.

6. Her clothes **are / aren't** in style now.

> ❝ I said her clothes are casual because she's wearing sneakers.

What's in *style*?

CHECK WITH A FASHION INFLUENCER!

- Most influencers are regular people with a unique and interesting style.

- Millions of people follow influencers on social media to learn about popular clothing brands.

- "I follow Lois Opoku," says one Instagram user, "because she's very stylish. She looks great in anything—an expensive jacket or an inexpensive pair of casual jeans. When something looks good on her, it usually suits me, too. So I buy it."

Lois Opoku is a fashion influencer and blogger living in Berlin, Germany.

THE FACTS ABOUT FAST FASHION

It's really cheap.

Designer brands (like Gucci or Supreme) sell stylish, expensive clothing. Fast-fashion brands (like Zara and H&M) also sell trendy[1] clothes, but for much less. A designer shirt, for example, might cost nearly $1,300. A similar shirt—made of cheaper material[2]—may sell for $13 at a store like H&M.

We're buying more.

Shopping for stylish clothes is cheaper than ever. It's easier, too. A person can learn about something on social media and then buy it online right away. For these reasons—and because fashion trends change quickly—people now buy almost twice as many clothes as ten years ago, especially casual items. Because of this, fast-fashion companies are also making a lot more clothing. One of the world's most popular clothing items is the cotton T-shirt. People buy almost two billion every year.

A lot goes in the garbage.

People are buying more clothing, and they are throwing away a lot, too. In the US alone, Americans put over eight million tons of clothes in the garbage each year because the items are worn[3] or they aren't in style anymore.

Many shoppers don't worry about throwing away inexpensive items. But doing this has a cost, experts say. For example, it takes 2,700 liters of water to make one cotton T-shirt. But after a few uses, we throw it away. Also, a lot of fast-fashion clothing is made of plastic. This hurts the planet.

Luckily, things are changing. Some stores—like Zara and H&M—now take people's used clothes and then resell or recycle them. This way, the items don't go in the garbage. All clothing stores should do these things, says one expert. But for now, it's a good start. 🎧29

[1] If something is **trendy**, it is popular or in style.
[2] **Material** is cloth; it is used to make clothes.
[3] If clothing or shoes are **worn**, they are damaged from use; they may be broken or have holes in them.

Over $450 billion worth of material is thrown in the garbage every year. Companies in Italy are trying to change this by making designer dresses from recycled clothing.

A Tell a partner: how many T-shirts do you have? Where did you buy them? How much were they?

B **Make predictions.** Read the title of the article and the sentences in bold. Guess the answers to the questions.

1. What is "fast fashion"?

2. In the author's opinion, is fast fashion mostly good or bad for us?

C Read the article. Check your ideas in **B**.

D **Scan for numbers.** Complete the sentences with numbers from the article.

1. A designer shirt might cost _____.

2. A similar shirt at H&M may cost _____.

3. Today, people buy almost _____ as many clothes as _____ years ago.

4. Every year, people buy _____ cotton T-shirts.

5. Every year, Americans throw away _____ tons of clothes.

6. You need _____ liters of water to make _____ cotton T-shirt.

E In pairs, role-play an interview between the two people below. Use ideas from **D** and other information from the reading. Switch roles. Then do your role play for another pair.

Student A: You're a journalist doing a report on fast fashion. You are meeting with the CEO of a large clothing company. Tell the CEO about some of the problems with fast fashion. Ask what the company is doing about them.

Student B: You are the CEO. Explain some good things about fast fashion. Describe what your company is trying to do about the problems.

LISTENING

A **Make predictions.** Answer the questions with a partner.

1. What is happening in the four photos?

2. Read the sentences below the photos. Can you guess any of the missing words?

You answer questions about your
(1.) _____ and your favorite
(2.) _____.

A personal (3.) _____
chooses items.

You get the items in the
(4.) _____.

You (5.) _____ for the clothes.
If something doesn't (6.) _____
you, you (7.) _____ it.

B Read the sentence. Then listen and choose the correct answer. 🎧30

Carla is telling Max about an online service. The service _____.

a. cleans your clothes   c. buys your old clothes

b. sends clothes to you

C Listen again. Complete 1–7 in **A**. Write one word in each blank. 🎧30

D **Infer meaning.** Listen one last time and circle the best answer. 🎧30

1. The site has **casual / formal / both casual and formal** clothes.

2. Carla gets new items every two **weeks / months**.

3. The service is for **women only / both men and women**.

4. In Carla's opinion, the service is **expensive / inexpensive**.

5. Carla is **mostly happy / a little unhappy** with the service.

E **Summarize.** Answer the questions with a partner.

1. How does the clothing service work? Cover the sentences below the photos in **A** and explain.

2. Would you like this service? Why or why not?

ACADEMIC SKILL
Infer meaning from context
Sometimes the speaker doesn't say exactly what they mean. You might have to infer the meaning by thinking about the person's situation and feelings.

GRAMMAR

A Read the Unit 4, Lesson B Grammar Reference in the appendix. Complete the
exercises. Then do the exercises below.

ADVICE WITH *COULD, SHOULD, OUGHT TO,* AND *HAD BETTER*			
You	could	buy	it online (or at a store).
	should / ought to		it online. It's cheaper.
	shouldn't		it at a store. It's more expensive.
	'd better		it now. Tomorrow, the price increases.
	'd better not		it now. It's too expensive.

B Work with a partner. Choose a role (A or B).

Student A: You have a job interview at a fashion magazine next week.

Student B: You're going on a trip to the beach. It's hot in the afternoon, but cool
at night.

C Give four pieces of advice to your partner about his or her situation. Use *could*,
should (*not*), *ought to*, or *had better* (*not*) and the items in the box.

bring a book to read	get dressed up	wear casual clothes
bring a jacket	iron your clothes	wear something unique
buy clothes there	wear a lot of cologne or perfume	wear sunglasses

“ Job interviews are formal, so I think you should get dressed up.

Yes, but this interview is at a fashion magazine. ”

“ Oh, then you'd better wear something unique. For example, you could . . .

Is this clothing appropriate
for a job interview?

ACTIVE ENGLISH Try it out!

A **WRITING** Imagine you signed up for an online clothing service. Complete the information about your personal style. Turn to the Unit 4 Writing appendix to see an example profile.

> ## My Style Profile
>
> 1. For school or work, I usually **get dressed up** / **wear casual clothes**.
> 2. It's important for clothes to be **comfortable** / **stylish** / **inexpensive** / **unique** / **other:** _____.
> 3. My two favorite clothing items are my _____. They suit me.
> 4. I look good in these colors: _____
> 5. My two favorite brands or clothing stores are _____
> 6. What else should your personal shopper know? Write about your daily routine or special clothes you need. _____
>
> _____
> _____
> _____

B Exchange books with a partner and read his or her profile in **A**. As your partner's personal shopper, think of six items for him or her. Write your ideas below.

Personal Shopper's Suggestions

clothes: _____

shoes: _____

accessories: _____

WORD BANK
accessory something extra you wear: a watch, belt, bag, hat, tie, etc.

C Return your partner's book to him or her. Then do the following:

Student A: Use the Useful Expressions to explain your suggestions to your partner.

> 66 You said you usually get dressed up, so I think you should buy a dark blue suit. You'll look great in it!

Student B: Do you agree with your partner's choices? Which are your favorites?

> 66 Really? A blue suit? I usually wear black, but maybe I'll try it!

> My favorite is the yellow sweater. Yellow usually looks good on me! 99

USEFUL EXPRESSIONS
You said you . . . , so I think you should buy . . .
You could wear . . .
. . . is / are in style now.
I think . . . will suit you.
You'll look great in . . .

D Switch roles and repeat the steps in **C**.

4B GOALS   Now I can . . .

Describe different personal styles _____

Give advice _____

1. Yes I can.
2. Mostly, yes.
3. Not yet.

GLOBAL VOICES

A Where do you usually buy clothes? Have you ever rented clothing? Tell a partner.

B Watch a video about clothing rental with Amanda Cosco, a fashion reporter. Check (✓) the questions she answers in the video.

☐ **1.** What is rental fashion?

☐ **2.** How does rental fashion work?

☐ **3.** Why would a customer rent clothes instead of buying them?

☐ **4.** When did rental fashion become popular?

☐ **5.** What will be the future trends in rental fashion?

☐ **6.** How should I get started?

☐ **7.** How long does it take for the clothing to arrive in the mail?

C Watch the video again and number the steps in the process of renting clothes (1–6).

_____ a. Receive the clothes at your house.

_____ b. Agree to pay an amount each month.

_____ c. Keep them for about a month and then return them.

_____ d. Sign up for a subscription.

_____ e. Choose a few items of clothing.

_____ f. The company cleans the clothes and rents them again.

D Work in pairs and imagine you are a new rental fashion company. Write a short ad for your company. In the ad, explain:

- how the service works
- the types of clothes you offer
- the benefits of the service

Then exchange ads with another pair. Would you like to use their service? Why or why not?

Some rental fashion companies started with formal clothing only, but now most have casual clothes, too.

Tourists and locals come together in Chorro de Quevedo, a small plaza in the La Candelaria neighborhood of Bogota, Colombia.

GOALS

Lesson A
/ Talk about chores and errands
/ Make appointments and requests

Lesson B
/ Compare ways of getting around
/ Describe your neighborhood

MY NEIGHBORHOOD

LOOK AT THE PHOTO. ANSWER THE QUESTIONS.

1. Do you live in a city like this?
2. Where do you think these people are going?
3. What is a popular neighborhood in your city?

WARM-UP VIDEO

A You are going to watch a video showing different neighborhoods in Shanghai, China. Write down a list of five things you think you will see in the video (for example, *a traffic jam*). Then share your list with a partner.

B Watch the video and check (✓) the things you see on your list from **A**.

C Watch the video again and number the activities (1–8) in the order you see them.

  1   a. Someone is taking an elevator.

_____ b. A girl is learning to play a musical instrument.

_____ c. A young woman is washing her hair.

_____ d. Someone is doing laundry.

_____ e. A young man is listening to music on the subway.

_____ f. Someone is sweeping the sidewalk.

_____ g. A man is brushing his teeth.

_____ h. People are waiting on their bicycles and scooters.

D In pairs, discuss the questions.

1. What three adjectives do you think best describe the city of Shanghai?
2. If you made a similar video of your town or city, what places and activities would you show? Why?

5A CHORES AND ERRANDS

VOCABULARY

A Look at the photo below. What household chore is Janice doing? What does "the good old Kansas wind" do?

You **do household chores** like cleaning and washing in your home. You **run errands** around your neighborhood (for example, going to the post office).

B Work with a partner. Match the sentence parts.

1. You **do the dishes** _____
2. You **do laundry** _____
3. You **drop off** your younger brother or sister _____
4. You **go grocery shopping** _____
5. You **make a reservation** _____
6. You **make a** doctor's **appointment** _____
7. You **make dinner** _____
8. You **pick up** your younger brother or sister _____
9. You **sweep** _____ to remove dust and dirt.
10. You **vacuum** _____ to remove dust and dirt.

a. at school in the morning.
b. for dinner at a restaurant.
c. after you eat.
d. the floors
e. in the evening.
f. when you feel sick.
g. when your clothes are dirty.
h. the rugs
i. when you have no food in the house.
j. from school in the afternoon.

C Which of the phrases in blue are *chores*? Which are *errands*? Some don't fit in either group.

D Complete the questions with verbs from **B**. Use the correct form of each verb.

1. Do you ever _____ the dishes?
2. When was the last time you _____ dinner for yourself? What did you eat?
3. Who usually _____ the laundry in your house?
4. How often do you _____ the floor or _____ the rug in your bedroom?
5. When was the last time you _____ an appointment for yourself? Who did you see?
6. When you _____ grocery shopping, what's something you always buy?
7. What's your favorite place to eat out? Do you have to _____ a reservation?
8. Do you ever _____ off or _____ up someone at school?

E Take turns asking and answering the questions in **D** with a partner.

Janice Haney, from Greensburg, Kansas (US), is doing laundry. She hangs her clothes outside so "the good old Kansas wind" can dry them.

62 | UNIT 5

LISTENING

A **Listen for gist.** Read the sentences. Then listen to four different phone calls. Circle the correct words to complete each sentence. 🎧31

1. The woman is calling to **make** / **change** a **hotel** / **restaurant** reservation.

2. The man wants to **drop off** / **pick up** his **pants** / **shirts** at the dry cleaner.

3. The man is calling to **make** / **change** an appointment with a **doctor** / **dentist**.

4. The girl needs a ride to **school** / **the doctor's office**.

B What would the speaker say next in each conversation? Listen again and circle your answers. Some items have two correct answers. 🎧31

1. a. Sorry, but the only other time available is 9:00 pm.

   b. Yes, we can add two more people to the reservation.

   c. Sure, no problem. How is 7:30 for you?

2. a. No, tomorrow's better.

   b. Perfect. I'll see you at 5:00.

   c. Okay, I can drop them off later.

3. a. Ten works for me. See you then.

   b. Great. See you tomorrow afternoon.

   c. That doesn't work for me. Do you have anything later?

4. a. OK, I'll see you at school later.

   b. Sure. I'll pick you up in fifteen minutes.

   c. Yes, it is.

C **PRONUNCIATION: Reduced forms of *could you* and *would you*** Listen. Notice the reduced pronunciation of *could you* and *would you* in each question. Then repeat the questions. 🎧32

1. Could you open the window, please?

2. Could you drop me off at school?

3. Would you mind making dinner tonight?

4. Would you pick up your socks from the floor?

D **PRONUNCIATION: Reduced forms of *could you* and *would you*** Listen to the questions. Circle the words you hear. 🎧33

1. **Could you** / **Would you** turn down the TV, please?

2. **Could you** / **Would you** make a dinner reservation for four people?

3. **Could you** / **Would you** spell your last name, please?

4. **Could you** / **Would you** take notes for me in class today?

E With a partner, take turns asking the questions in **C** and **D** with the reduced forms of *could you* and *would you*. Reply to the questions.

> Could you open the window, please?

> Sure! No problem.

> Sorry, but I'm too cold.

SPEAKING

A Listen to the conversation. Then answer the questions with a partner. 🎧34

Martina: Hello, Metro Salon. This is Martina.

Minh: Yeah, hi. I'd like to make an appointment for a haircut on Friday. Is Carlos working that day?

Martina: I can help you with that! Let's see . . . Yes, Carlos is available on Friday. Can you come in at 10:30?

Minh: No, that time isn't good for me. Do you have anything later in the day?

Martina: Let me check. OK, how's 4:15?

Minh: That's perfect.

Martina: Great. Now, I just need to get your name.

Minh: It's Minh Nguyen.

Martina: Could you spell your last name for me, please?

Minh: Sure, it's N-G-U-Y-E-N.

1. Why is Minh calling the salon?
2. When is he planning to go there?

Hairdresser Mario Hvala creates a "hair tattoo" of Lionel Messi for a soccer fan in Serbia.

B Practice the conversation with a partner.

C With a partner, create a new conversation like the one in **A**. Use the situation below and at least two expressions from the Speaking Strategy.

Student A: You want to make an appointment with a student counselor on Tuesday afternoon.

Student B: You work at the student counselor's office. On Tuesday, the counselor is free at 11:30 am. She is also free after 12 pm on Wednesday and Thursday.

SPEAKING STRATEGY 🎧35
Making appointments

I'm calling to . . . / I'd like to . . .
  make an appointment with a counselor /
  Dr. Smith / the dentist.
  make a doctor's / hair appointment.
  reschedule my appointment / our meeting.

Scheduling the time
Can you come in / Could we meet /
How's tomorrow at 2:00?
That's perfect. / That works for me.
No, that (time / day) doesn't work for me.

D Switch roles and repeat with the situation below.

Student A: You and your classmate usually meet on Tuesday to study. You want to reschedule for Wednesday at 1:00, but you can also meet on Friday.

Student B: You can only meet on Thursday or Friday after 1:00.

GRAMMAR

A Read the Unit 5, Lesson A Grammar Reference in the appendix. Complete the exercises. Then do the exercises below.

REQUESTS WITH MODAL VERBS AND *MIND*			
Making requests			**Responding to requests**
Can / Will you **Could / Would** you	help	me, please?	Sure, no problem. / I'd be glad to. / Of course. / Sure thing. Sorry, / I'd like to, but I can't.
Would you **mind**	helping		No, not at all. / No, I'd be glad to. Sorry, / I'd like to, but I can't.

B Complete the conversations with the missing words. Some items have more than one possible answer.

1. **A:** Hey, Jin! (1.) _____ you do me a favor? Would you
   (2.) _____ helping me move this box? It's really heavy.

   B: No, not at (3.) _____!

   A: Great, thanks!

2. **A:** Sura, (4.) _____ you take notes for me in class tomorrow? I have a dental appointment.

   B: Sorry, I'd (5.) _____ to, but I won't be in class tomorrow, either.

   A: No (6.) _____. I'll ask someone else.

C Work with a partner and follow the steps.

1. Take sixteen small pieces of paper. On eight of them, write the numbers 1 to 8. Shuffle these and put them facedown on the desk. Then on four pieces of paper, write the word *Yes*. On the other four, write *No*. Shuffle these and put them facedown in a different pile.

2. Imagine that you and your partner are college roommates. Read the list of activities in the box.

   1. make dinner tonight
   2. take notes for me in class tomorrow
   3. pick up my clothes at the dry cleaner
   4. drop me off at the mall
   5. loan me some money for lunch
   6. be a little quieter after 11:00 pm
   7. do my laundry
   8. introduce me to your cute friend

3. **Student A:** Turn over a number (1–8). Ask your roommate to do this activity from the list. Explain why you need the favor.

4. **Student B:** Turn over a *Yes / No* paper and respond in an appropriate way. Remember, when responding to a *Would you mind . . .?* request, you should say, *No, not at all.* or *No, I'd be glad to.* if you can do what they asked.

5. Switch roles and repeat steps 3 and 4. Take turns and continue until you discuss all eight favors.

D Think about the requests you made in **C**. For any of them, did you use *Would you mind . . .?* Why or why not?

Don't feel like waiting? Hire a *benriya* to stand in line for you.

In Japan, you can hire a *benriya*. This is a person who fixes things, does household chores, and runs errands. A benriya can also help you study, be your travel partner on a trip, or even break up with your boyfriend or girlfriend for you.

ACTIVE ENGLISH Try it out!

A Look at the photo and read the information. What would you pay a *benriya* to do for you?

B Work with a partner and create your own benriya service. Answer the questions.

- What services do you offer (doing housework, running errands, fixing things, etc.)?
- How much do you charge for each service?
- What is your company's name, and when do you work?

C Find a new partner and follow the steps below. Use the example conversation to help you. Then switch roles and repeat.

1. Call your new partner's benriya service.
2. Use your idea from **A**. Explain what you want the service to do for you.
3. Ask what your partner's service charges.
4. Make an appointment with the service.

A: Hello, Handy Helpers Service. How can I help you?

B: Hi. I'd like some information about your service.

A: Sure, what exactly do you need us to do?

B: I want to break up with my boyfriend.

A: No problem! We can do that for you.

B: Great. Could you tell me how much you charge, please?

D Repeat **C** with three other partners. Of the four benriya services you talked to, which is the best? Tell the class.

5A GOALS Now I can . . .

Talk about chores and errands _____

Make appointments and requests _____

1. Yes, I can.
2. Mostly, yes.
3. Not yet.

VOCABULARY

A Read the text and match the words in blue to the definitions (1–7). Then look at the photo. Do you think this a *walkable* area? Why or why not?

> Is your neighborhood **walkable**? In a walkable neighborhood:
>
> a. It's easy to **get around** the city **on foot** because **sidewalks** are in good condition.
>
> b. It's safe for **pedestrians** to cross the street because there isn't a lot of **traffic**.
>
> c. There are **bike lanes** so **cyclists** can ride safely.
>
> d. It's easy to **get to** other parts of the city by bus or subway.

1. easy to walk around: _____ walkable _____

2. special places to walk or cycle: _____, _____

3. people who walk or ride on bikes: _____, _____

4. vehicles (cars, trucks, etc.) on the road: _____

5. to go from place to place in a town or city: _____

6. to travel somewhere: _____

7. by walking: _____

B Ask a partner the questions. Answer in two ways: with *by / on* and with a verb.

1. How do you usually get around your neighborhood?

   66 I usually get around my neighborhood by car.

2. How do you get to school or work?

   66 I usually drive.

3. How do you go to other towns or cities?

WORD BANK
Describing ways of going places

by / on		verbs
	bike	(ride my) bike
by	bus / subway	take the bus / subway
	car	drive
	taxi	take a taxi
	train	take / catch a train
on	foot	walk

Cyclists ride their bikes on Avenida Vieira Souto, a busy street with bike lanes and wide sidewalks in the Ipanema neighborhood of Rio de Janeiro, Brazil.

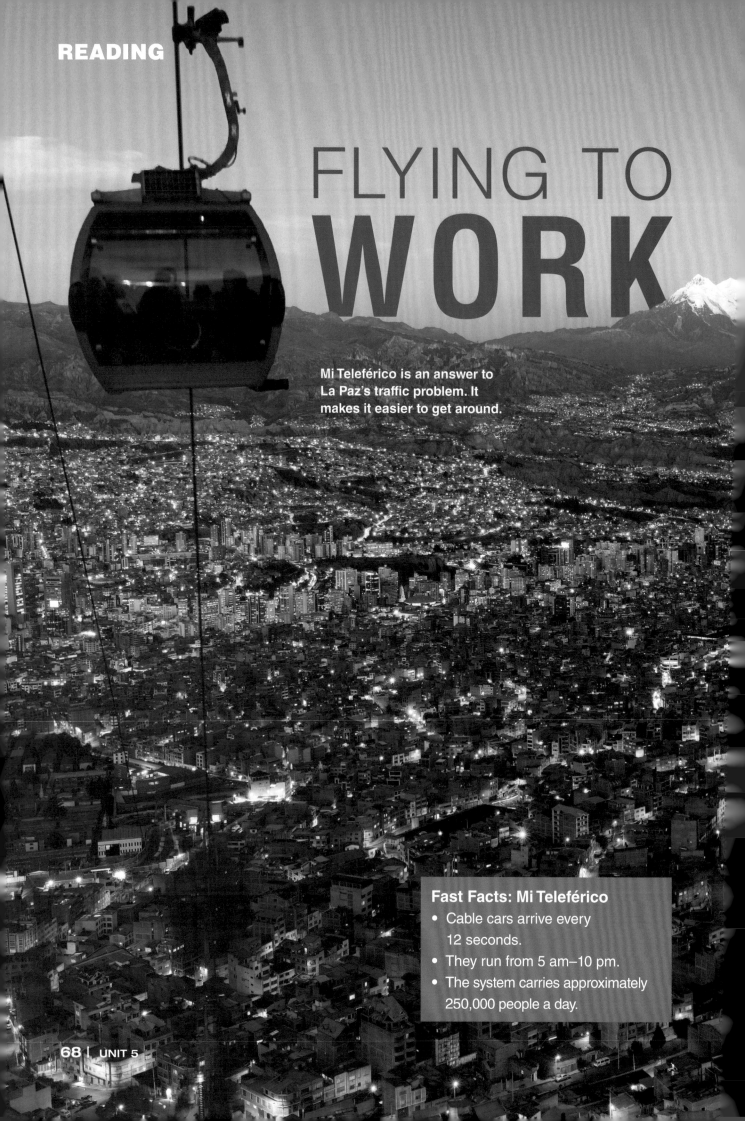

FLYING TO WORK

Mi Teleférico is an answer to La Paz's traffic problem. It makes it easier to get around.

Fast Facts: Mi Teleférico
- Cable cars arrive every 12 seconds.
- They run from 5 am–10 pm.
- The system carries approximately 250,000 people a day.

La Paz, in Bolivia, is a city that is nearly 12,000 feet (3,650 m) above sea level. The streets are steep, and getting around on foot can be challenging. It also has heavy traffic that moves slowly, so it isn't a very walkable city.

Near La Paz is the city of El Alto, 13,615 feet (4,150 m) above sea level. Every day, people take the bus between the two cities. It costs five bolivianos (about fifteen cents) and takes about an hour. The buses run frequently, but they are crowded. So the daily commute by bus can be a frustrating experience.

Now there's another way to travel from El Alto to La Paz. You can catch a ride on Mi Teleférico, La Paz's high-altitude[1] cable car system. For only three bolivianos, you can float[2] above the city, watching as one neighborhood changes to the next. After a peaceful ride in the high-tech car with eight or nine other passengers, you reach La Paz in ten to fifteen minutes.

Mi Teleférico is not like other transportation systems. First, it is very popular, so it doesn't need any money from the city. It pays for itself. Second, Doppelmayr, an Austrian company that usually builds cable car systems for ski resorts, built the system in La Paz without destroying[3] a lot of homes or green spaces. It was much easier than building a subway or train system.

Thanks to Mi Teleférico, locals now enjoy an easier commute to school or work. Tourists use it to visit difficult-to-reach areas of the city. Everyone is happy to have this new and convenient way to get around the city.

[1] The **altitude** of an object is its height (above sea level).
[2] To **float** is to move easily on water or through air.
[3] **Destroying** means ending something by damaging it; for example, knocking down a house or building.

A Answer the questions in pairs.

1. How long is your daily commute to work or school?
2. What kind of transportation system do you use (for example, a bus or train)?
3. How many passengers does it carry?

B Read the article and the Fast Facts box on the left. Answer each question about both the bus and cable car systems. If the information isn't given, write *DK* (don't know).

1. How much does it cost?
2. How long does it take from La Paz to El Alto?
3. How often does it run?
4. How many people ride it each day?

C Read the article again and circle the adjectives described below. Look up any words you don't know.

1. In paragraph 1, words that describe La Paz (the streets, the traffic, getting around)
2. In paragraph 2, words that describe bus rides
3. In paragraph 3, words that describe cable car rides

D Why did the city of La Paz build a cable car system? Write two or three sentences in your notebook. Use at least three adjectives from **C** in your answer. Then tell a partner.

E Answer the questions in pairs.

1. How is building a cable car system different than building a subway?
2. What type of cable car systems does Doppelmayr usually build?
3. Who uses Mi Teleférico?

F **Think critically.** Compare the buses and cable cars, using the information from **B**. Which system do you think is better?

❝ The buses are more expensive than . . .

Because of this, I think the . . . are better. ❞

LISTENING

A Where is the neighborhood in the photo? What do you think it's like? Tell a partner.

B Listen to a podcast about Hongdae and check (✓) the two main ideas. 🎧37

☐ a. Hongdae is very walkable and easy to get to.

☐ b. The neighborhood of Hongdae has a lot of problems.

☐ c. Being a student at Hongik University is great.

☐ d. You can do a lot of different things in Hongdae.

C **Infer meaning.** Read the sentences and listen again. Circle the correct answer. 🎧37

1. Hongdae **has** / **doesn't have** many places to shop and eat.

2. The area **is** / **isn't** easy to get to by bike.

3. It's best to go to Hongdae **by car** / **on public transportation**.

4. Hongdae **is** / **isn't** easy to get around on foot.

5. There **are** / **aren't** a lot of things to see in Hongdae.

6. You **need** / **don't need** to bring your own food to Hongdae.

> **ACADEMIC SKILL**
>
> **Listening for words connected to a topic**
>
> In listening tests, the words you hear in the recording are rarely the same words used in the questions. Read the questions first; then listen for words connected to the topic of the question. For example, in the first item in **C**, *places to shop and eat* means the *stores, restaurants, and clubs* discussed in the listening.

D **Identify key details.** What information helped you choose your answers in **C**? Listen one more time and write the words you hear. 🎧37

1. ". . . a neighborhood that has lots of _____, _____, and clubs . . ."

2. ". . . there aren't many _____ for cyclists, so I'd definitely take the _____ or a _____."

3. "Once you arrive, you _____ get around on foot. It's very _____."

4. "It's a _____ place to see _____ of art and street performers."

5. "You might not know what everything is, but you should _____ of it!"

E What is one of your favorite places in your town or city? What is it like? How do you get there? Tell a partner.

A busy street in the Hongdae neighborhood of Seoul, South Korea

GRAMMAR

A Compare sentences 1 and 2 with sentence 3. How does the writer join the sentences?

1. La Paz is a city.

2. La Paz is nearly 12,000 feet (3,650 m) above sea level.

3. La Paz is a city that is nearly 12,000 feet (3,650 m) above sea level.

B Read the Unit 5, Lesson B Grammar Reference in the appendix. Complete the exercises. Then do the exercises below.

SUBJECT RELATIVE CLAUSES WITH *THAT*		
La Paz has heavy traffic		moves slowly.
Doppelmayr usually builds cable car systems	**that**	don't affect nature.
Mi Teleférico is a transportation system		pays for itself.

C Read the clues and underline the subject relative clauses. Then work in pairs to complete the crossword puzzle with the words from the box.

chores	cyclists	neighbor	taxi
commute	get	subway	~~traffic~~

Across:

1. It's all the vehicles <u>that are on the roads</u>.

2. They are people that ride bikes.

3. It's the person that lives next to you.

4. It's a type of train that travels underground.

Down:

5. It's a car that takes you around town quickly.

6. It's a regular trip that goes from your home to work or school.

7. They are jobs that are around the house.

8. It's a verb that goes before *to* or *around*.

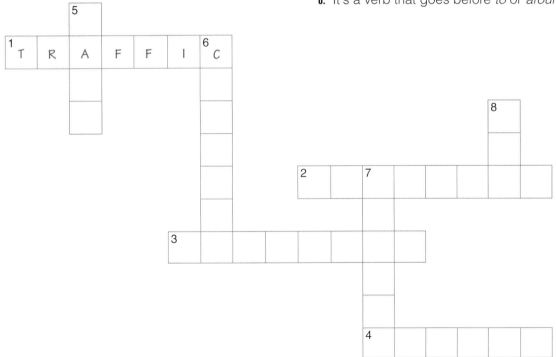

D Work in pairs and write five similar clues for different objects, places, or people, using subject relative clauses. Then join another pair and read your clues. Can they guess the answers?

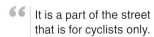

66 It is a part of the street that is for cyclists only.

Is it a bike lane? 99

ACTIVE ENGLISH Try it out!

A Work in pairs and follow the steps below.

Student A: Close your book. Student B is going to read different prompts and you have to say a word or phrase for each one; for example, if Student B says *verb*, you could say a verb like *go* or *get to*. If Student B says *length of time*, you could say *five minutes* or *ten hours*.

Student B: Read the prompts (1–10) to Student A and write down the words they give you. For example, if you say *verb*, Student A might say *go* or *get to*.

1. Name of a city: _____
2. Adjective: _____
3. Type of transportation: _____
4. Another type of transportation: _____
5. Adjective: _____

6. Places to go in a city: _____
7. Length of time: _____
8. Adjective: _____
9. Verb: _____
10. Opposite of *busy* or *noisy*: _____

B Now repeat the activity in **A** but switch roles. (Student A reads items 1–10 and Student B provides the words.)

C Put your partner's ten new words into this description and read it to your partner.

I live in a city called (1.) _____. I like living here for three reasons. First, my neighborhood is (2.) _____ because it's easy to get around by (3.) _____. I can go anywhere in the city, and I don't need a / an (4.) _____. It is also a very (5.) _____ neighborhood that has a lot of (6.) _____. I can walk to the supermarket or my favorite cafe in (7.) _____. There's also a / an (8.) _____ park that's a great place to (9.) _____ with friends. And finally, I live on a busy street that's noisy during the day, but at night it's (10.) _____; I like that.

D Which of your partner's words sound natural in the description? Which words would you change?

E **WRITING** Using the paragraph in **C** as an example, write a description of your neighborhood, town, city, or a place you know well. Include these four items:

- reasons why you like it
- information about transportation, places to go, ways to relax
- a lot of different adjectives
- at least one subject relative clause

USEFUL EXPRESSIONS

I like living here because . . . / for three reasons . . .
First, . . . / It's also . . . / There's also . . . / And finally, . . .
It's a place / city / neighborhood that has . . .
I live on a street / in a neighborhood that . . .
It's convenient / walkable / quiet / busy.
It's easier to get around by . . . than by . . .
There's a . . . that's a great place to . . .

F Exchange descriptions with a partner and read his or her paragraph. Does it include the four items in **E**?

5B GOALS Now I can . . .

Compare ways of getting around _____

Describe my neighborhood _____

1. Yes, I can.
2. Mostly, yes.
3. Not yet.

GLOBAL VOICES

A Watch a video about neighborhoods in the capital city of Lima, Peru. Check (✓) what you can do in each neighborhood. Check some answers more than once.

	Downtown Lima	Barranco	Miraflores
1. Meet friends in Plaza San Martín.			
2. Visit the Bridge of Sighs.			
3. Visit historic buildings and museums.			
4. See government buildings.			
5. See street art.			
6. Eat out.			

WORD BANK
A **magical** place is beautiful and very different from normal places.
A **bohemian** neighborhood looks artistic and unique.

B Read the sentences from the video and guess the missing adjectives. Then watch the video again and check your answers.

1. "You should visit Lima downtown because it's a h<u>istoric</u> district here."

2. "You should go to Lima downtown because it's a m_____ place."

3. "Downtown Lima is a beautiful and w_____ area that is very important . . ."

4. "You can see the statue of José de San Martín and visit the f_____ Hotel Bolívar."

5. "There are a number of i_____ government buildings . . ."

6. "You can go to have some drinks or food. They have d_____ food."

7. "In the evening . . . you will see a l_____ sunset."

8. "If you're planning to visit a p_____ restaurant, remember to make a reservation!"

9. "The beaches of Punta Hermosa . . . are w_____ k_____ for surfing."

10. "Lima is a city with so many w_____ neighborhoods to explore."

C In pairs, role-play a conversation between a tour guide (Student A) and a tourist (Student B) in Lima. Watch the video again with the sound off. Student A will describe the different places around Lima that you can see. Student B can ask questions about the different places. About halfway through the video, switch roles. You can use words from the video and the phrases below.

Tour guide:
Welcome to this tour of Lima!
At the moment, we're standing in . . .
This is a / an . . . neighborhood . . .
Look at the . . .
This area is famous / popular for its . . .
You can eat / see / visit . . .

Tourist:
What are we looking at now?
What's this neighborhood famous for?
Is that an important building?
Is this area very walkable / popular?
What is there to do here?
Are there any good restaurants near here?

El Malecón, a walkway that goes through the Barranco and Miraflores neighborhoods of Lima, has beautiful views of the ocean.

GOALS

Lesson A

/ Discuss future plans and decisions

/ Respond to bad news and offer help

Lesson B

/ Describe educational and work goals

/ Make predictions about the future

People work together in the offices of Barbarian, an advertising company in New York City, US.

6

GOALS

LOOK AT THE PHOTO. ANSWER THE QUESTIONS.

1. How would you describe this workplace?
2. Would you like to work in a place like this? Why or why not?

WARM-UP VIDEO

A What will you do (or did you do) after leaving school? Tell a partner.

B You are going to watch a video showing different choices after high school in the US. Match the goals to the three types of schools.

_____ 1. Improve your school grades.

_____ 2. Learn new skills.

_____ 3. Get a bachelor's degree.

a. four-year college (or university)

b. two-year community college

c. technical or trade schools

C Watch the video again and answer the questions.

1. What are three reasons for getting a bachelor's degree?

2. What can a two-year college give you some time to do?

3. When can you use the skills you learn at a technical or trade school?

4. What do you need to know for whatever school you choose? Why?

D Discuss the questions in groups.

1. What do you call "high school" in your country? When do students usually finish?

2. What types of schools can you choose from afterward?

3. What are the differences between the choices?

VOCABULARY

A Read the information about applying to colleges in the US. Complete the words using the correct word form (verb or noun) from the Word Bank.

If you (1.) pl_____ to go to college after high school, there are a lot of great choices out there. If you do your research well, you'll be fine! Make the right (2.) ch_____ by following these instructions:

- Look at different college websites. (3.) Co_____ questions like: Where is the school located? How big are the classes?

- If you (4.) in_____ to visit a school, (5.) ar_____ a time to watch some classes and meet some of the students. Find out what they think.

- Ask your high school teachers to write letters of (6.) re_____ for you.

- Decide which schools to apply to and send your (7.) ap_____s in on time.

- Most schools will give you their (8.) de_____ within a few months.

Good luck!

WORD BANK	
verb	**noun**
apply (to)	application
arrange	arrangement
choose	choice
consider (doing)	consideration
decide (to do)	decision
intend (to do)	intention
plan (to do)	plan
recommend (doing something)	recommendation

B Review the steps in **A** with a partner. How is applying to college different in your country? How is it similar?

C Read three messages from an online forum about college. What does each person hope to do? What advice would you give each person? Discuss in small groups.

Difficult College Decisions

Kento
My parents want me to apply to Tokyo University. It's one of the best, but I'm not sure I want to go to college right now. I'd like to travel.

Margarita
All my friends intend to go to college, but I hope to become a chef. So I need to decide between applying to a community college and learning on the job.

Paulo
I didn't get the grades I need for my top-choice school. I could consider a different college, or I could take my exams again.

❝ He intends to . . .

❝ He doesn't have to apply to . . .

She should consider . . . ❞

There are other choices . . . ❞

LISTENING

A You're going to hear a podcast about an unusual school. How do you think Green School Bali is special? Look at the photo and the profile below and guess.

B **Listen for details.** Listen to the podcast and complete the profile. 🎧38

> ### Green School Bali
>
> **The students:** The school has over (1.) _____ students of all ages including early years (ages 3–6), primary (ages 7–11), middle (ages 11–14), and (2.) _____ school (ages 14–18).
>
> **Location:** On the (3.) _____ of Bali, in Indonesia
>
> **Classrooms:** Made from bamboo and close to (4.) _____
>
> **Subjects and lessons:** These include mathematics, reading, science, and "green (5.) _____."

WORD BANK
environmental relating to the natural world
mission a goal or a task that a person or group of people work on

C Listen again and answer the questions. 🎧38
1. What type of person is the podcast for?
2. What plans and decisions are these people making?
3. What kind of fuel does the school bus use at Green School Bali?
4. Do the lessons always take place inside a classroom?
5. Where does the food come from for school lunches?
6. What is Wayan's Greenstone project going to be about?
7. What type of mission does the school have?

D In pairs, compare Green School Bali to the school you currently attend or a school you went to in the past. Tell your partner about any similarities and any differences.

High school students at Green School Bali study in one of the bamboo classrooms.

SPEAKING

A Listen to the conversation and answer the questions with a partner. 🎧39

Kai: Hey, Li. How's it going with the grad school applications?

Li: Not so great. I didn't get into Tsinghua University.

Kai: Oh, no! I'm sorry to hear that.

Li: Yeah, and it was my first choice.

Kai: You must be disappointed. What are you going to do instead?

Li: Well, I applied to one other school, but I'm waiting to hear back from them.

Kai: I'm sure you'll get in.

Li: Thanks. If not, I'll take a gap year and apply again next year.

Kai: Well, good luck. And if you want to talk, just call me.

Li: Thanks, Kai. I really appreciate it.

1. Li is unhappy about something. What?

2. How does Kai respond to Li's bad news? Underline Kai's responses.

3. Do you think Kai is a good friend? Why or why not?

Tsinghua University, located in Beijing, China, is one of the top universities in the country.

B Practice the conversation with a partner.

C Do the role play below with a partner. Practice responding to bad news and offering to help. Use the Speaking Strategy and the conversation in **A** to help you.

Student A: You just received an exam back. You didn't fail the test, but your grade is much lower than expected.

Student B: Respond to Student A's news and offer to help.

D Switch roles and do the role play again.

GRAMMAR

A Read the Unit 6, Lesson A Grammar Reference in the appendix. Complete the exercises. Then do the exercises below.

PLANS AND DECISIONS WITH *BE GOING TO* AND *WILL*		
Plans	I'm going to study science in college. I'm not going to apply to school next year.	
Decisions	A: Oh, no, I forgot my wallet! B: Don't worry! I'll pay for lunch. A: We're having a surprise party for Mark. B: OK, I won't say anything to him!	
Question forms with *be going to*		
Yes / No questions	Are you going to study science?	Yes, I am. / Maybe. No, I'm not.
Wh- questions	What are you going to do after graduation?	I'm going to take a gap year.

B Circle the best answer to complete each conversation.

1. **A:** What are your plans for tonight?

   B: **I'll** / **I'm going to** study.

2. **A:** We need your application by 5:00 pm today.

   B: Sorry, I didn't know that! **I'll** / **I'm going to** do it right now.

3. **A:** When's your interview tomorrow?

   B: **It'll** / **It's going to** start at 9:00 am.

4. **A:** Oh, no! I just spilled water all over the floor.

   B: Don't worry! **I'll** / **I'm going to** get some towels.

5. **A:** What are your plans for this afternoon?

   B: **I'll** / **I'm going to** do some homework.

6. **A:** Who's writing your letter of recommendation?

   B: Hmm, I'm not sure . . . Oh, I know! **I'll** / **I'm going to** ask Mr. Stuart, my math teacher.

C PRONUNCIATION: Reduced forms of *going to* and *will* Listen and check your answers in **B**. Notice how the speaker pronounces *going to* and *will* in the sentences. Then, in pairs, practice reading the conversations in **B** aloud. 🎧41

D Imagine you can go to any school in the world. Choose a school and complete the sentences.

1. I'm going to apply to _____ school(s).
   (number)
2. I'm going to go to _____.
   (name of school)
3. I'm going to live at / in _____.
   (home / a dorm room / an apartment)
4. I'm going to study _____.
   (name of major)

5. I'm going to graduate in _____ years.
   (number)
6. After graduation, I'm going to become _____.
   (a / an + job)

E Ask questions to get a partner's answers to **D**. On a piece of paper, write six questions with *be going to* or *will* and the question words below. Take turns asking and answering the questions.

1. How many . . .?
2. Where . . .?
3. Where . . .?
4. What . . .?
5. When . . .?
6. What . . .?

ACTIVE ENGLISH Try it out!

A Read the questions on the left side of the chart. In the *Me* column, check (✓) the activities you're planning to do in the future. Then add your own question at the bottom.

Are you going to . . .	Me	Classmate's name	*Wh-* Question	Answer
graduate from high school or college soon?			When . . .?	
take a trip somewhere this summer?			Where...?	
go out this weekend?			Who . . .?	
study after class today?			What . . .?	
take a test in English (like the TOEFL or IELTS) soon?			Which . . .?	
keep studying English after this class?			Where . . .?	
_____?				

B Interview your classmates. For each question, find a different person who answers *Yes*. Write the classmate's name in the chart above. Then ask a *Wh-* question to get more details and write down their response.

❝ Are you going to take a trip somewhere this summer?

Yes, I am. ❞

❝ Where are you going to go?

To the beach. ❞

C Look at the answers you got above. Which one was the most interesting? Tell the class.

D Work in pairs and look at your plans again in **A**. Imagine you receive some bad news, so you aren't going to do one of these things. Complete the steps below.

1. Tell your partner the bad news.

2. Your partner responds and offers help.

3. Make a decision about what you'll do next. Then switch roles and repeat the steps.

6A GOALS   Now I can . . .

Discuss future plans and decisions _____

Respond to bad news and offer help _____

1. Yes, I can.
2. Mostly, yes.
3. Not yet.

VOCABULARY

A The people below are college seniors or recent graduates. Take turns reading their plans aloud with a partner.

"I want to **do an internship** this summer. At some point before then, I have to **create a resume**." —Linh

"I'm going to **take time off** in the near future, maybe after graduation, and go on vacation." —Martina

"I'm working now, but eventually, I'd like to **go back to school** and get my PhD." —Roberto

"Someday, I'd like the **opportunity** to set up a company and **be my own boss**, but not yet. I have a lot to learn still." —Simon

WORD BANK

Definite future time
after graduation
in a month
next year
this summer

Indefinite future time
soon
in a few days / weeks
in the near future
at some point
someday / eventually

B Look at the blue expressions in **A**. Answer the questions. Then tell a partner.

Which person . . .

1. wants to return to school? _____

2. wants to get some work experience over the summer? _____

3. would like to work for himself / herself? _____

4. is planning not to work or study for a short time? _____

5. needs to create a summary of his / her education and job experience? _____

6. wants the chance to start a business? _____

C When do the people in **A** want to do these things? Do they give a definite future time or not? Tell a partner.

D Look again at the blue expressions in **A**. Do you want to do any of these things? If so, when? Use the future time expressions to tell a partner.

Fousseyni Djikine, originally from Mali, is his own boss at BMK, a popular restaurant that he opened in Paris, France.

LIFE'S ESSENTIAL
QUESTIONS

Wait, what?
In this question, *wait* reminds us to stop and think. Before we make an important decision, we need to understand the situation fully.

How can I help?
When someone needs help, it's good to ask, *How can I help?* Then the other person can give you a specific answer, and you will be more useful.

What truly matters?
Sometimes it's hard to make a decision. When this happens, it helps to ask yourself: *What is most important?*

Students cheer during a Harvard University graduation ceremony in Cambridge, Massachusetts (US).

In a Harvard University graduation speech, speaker James Ryan talked about "life's essential questions." By asking these simple but important questions, we can make better choices in our lives. We can help others, too, Ryan believes. But how can these questions actually help us in our everyday lives? Here is one example:

Imagine. It's the summer after graduation, and you're doing an interesting internship at a company you like. The only problem is the internship is part time and unpaid. But, after a month of working hard, your boss offers you a full-time job. You are excited about the opportunity until your boss tells you the starting pay. You stop and think, ***Wait, what?*** The pay is very low. You really want the job, but you wonder, *How will I support myself?*[1] It won't be easy.

Your boss gives you a few days to think over the offer, so you talk to a friend about it. You tell your friend you're not sure whether you should accept the low pay or quit and apply for other jobs. You're even considering taking some time off to do something else, like travel. Your friend listens and asks, ***How can I help?***

You ask your friend for some advice and she suggests that first you ask your boss for higher pay. However, if the company can't pay more, she says that you should ask yourself, **What truly matters?** *What is most important right now: the money or the opportunity to work for this company? How will your choice help you in the future?* You thank your friend and smile because you know that with the help of "life's essential questions," you'll make the right decision.

[1] *If you **support yourself**, you make your own money and live on your own.*

A Read the title of the article. What do you think is one of "life's essential questions"? Tell the class.

B Read about the three essential questions in the box below the title. Then match each question (1–3) with its purpose (a–d). One purpose is extra.

_____ 1. Wait, what?

_____ 2. How can I help?

_____ 3. What truly matters?

a. to help you make a difficult choice

b. to be sure you understand something well

c. to ask why something is true

d. to offer useful assistance

C Read the whole article. Then circle **T** for *true* or **F** for *false*. Correct the false statements.

1. James Ryan was a speaker at the University of Massachusetts.　　**T**　**F**

2. In the article, you were offered a full-time job after four weeks at an internship.　　**T**　**F**

3. You are excited about the starting pay.　　**T**　**F**

4. Your friend says you should ask for higher pay.　　**T**　**F**

5. Asking the question *What truly matters?* helps you make a hard decision.　　**T**　**F**

D With a partner, take turns answering the questions to retell the story.

ACADEMIC SKILL

Retelling

Retelling a story helps you remember the main points and check your understanding.

1. What happened after a month at your internship? Was this a good thing or bad thing? Why?

2. What choices did you consider after you got the job offer?

3. What was your friend's advice? Was it helpful?

E Imagine you are going to respond to your boss about the job offer. In pairs, role-play a conversation between you and your boss. Use ideas from the reading and some of your own, too. Switch roles and do the role play again.

LISTENING

A **Listen for gist.** You are going to hear three different conversations. In each, which sentence is true? Listen and circle the best answer. 🎧43

1. a. She's going to graduate soon.
   b. She is applying to graduate school.
   c. She just got accepted to a good school.

2. a. She's working on her resume.
   b. She's going to be her own boss.
   c. She just got a summer internship.

3. a. She wants to take time off from college.
   b. She's planning to do an internship.
   c. She wants to change her major.

B **Listen for details.** Read the sentences below. Then listen again. Write one word in each blank and circle the correct answers. 🎧43

Conversation 1

1. The woman wants to get a degree in _____.

2. She's planning to go **this July** / **in the spring**.

Conversation 2

3. The internship is _____.

4. She hopes to make money **at some point** / **right away**.

Conversation 3

5. The woman wants to _____ in New York.

6. She plans to do this **after graduation** / **in the near future**.

7. She **will** / **won't** return to regular classes in September.

> **WORD BANK**
> A **paid position** is a job in which you make money.
>
> A school year is divided into **terms** (for example, the spring and fall terms).

C What are the women in each conversation doing or planning to do? Do you know anyone who did any of these things? Tell a partner.

> 66 | The third woman wants to . . . My older brother is doing that now.

Many people move to big cities such as New York after graduation.

GRAMMAR

A Read the Unit 6, Lesson B Grammar Reference in the appendix. Complete the exercises. Then do the exercises below.

PREDICTIONS WITH *BE GOING TO* AND *WILL*
She**'s going to** / She **will** be very successful. Some students **aren't going to** / **won't** pass the exam.
He <u>definitely</u> **won't** study history in college. He**'ll** <u>probably</u> study business. <u>Maybe</u> he**'ll** study economics, too.
Is she **going to** / **Will** she go to graduate school? <u>Maybe</u>. / <u>Probably not</u>.

B Read the text and underline examples of *be going to* and *will*.

A Robot for a Teacher

In a primary school in Finland, the teachers have a new assistant. His name is Elias, and he's a robot. Elias speaks 23 languages, and he's going to help the students with their language learning. The teachers also think Elias will motivate the children.

But are the teachers worried about their jobs? Will robots like Elias replace them in the future? Probably not. Robots can help with subjects like languages and mathematics, but they definitely won't be able to manage a classroom of young students!

C Circle the correct words to complete the sentences about the text in **B**. In one sentence, both answers are possible.

1. Elias **will** / **won't** help the students with language learning.

2. The children **are going to** / **will** be more interested in learning because of Elias.

3. In the future, robots **will probably** / **probably won't** replace teachers.

4. Robots **are** / **aren't** going to manage classrooms in the future.

D What's your opinion? Will robots do more teaching in the future? What else do you think robots are going to do in the future? Tell the class.

E Work in pairs and write three predictions about your partner's future using *be going to* and *will*. You can write sentences about his / her future education, job, home, or travel experiences. Then take turns reading your predictions to each other. Do you think your partner's predictions will come true?

❝ I think you'll probably study biology and become a doctor.

I probably won't. I'm not interested in science! ❞

The Universidad Nacional Autónoma de México (UNAM) campus in Mexico City, Mexico

ACTIVE ENGLISH Try it out!

A Did you ever write a personal profile on . . .

- social media?
- a school application?
- a website?
- a job application or resume?
- anywhere else?

What information did you include? Tell the class.

> **i** A personal profile is a short summary (about 100–150 words) of your life. It might include information about your school / work experience, your abilities, where you live, your interests, goals, etc.

B Turn to the Unit 6 Writing appendix to read an example personal profile. Take notes on the information below in your notebook.

1. Miguel's school
2. major / subject
3. work experience
4. school activities
5. other abilities / interests
6. future plans and goals

C You are going to write a personal profile for a partner. Interview him / her and ask for the information in 1–6 in **B**. Take notes.

66 Are you in school now? Where?

66 Do you have any work experience?

66 What are you studying?

USEFUL EXPRESSIONS
I'm a student / employee at . . .
I am going to graduate / I graduated with . . .
Last year, I did an internship / got a job at . . .
I studied / worked with . . .
In addition, . . . / I also like . . .
After graduation / leaving school, I'm going to . . .
I intend to / plan to / hope to . . .

D **WRITING** Using your notes from **C**, write a personal profile for your partner. Use *I* and *my* in your writing.

E Exchange profiles with your partner and read his or her profile about you. Circle any information that is incorrect or incomplete and make changes to the profile if necessary.

6B GOALS   Now I can . . .

Describe educational and work goals _____

Make predictions about the future _____

1. Yes, I can.
2. Mostly, yes.
3. Not yet.

GLOBAL VOICES

A Watch a video about achieving your goals. Match the three people with their present and future goals (a–e). Some items will have more than one correct answer.

1. Ricardo _____   2. Pedro _____   3. Maite _____

    a. To do a master's degree in a foreign country

    b. To take care of the environment

    c. To start a new business

    d. To find financial support to make a movie

    e. To work in a design studio for a few more years

> **WORD BANK**
> **achieve your dreams**
> reach your goals
> **face challenges** deal
> with difficult problems
> **financial support**
> when someone helps
> you by giving or lending
> you money
> **overcome** deal with
> and get past something
> difficult

B Complete the sentences from the video with the missing verbs. Then watch the video again and check your answers.

achieve	become	do	face	get	learn	make	overcome

1. "A lot of us have career goals and plans for the future. The problem is knowing how to _____ started."

2. "He's getting some real work experience before he goes back to school to _____ his dream of making movies."

3. "Someday, I would like to _____ a famous Hollywood photographer . . ."

4. "What challenges do Pedro and Maite think they will _____ in the future?"

5. ". . . you need a lot of money to _____ a movie, a lot of time, teamwork, and sacrifices."

6. "First, decide what you want and _____ your research."

7. ". . . get some work experience and _____ on the job."

8. "Finally, identify the challenges and be prepared to _____ them with some hard work."

C Work in pairs and interview each other about your goals and dreams with the questions below.

1. What are your career goals and dreams?

2. How can you do more research about them?

3. How can you get started?

4. Are you going to go back to school in the future? Or are you going to get work experience and learn on the job?

5. What challenges will you face in the future?

6. How will you overcome the challenges and achieve your dreams?

One of Pedro's goals is to win an Oscar someday. The Oscars are famous awards for filmmakers and actors.

REAL WORLD LINK DESIGN A SURVEY

Residents of Vancouver, Canada have easy access to nature with the 405-hectare (1,000-acre) Stanley Park located right outside the city.

FUTURE CITIES SURVEY RESULTS

What do young people today want their future cities to look like? What types of neighborhoods do they hope to live and work in someday? According to one new survey of young people (ages 18–35), only 12% intend to live in cities with more than one million people. It was a survey of 5,624 young people from different European countries. Here are some of the key results.

Question 1: What will be most important for you to live near?

In the survey, young people chose two items from a list of choices; the graph shows the percentage of people that chose each item. Most of them plan to live in neighborhoods near their friends and family, their work, and—interestingly—nature.

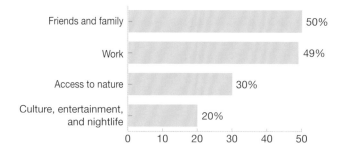

Question 2: Which type of transportation do you prefer for getting to work / school?

The most common answers were going by car, taking public transportation, riding a bike, and going on foot.

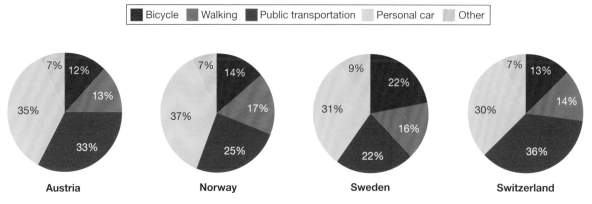

UNITS 4–6

Question 3: Does your city have enough green spaces?
More than half of the young people in the survey think their city has enough green spaces, but many young people also think future cities will need more.

Country	Percentage of people that think their city has enough green spaces
Austria	55
Norway	57
Sweden	58
Switzerland	52

A A survey is an activity in which many people are asked the same question(s) to get information about what they think or do. Read the survey results and circle the correct word in each sentence.

1. In the future, **less / more** than 10% of the young people in the survey plan to live in cities of over one million.

2. **Exactly / Approximately** half of young people in the survey want to live in neighborhoods near their friends and family.

3. **Over / About** a third hope to live somewhere with access to nature.

4. **Exactly / Nearly** a quarter of the young people from Sweden prefer to get around by bicycle.

5. **Over / Under** half of the young people in Switzerland think their city has enough green spaces.

B Work in groups and answer the three questions from the survey. Are your answers similar to the survey results? Why or why not?

C **You Choose** In your groups, you will prepare a survey about life in the future. Follow the steps.

1. Choose one of these topics to research:

   • Shopping in the future   • Education in the future   • Transportation in the future

2. Write five questions for your survey. Then, as a group, choose one of the options for giving your survey to the rest of the class.

   Option 1: Make copies of the questions on paper and hand out the survey to everyone in the class.

   Option 2: Put your survey online and ask your classmates to fill it out online.

   Option 3: Interview each person individually and write down their answers.

   " Do you think people will . . . ?

   " Are you going to . . . ?

   " What will be the most important . . . ?

D In your groups, study the results from your survey and prepare a group presentation for the rest of the class. If possible, show slides or a poster of the results.

USEFUL EXPRESSIONS
We'd like to present the results of our survey.
The topic of the survey was . . .
Question 1 was . . . and here are the results.
As you can see from the slide / chart / graph, . . .
Most people think . . .
Half of us will . . .
None of us are going to . . .
Thank you for listening to our presentation.
Do you have any questions?

E Take turns giving your presentations to the class. When you are listening, ask questions and make comments at the end.

" Thanks for your presentation. I have a question . . .

It's really interesting that most people . . . "

89

CELEBRATIONS

7

LOOK AT THE PHOTO. ANSWER THE QUESTIONS.

1. What is this festival? How are people celebrating?

2. Do you know of a similar festival in your country or another country? If yes, what happens?

WARM-UP VIDEO

A Watch the video. What important sporting event are the people watching?

> **WORD BANK**
> **Fans** are people who enjoy something (for example, a sport or a team).
> An **inspiration** is something or someone that makes a person want to do something.
> If you watch a game **live**, you watch it in person or at the time it happens.

B Read the questions and guess the answers. Then watch again and check your answers.

1. How do most fans watch big sporting events?

2. How do "a few lucky ones" watch the game?

3. What happens when one team wins?

4. When a favorite team wins an important game, why do people feel happy?

5. When the team scores a point, what do the fans do?

C Answer the questions in pairs.

1. What was the last sporting event you watched? How did you watch it? Who won?

2. Are you a fan of any team? If yes, which one?

3. When you watch your team play, do you get emotional (do you yell or jump up and down)?

Thousands of dancers in handmade costumes parade through the streets during the Carnival of Oruro, a cultural and religious festival in Oruro, Bolivia.

GOALS

Lesson A
/ Make and respond to invitations
/ Agree with someone

Lesson B
/ Talk about parties, festivals, and holidays
/ Describe what people do on those days

7A PARTIES

Celebrations begin on the field at the end of a Super Bowl game in East Rutherford, New Jersey (US).

VOCABULARY

A What do you know about an event called the Super Bowl? Take the quiz and find out! Compare your answers with a partner's. Then check your answers at the bottom of the page.

1. The Super Bowl is the championship game for **American football** / **soccer** in the US.
2. It is currently held on the first **Monday** / **Sunday** in February.
3. More than **two hundred million** / **one hundred million** people watch it every year.
4. Not all of the viewers are football fans. Many watch to see the **commercials** / **fireworks**.
5. There is a big halftime show with famous **athletes** / **singers**.

B Read the information about how people celebrate the Super Bowl. Then match five of the words in blue to the definitions below. One item has more than one possible answer.

Many people **celebrate** the day by **throwing a party**. They **invite** friends to come to their home. Everyone **gets together** in the afternoon, and the game begins in the late afternoon or early evening.

Having your own Super Bowl **party**? Here is some advice on how to **plan** one:

* **Decorate** your home or bake a cake with the teams' colors.
* Play games. Have your **guests** try to guess the final score of the game.
* Buy plenty of "finger foods"—like chips and salsa—for the **occasion**.
* Don't forget to **have a good time**!

> **WORD BANK**
> attend / go to /
> host / organize a party

   a. do something special and fun for an important event or holiday: _____
   b. to meet and do something fun with other people: _____
   c. to make something look nice for a special occasion: _____
   d. an important time or celebration: _____
   e. the people you invite to your party: _____

C Complete the questions with words in blue from **B**. Then ask and answer the questions in pairs.

1. When do people usually t_____ a party in your country?
2. What is one special day that you c_____ and p_____ a party for?
3. Who do you normally i_____ and get t_____ with?
4. How do you d_____ your home?
5. What food do you serve to your g _____ for the o _____?

1. American football 2. Sunday 3. one hundred million 4. commercials 5. singers

LISTENING

A **Listen for gist.** Two people are going to talk about an important celebration in their country. Read the sentence. Then listen and complete it. 🎧44

Both speakers are talking about special days that celebrate _____.

a. getting a driver's license

b. graduating from college

c. growing up

d. getting married

B **Listen for details.** Read the sentences below. Then listen and check (✓) the correct celebration. Some sentences are true for both celebrations. 🎧45

	La Fiesta Rosa	Coming of Age Day
a. You are 20.	☐	✓
b. You are 15.	☐	☐
c. It happens in Japan.	☐	☐
d. It happens in El Salvador.	☐	☐
e. It's only for young women.	☐	☐
f. You wear special clothes.	☐	☐
g. Everyone celebrates together on a day in January.	☐	☐
h. There's a ceremony at City Hall first.	☐	☐
i. There's a religious ceremony first.	☐	☐
j. You get a gift or gifts.	☐	☐
k. There is a lot of food and dancing at a party.	☐	☐
l. You go with friends to different clubs and parties.	☐	☐

C **Summarize.** Choose one of the celebrations above. Use your answers from **A** and **B** to describe it to a partner.

D **Make connections.** Discuss the questions with a partner.

1. Is there a similar celebration in your country?

2. When does it happen, and what do people do on that day?

ACADEMIC SKILL

Make connections

After you learn something about another part of the world, make connections with your own life and country. This can help you remember new things you learn.

A group of 20-year-old women in traditional kimonos celebrate Coming of Age Day in Urayasu, Japan.

Have you ever been to a costume party? If so, what costume did you wear?

SPEAKING

A Listen to the conversation. Then answer the questions with a partner. 🎧46

Omar: Hey, Lane. My classmate Sayuri is having a party this weekend.

Lane: Really?

Omar: Yeah, it's a costume party.

Lane: Sounds like fun.

Omar: Do you want to go with me?

Lane: Are you sure? I don't really know Sayuri.

Omar: No problem. She said I could invite a friend.

Lane: OK, then. I'd love to go. When exactly is it?

Omar: On Saturday night.

Lane: Wow, that's the day after tomorrow! I need to get a costume.

Omar: Me, too. There's a good place near here that rents them. Let's go there after school.

Lane: Sounds good!

1. Omar is going to a party. What kind of party is it? How does Omar invite Lane?

2. Does Lane accept? What does she say?

B **PRONUNCIATION: Reduced *want to*** Listen and complete the conversation. Notice the pronunciation of *want to*. Then practice the conversation with a partner. 🎧47

A: _____ do you _____ do this weekend?

B: I don't know. Maybe see that new sci-fi movie. _____ you _____ come with me?

A: Sorry, but I don't really _____ see that movie.

C Practice the conversation in **A** with a partner.

D Write four invitations using the activities and times in the box below. Use the expressions in the Speaking Strategy to help you.

SPEAKING STRATEGY 🎧48

Inviting someone to do something		Accepting or refusing an invitation
Do you want Would you like How'd you like	to go with me?	Sure, I'd love to. That sounds great. I'm sorry, but I can't. I have plans. Unfortunately, I can't. I have to work. I'd love to, but I'm busy (then / that day).
When refusing an invitation, it's polite to give a simple explanation.		

come to a party	study together	after class	tomorrow
see a movie	your idea: _____	this weekend	tonight

E Take turns inviting a partner to the events in **D**. Refuse two of your partner's invitations. Give a simple explanation.

 We have an English test this Friday. How'd you like to study for it after class?

I'd love to, but . . . 99

GRAMMAR

A Read the Unit 7, Lesson A Grammar Reference in the appendix. Complete the exercises. Then do the exercises below.

AGREEING WITH OTHER PEOPLE'S STATEMENTS: *SO, TOO, NEITHER,* AND *EITHER*		
	Affirmative	**Negative**
With *be*	I'm going to Emi's party. So am I. / I am, **too**. / Me, **too**.	I'm not going to Emi's party. **Neither** am I. / I'm not **either**. / Me **neither**.
With other verbs	I have a costume for the party. So do I. / I do, **too**. / Me, **too**.	I don't have a costume for the party. **Neither** do I. / I don't **either**. / Me **neither**.

B Match each statement with the correct response.

_____ 1. I'm having a party this weekend.

_____ 2. Sandra wasn't at the party last night.

_____ 3. I bought a present for Yukio.

_____ 4. I was so tired this morning.

_____ 5. I didn't have a good time at the party.

_____ 6. I don't like costume parties.

_____ 7. In my country, we have a big party for a teenager's fifteenth birthday.

_____ 8. I'm not going to Diana's party.

a. Neither was I.

b. Neither did I.

c. So do we.

d. So did I.

e. I was, too.

f. So am I.

g. I'm not either.

h. Neither do I.

> **i** *Me, too* and *me neither* are common in casual spoken conversation.

C Complete the sentences. Make them true for you.

1. I **like** / **don't like** to stay home on the weekend.

2. I **like** / **don't like** to talk during class.

3. I **need** / **don't need** to study harder.

4. I **think** / **don't think** big parties are fun.

5. I'm **good at** / **not good at** remembering new vocabulary.

6. I **finished** / **didn't finish** my homework last night.

7. I'm **going to** / **not going to** apply to college in the future.

8. In my country, we **usually** / **never** have a cake on someone's birthday.

D Compare your opinions in **C** with a partner's.

“ I like to stay home on the weekend.

So do I. What do you like to do? ”

“ Play games on my computer.

“ I like to stay home on the weekend.

Really? I don't. I like to go out with my friends. ”

Around the world, people light candles on birthday cakes, make wishes, and blow the candles out.

ACTIVE ENGLISH Try it out!

A Plan a party with a partner. Choose an item from each category or think of an idea of your own.

Type of party

a. a costume party   b. a pool party   c. a birthday party   d. your idea: _____

Place

a. a friend's house   b. a nightclub   c. a park   d. your idea: _____

Type of food

a. finger foods   b. barbecue   c. pizza   d. your idea: _____

B Stand up and invite four other pairs to your party. Ask and answer questions about each other's parties and make notes in the invitations below.

“ Would you like to come to our party next week?

What kind of party is it? ”

“ It's a surprise birthday party for Antonio. He turns 22 next Friday.

Type of party: _____
Place: _____
Food: _____

Type of party: _____
Place: _____
Food: _____

Type of party: _____
Place: _____
Food: _____

Type of party: _____
Place: _____
Food: _____

C Discuss the parties in **B** with your partner. What do you think of each one? Choose your favorite.

“ I really like the surprise birthday party.

So do I. The costume party sounds fun, too. ”

D Go back to each pair from **B** and either accept or refuse their invitation.

“ We'd love to come to the surprise birthday party!

I'm sorry, but we can't come to the costume party. We have plans. ”

7A GOALS   Now I can . . .

Make and respond to invitations ____

Agree with someone ____

1. Yes, I can.
2. Mostly, yes.
3. Not yet.

VOCABULARY

A Take turns reading the information about the festival aloud with a partner.

> **The International Festival of the Sahara** takes place in December for four days in Douz, a town in Tunisia near the Sahara Desert. Thousands of people gather to celebrate the traditions of the desert people.
>
> **Events**
>
> - Watch people compete in games to win prizes. Be sure to see one of the horse or camel races.
> - Love words? Don't miss the festival's poetry competition.
> - Local musicians and DJs from around the world perform every night.
> - Participate in activities outside of Douz. Visit the dunes (large sand hills) for sand skiing.

B Match the correct forms of the words in **blue** to the definitions.

1. To play a game or other activity and try to be the best: _____*compete*_____

2. A type of activity (running, driving) that you try to be the fastest in: _____

3. To sing, dance, or play music in front of others: _____

4. To come together in a group: _____

5. To happen: _____

6. Something (like money) given to the winner of a game or activity: _____

7. To join in and do something together with others: _____

8. Customs or ways of doing something for a long time: _____

WORD BANK

Verb	Noun	Noun (person)
compete	competition	competitor
participate	participation	participant
perform	performance	performer

C Cover the information about the festival. Ask and answer the questions with a partner.

1. Where and when does the festival take place?

2. What happens at the festival?

A traditional show of horseback riding at the International Festival of the Sahara

GET READY TO
GET MESSY

The Orange Festival

It's a cool February afternoon in the small town of Ivrea, in Northern Italy. The streets are usually quiet, but today they're full of people as the four-day Orange Festival begins. The "Carnevale di Ivrea" is over 900 years old. It celebrates the story of a girl named Violetta. She killed the town's evil[1] leader and freed[2] the people of Ivrea. The festival remembers the fight that took place between the people of Ivrea and the evil leader's soldiers. In the original fight, people threw rocks at the soldiers. Today, participants throw oranges at each other. Before they start, a young woman dressed as Violetta speaks to the people and gives them candy. After that, the orange fight begins! To participate, you need to join a team—you can be on a team of "freedom fighters" or soldiers. If you don't want to fight, you must wear a red hat. Then no one will throw oranges at you. When the fighting ends, there are oranges everywhere!

The Festival of Color

The Festival of Color, also called Holi, is a popular spring celebration from India. It takes place every year, usually in early or mid-March, and lasts at least two days. In Indian mythology,[3] an evil woman tried to kill a young man named Prahlad by burning him in a fire. Because Prahlad was a good person, he escaped[4] from the fire unhurt.

People throw colorful powder during Holi.

Today, people remember this event by lighting large fires in the streets on the night before Holi. The fire is a symbol[5] of the end of all bad things. The next day, Holi celebrates the start of spring and a new beginning. To celebrate, people gather in the streets, and when they throw colored powder into the air, they say, "Holi Hai!" Others throw colored water or powder at each other. After the festival ends, the streets are filled with color and smiles! 🎧49

[1]Something **evil** is very bad.
[2]To **free** someone means to release them from something bad.
[3]**Mythology** is a collection of very old traditional stories.
[4]If you **escape** from something bad, you get away from it.
[5]A **symbol** is something that represents something else. For example, a heart shape is a symbol of love.

A Make predictions. Read the title and look at the photo. What do you think happens at this festival? Tell a partner.

B Read for details. Work with a partner. Answer questions 1–3 about your festival only.

Student A: Read about the Orange Festival.

Student B: Read about the Festival of Color.

1. Where and when does it take place?

2. What is the purpose of the festival? What event does it celebrate?

3. What do people do at the festival?

C Ask your partner the questions in **B** about his or her festival. Then read about the festival. Check your partner's answers.

D Categorize information. What festival is each sentence about? Write *O* for Orange Festival or *H* for Holi. Write *B* if both answers are possible.

_____ 1. It's celebrated in the spring.

_____ 2. It's about an old story.

_____ 3. It celebrates good over evil.

_____ 4. You throw things at other people.

_____ 5. You need to join a team.

_____ 6. The day before, people light a fire.

_____ 7. The celebration lasts more than one day.

_____ 8. Wearing a red hat means you don't want to participate.

_____ 9. The festival remembers a good person from the past.

_____ 10. The festival is in the photo.

E Answer the questions with a partner.

1. Imagine you can go to Holi or the Orange Festival. Which one do you want to go to? Why?

2. Think of a traditional festival in your country and answer the questions in **B** about it.

LISTENING

A Listen for the main idea. Listen to a news report from Cameroon and answer the questions. 🎧50

1. What type of competition is it?
2. Is it difficult? Why or why not?
3. What is the town getting ready for?

B Listen for details. Listen again and complete the notes about the event. 🎧50

1. **When the event takes place:** every year, usually in _____
2. **Number of participants this year:** _____
3. **Distance:** _____ kilometers
4. **What the competitors do:** They run up a _____ and then back down.
5. **Prize:** over $ _____
6. **Other events:** During the weekend, there's also a festival with _____.

C Imagine you and a partner work for an advertising agency. You are helping the government of Cameroon tell the world about this special event. Create a print or video advertisement for the event. Use your notes from **A** and **B**.

D Share your advertisement with two other pairs. Which one is the best? Why?

Jenevarius Bongkiyung, who won the Mount Cameroon Race of Hope in 2007, holds one of his prizes.

In Spain and many Latin American countries, January 6 is Three Kings' Day. To celebrate, people often eat *rosca de reyes*, a special sweet bread.

GRAMMAR

A Read the Unit 7, Lesson B Grammar Reference in the appendix. Complete the exercises. Then do the exercises below.

TIME CLAUSES WITH *BEFORE, AFTER, WHEN*	
Time clause	**Main clause**
Before the festival starts,	Violetta speaks.
After the party ended,	we went home.
When you throw powder in the air,	you say, "Holi Hai!"
Main clause	**Time clause**
Violetta speaks	**before** the festival starts.
We went home	**after** the party ended.
You say, "Holi Hai!"	**when** you throw powder in the air.

B Look at the photo. Then read about Paloma's activities on Three Kings' Day. With a partner, combine the different sentences using *before*, *after*, and *when*. Multiple answers are possible.

> **January 5**
> 9:00 pm   Paloma and her family go to the Three Kings' Parade.
>
> **January 6**
> 7:00 am   Paloma's younger brothers get up.
> 7:00 am   They wake Paloma up.
> 7:15 am   The family gathers in the living room.
> 7:20 am   They open presents.
> 8:00 am   Everyone relaxes and enjoys the morning.
> 11:00 am   Paloma and her mom prepare lunch.
> 2:00 pm   Paloma's grandparents arrive at her house. Everyone has lunch.
> 3:00 pm   The family eats a special sweet bread called *rosca de reyes*.
> 3:30 pm   The adults talk, and the children play games.

““ When Paloma's brothers
get up, they . . .

C Think of a holiday you know. What happens on this day? Use *after*, *before*, and *when* to describe the day's events. Tell a partner.

ACTIVE ENGLISH Try it out!

Clean Your Desk Day (Second Monday in January)

A Look at the photos of three special days. Then ask and answer the questions with a partner.

1. What do you think happens on each day?
2. Which one(s) would you like to celebrate? Why?

B With your partner, use the questions below to invent an unusual holiday.

- What is the name of the holiday?
- When does it take place?
- What is the reason for the holiday?
- Who celebrates it?

- What do people do on the holiday?
- What do people wear?
- Are there any special foods or decorations?
- Do people celebrate it at home or out somewhere?

National Pet Day (April 11th)

C Take turns presenting your unusual holidays to the class and taking notes. Then, as a class, decide which of the holidays you would like to celebrate every year.

D Turn to the Unit 7 Writing appendix and read the text. Then answer the questions with a partner.

1. Is the person writing about a festival or holiday?
2. What is it called?
3. Where and when does it happen?
4. What do people do, and when?

World Tourism Day (September 27th)

E **WRITING** Think of an important holiday or festival in your city or country. Answer the questions in **D** about it. Then use your ideas and the Useful Expressions to help you write a paragraph or two about it.

F Exchange papers with a partner. Answer the questions in **D** about your partner's writing. Circle any mistakes. Then return the paper to your partner. Make corrections to your own writing.

USEFUL EXPRESSIONS

We have a holiday called . . .
It takes place in / on . . .
It is a holiday for . . .
Many people travel / celebrate . . .
In the morning / evening, . . .
Before / After / When . . .

7B GOALS   Now I can . . .

Talk about parties, festivals, and holidays _____

Describe what people do on those days _____

1. Yes, I can.
2. Mostly, yes.
3. Not yet.

GLOBAL VOICES

A When is New Year's in your country? How important is it? How do you celebrate it?

B Watch a video about how people celebrate New Year's. Circle **T** for *true* or **F** for *false*.

1. The people in the video celebrate New Year's at different times of the year.   **T**   **F**

2. Many of them think New Year's is important in their country.   **T**   **F**

3. They all watch fireworks at midnight.   **T**   **F**

4. Most people celebrate with family and friends.   **T**   **F**

5. Everyone thinks New Year's in the US is very similar to their own country.   **T**   **F**

> **WORD BANK**
> A **charm** is an object that brings luck.
> A **shrine** is a religious place.
> To **wish** / **make a wish** means to hope for something good to happen.

C Watch the video again and answer the questions.

1. In which country do some people go to a shrine on New Year's?

2. In Brazil, what do some people wear on New Year's?

3. How late do some Brazilians stay awake on New Year's Eve?

4. In Brazil, when people jump over waves seven times in the sea, what do they make?

5. On New Year's, what is the difference between the seasons in Brazil and the US?

6. What are two differences that Chiyuki noticed between New Year's in Japan and the US?

7. Jaqueline has celebrated New Year's Eve in the US and Colombia. What is similar and different about the celebrations in these countries and in her country of Brazil?

D Work in pairs and plan a two-minute video about New Year's in your country or different countries. Make notes about your video in a table, like this:

What you see	What you hear
Fireworks in the sky	Narrator: "In many countries, people celebrate New Year's with fireworks . . ."
A family eating together	Narrator: "and they often have a meal with family and friends . . ."

Then join another pair and present your plans for the video.

New Year's Eve fireworks in Rio de Janeiro, Brazil

People often describe
Neuschwanstein Castle
near Schwangau, Germany
as a "fairy-tale" castle.

GOALS

Lesson A
/ Tell a story
/ Ask questions to find out what happened

Lesson B
/ Talk about the meaning of stories
/ Describe how something is done

ONCE UPON A TIME

LOOK AT THE PHOTO. ANSWER THE QUESTIONS.

1. What do you see in the photo? How would you describe this place?

2. Which books, movies, or TV shows does this place remind you of?

WARM-UP VIDEO

A You are going to watch a short film called *Snack Attack*.* Number the events (1–8) in the order you think they will happen.

   1   a. An old woman arrives at the train station.

       b. She gets very angry with the young man and starts shouting.

       c. The young man also eats a cookie.

       d. She sits down next to a young man, eats a cookie, and reads a newspaper.

       e. He shares the last cookie with her.

       f. Angrily, she gets on her train.

       g. She buys a snack from a vending machine.

       h. The old woman moves the cookies away from him, but he takes another.

*A **snack attack** (slang) is when you suddenly feel very hungry and have to eat.*

B Watch the first part of the video and pause when the woman gets on the train. Check your answers in **A**.

C What do you think happens next? How does the story end? Tell the class your ideas.

D Watch the end of the video. What do you think is the message of the story?

8A WHAT'S THE STORY ABOUT?

In this scene from the *Life of Pi* movie, the tiger was created using special effects.

VOCABULARY

A Do you know any movies that started as books? Do you prefer reading the book or watching the movie? Why?

B Read the text and check your understanding of the words in blue. Then answer the questions below.

Good movies need good stories, so many are **based on** famous **fiction**. For example, *Life of Pi* is a **best-selling** book by the author Yann Martel. It **tells the story of** a young man named Pi and his family. They own a zoo and move their animals from India to Canada. But on the journey, the ship sinks, and only the main **character** survives on a small boat with a tiger. The film **director** Ang Lee made a *Life of Pi* movie, and like the book, the story is **unpredictable** and a lot of it **takes place** at sea on the small boat. The movie is exciting to watch, and the special effects are very **realistic**. Sometimes, when a movie is based on a book, the story needs to change so the movie is **easy to follow**. But when Yann Martel saw *Life of Pi*, he liked it because the movie was fairly similar to the book.

1. What is the name of the book? Is it fact or fiction?
2. Who wrote the book? Was it successful?
3. Who is the main character?
4. What is the story about? Is it predictable?
5. Where does a lot of the story take place?
6. How realistic are the movie's special effects?
7. Who made a film based on the book?
8. Did Yann Martel like the film? Why or why not?

 The *Crazy Rich Asians* movie is based on a book.

I prefer the book. I didn't like the movie.

WORD BANK
The **main character(s)** in the story is / are . . .
The story is about . . .
easy to follow ⟷ hard to follow
predictable ⟷ unpredictable
realistic ⟷ unrealistic

C Work in pairs. Ask and answer the questions about your favorite book or movie.

1. What is the name of your favorite book or movie?
2. Who is the author or director?
3. Who are the main characters?
4. Where does it take place?
5. What is the story about?
6. Is it easy or hard to follow? Predictable or unpredictable?

LISTENING

A Answer the questions. Take notes and share your ideas with a partner.

1. Have you ever heard the word *crowdsourcing*?
2. Can you guess the meaning by looking at the two parts of the word: *crowd* and *source*?

B **Listen for details.** Listen to the conversation about using crowdsourcing to write a story. Circle the correct answer to complete each sentence. 🎧51

1. Jamal is working _____.
   a. alone
   b. with a couple of friends
   c. with a lot of people

2. Jamal met the other writers _____.
   a. at school
   b. in writing class
   c. online

3. Each person adds _____ at a time.
   a. one word
   b. one sentence
   c. one ending

4. The story is _____.
   a. unpredictable
   b. unrealistic
   c. hard to follow

5. Jamal is working on a _____ story.
   a. fantasy
   b. love
   c. crime

6. The story isn't _____.
   a. realistic
   b. true
   c. well known

ACADEMIC SKILL

Using parts of words to guess meaning
When you don't know the meaning of a new word, sometimes you can guess the meaning from its different parts.

WORD BANK
When you **contribute**, you help to make something happen.

C **Summarize.** Look at your notes from **A** and your answers in **B**. What is a crowdsourced story? Complete the summary below. Compare your answers with a partner's.

To create a crowdsourced story, (1.) _____ work together. They don't work in an office. They work (2.) _____. Everyone contributes (3.) _____ at a time. The people don't (4.) _____ each other, and they don't receive any (5.) _____ for their work.

D Discuss the questions with a partner.

1. Do you think crowdsourcing is a good way to tell a story? Why or why not?
2. What do you think are some other ways that crowdsourcing can be used?

Part of Jamal's story takes place in Madrid, Spain. What place do you think would make a good story setting?

SPEAKING

A Mia is telling Nico a story. Listen and then answer the questions below. 🎧52

Mia: Wow, I just heard an amazing story.

Nico: Yeah? What's it about?

Mia: It's a story about a waitress. She had a lot of money problems.

Nico: That sounds hard.

Mia: It is. Anyway, she found out she was losing her apartment. She had to move, but she didn't have enough money.

Nico: Oh, no!

Mia: As it turns out, she told one of her customers about the situation. This customer was special. He came to the restaurant often and knew the waitress well. And he wanted to help her.

Nico: So what did he do?

Mia: One day he paid his bill and left the restaurant, as usual. When the waitress went to collect her tip, she found a $3,000 tip . . . on a bill of $43.50!

Nico: Are you serious?

Mia: I am. It's a true story. And in the end, the waitress was OK.

Nico: What a heartwarming story. I'm glad it had a happy ending.

1. How many characters are in the story?
2. Where does it take place?
3. What happened? Was the story easy to follow?
4. This is an example of a *feel-good* story. What do you think that means?

When eating out in the US, people usually tip their server an extra twenty percent for service after finishing the meal.

B Practice the conversation with a partner.

C On a piece of paper, write a word or sentence for each item below. Then exchange papers with a partner. Use your partner's notes and the Speaking Strategy to write a story.

1. a person's name
2. another person's name
3. a place
4. how the two people met
5. what happened to the two people

D Work with a new partner.

Student A: Tell your story.

Student B: Listen. Show interest. Ask follow-up questions.

> " My story is about a student named Jonah. Something amazing happened to him.
>
> What happened? "

E Switch roles and do **D** again.

SPEAKING STRATEGY 🎧53

Tell a story

I just heard an amazing / interesting / unbelievable story.

It's a story about . . .

One day . . .

Later, . . . / After that, . . .

As it turns out, . . .

In the end, . . .

Show interest and find out what happened

What's it about?

Oh, no! / Really?

So what did he / she do?

What happened next?

Are you serious? / Wow!

GRAMMAR

A Compare the two underlined verbs in the sentence below. Which verb describes a long (continuous) action in progress? Which verb describes a short (simple) action?

The old woman <u>was waiting</u> for her train when a young man <u>ate</u> her cookie!

B Read the Unit 8, Lesson A Grammar Reference in the appendix. Complete the exercises. Then do the exercises below.

THE PAST CONTINUOUS: STATEMENTS				
Subject	was / were (not)	Verb + -ing		
I / He / She	was(n't)	studying	English	at four o'clock. last summer. after lunch.
You / We / They	were(n't)			

THE PAST CONTINUOUS: QUESTIONS						
	Wh- word	was / were	Subject	Verb + -ing		Answers
Yes / No Questions		Were	you	reading	a story?	Yes, I **was**. / No, I **wasn't**.
Wh- Questions	What	were	you	reading?		(I **was reading**) a story.

C Unscramble the questions and their answers.

1. **A:** were / doing / at / what / you / last night / 8:00 _____

   B: a TV show / watching / I / was _____

2. **A:** yesterday / friend / was / what / wearing / your _____

   B: wearing / school / her / she / uniform / was _____

3. **A:** the / were / phone / talking / earlier / you / on _____

   B: wasn't / no, / I _____

   lunch / was / I / eating _____

4. **A:** studying / was / your / last week / class / what _____

   B: were / *World Link* / grammar / we / studying / in _____

5. **A:** summer / family / was / your / traveling / last _____

   B: were / we / yes, _____

   to / went / Brazil / we _____

D Ask and answer the questions in **C** with a partner. Give answers that are true for you. Then think of a follow-up question to ask your partner.

" What were you doing at 8:00 last night?

I was studying at home in my room. "

" How long were you studying?

For about three hours. I was preparing for a big test. "

ACTIVE ENGLISH Try it out!

A You are going to hear two people talk about a car accident. One person is lying. Listen to each person's story and take notes below. 🎧54

	Jenna	Ryan
When did it happen?		
Where did it happen?		
What happened?		
What color was the car?		
Who was driving?		

B Circle your answers below. Discuss your ideas with a partner.

1. **Jenna** / **Ryan** remembers the details clearly.

2. **Jenna** / **Ryan** sounds more confident.

3. I think **Jenna** / **Ryan** is making up the story.

C Think about something funny or unusual that happened to you. Then follow the steps below with a partner.

1. **Student A:** Tell your story about the funny or unusual experience.
   Student B: Listen, show interest, and find out what happened. Take notes on *who, what, where, when,* and *why.*

2. Switch roles and repeat step 1.

3. Now choose one of your stories. You will tell this story to another pair.

4. Think of ways that you can make the story untrue (for example, changing the details). Write down another version of the story with the untrue parts.

D Get together with another pair.

- **Pair 1:** One of you will tell the story as it really happened to you. The other person will tell the story with the made-up parts. Begin with each person saying the first sentence of their story. Take turns telling the rest, one sentence at a time.

- **Pair 2:** Ask each person in pair 1 questions about his or her story. You have one minute. Then guess: Who is telling the truth and who is making up the story? How do you know?

" I was walking to work one day when I met someone famous.

I was walking to the store one day when I met someone famous. "

" OK, let me start with Alexei. You said you were walking to work. Where exactly do you work?

E Switch roles and do **D** again.

8A GOALS Now I can . . .

Tell a story _____

Ask questions to find out what happened _____

1. Yes, I can.

2. Mostly, yes.

3. Not yet.

8B MODERN FAIRY TALES

VOCABULARY

A Read the text about modern fairy tales. Then match the words in blue to the definitions.

> Every country has its own fairy tales. They are **traditional** stories for children, but sometimes adults read them, too. Often, they are set in **ancient** places with castles and forests, and they tell stories about characters such as lost children, talking animals, or people with **magic**. Some of the most famous fairy tales, such as *Cinderella* or *Sleeping Beauty*, have become films. Today, modern fairy tales like *Harry Potter* and *Star Wars* have new characters and take place in space and other new places. Whether old or modern, in most fairy tales . . .
>
> • there is a good character and an **evil** character.
>
> • the good character is often **clever** and **brave**.
>
> • the good character has a difficult challenge but always **succeeds**.
>
> • **incredible** things happen (e.g., animals talk, people have special powers).
>
> • the good character **discovers** something important about life and the story ends happily.

1. old, from past generations of people:
   ___traditional___

2. special powers to do impossible things:
   _____

3. very bad (usually describing a person):
   _____

4. intelligent; able to learn quickly:
   _____

5. amazing (and difficult to believe):
   _____

6. from a long time ago (often a place or building): _____

7. not scared of danger: _____

8. finds out something: _____

9. does something that is difficult:
   _____

B Work with a partner. Follow the steps below.

1. Choose a modern fairy tale (a movie, book, or TV show) to talk about.

2. Which information from the text in **A** is true for your story?

3. Do you like the story? Why or why not?

4. Choose a different modern fairy tale and repeat steps 1–3.

> " In *Star Wars: The Rise of Skywalker*, the main character is Rey. She's clever and brave.

Examples of modern fairy tales				
Frozen	*Spirited Away*	*Star Wars*	*Superman*	*The Lion King*

Pan's Labyrinth is a modern fairy tale. The movie's director, Guillermo del Toro, is famous for his creativity with magical characters and special effects.

THE CINDERELLA STORY

1. _____

The Cinderella story is a famous one. Cinderella was living happily with her family when her mother died. Her father remarried. Cinderella's new stepmother and two stepsisters treated her poorly. She had to wear old clothes and work hard while the sisters wore beautiful clothes and had fun.

You know the rest of the story. A good fairy[1] helped Cinderella. She turned Cinderella's old clothes into a beautiful dress. Cinderella went to a party, and a prince fell in love with her. Cinderella left the party quickly and didn't tell the prince her name. But she did leave a glass slipper, and the prince used that to find her. Eventually, Cinderella and the prince married and lived happily ever after.

2. _____

That's one telling of the story, but the Cinderella fairy tale is found in many different countries with some differences. In an African version, for example, there is one stepsister, not two. In a version from the Philippines, a forest spirit helps the Cinderella character. Settareh, a Middle Eastern Cinderella, goes to a New Year's party. And Cinderella is not always a woman. In an Irish story, a young boy, Becan, marries a princess and lives happily ever after.

3. _____

There are also modern retellings of the Cinderella story. In one, a girl named Cindy Ella is a student at a Los Angeles high school. Her fashionable stepmother and older stepsisters care a lot about shopping and money. Cindy doesn't. When she writes a letter to her school newspaper against a school dance, she becomes very unpopular with both students and teachers. Only her two best friends—and later the school's most handsome boy—support her.

4. _____

Why is the Cinderella story so popular and found in so many cultures? There are a few reasons. First of all, it's a romantic story, which is a popular style. Also, Cinderella is a kind girl with a hard life. People want her to succeed. But maybe the most important reason is that, in the Cinderella story, a person struggles,[2] but overcomes[3] the difficulties in the end. That's a story that everyone—boy or girl, young or old—wants to believe can happen. 🎧55

[1] A **fairy** is someone with magical power who often has wings.
[2] To **struggle** means to try hard to do something difficult.
[3] To **overcome** means to deal with a difficult situation successfully.

A **Use background knowledge.** Look at the title and the photo. What do you know about the fairy-tale character Cinderella? Tell a partner.

B **Identify main ideas.** Read the article. Then write the subheadings below in the correct places in the reading. Two are extra.

- One story, many cultures
- Why we love her
- Cinderella in the Philippines
- Cinderella online
- A present-day Cinderella
- A famous fairy tale

C **Scan for details.** Match the information to make true sentences. One answer is extra.

1. The African Cinderella _____
2. Becan _____
3. Cindy Ella _____
4. The Filipina Cinderella _____
5. Settareh _____

a. attends a New Year's party.
b. gets help from a forest spirit.
c. has only one stepsister.
d. is a boy "Cinderella."
e. is a movie version of the Cinderella story.
f. is an unpopular high school student.

D Answer the questions with a partner.

1. Why is the Cinderella story so popular? Find three reasons in the article. Do you agree with them?

2. Is there a Cinderella story in your country? If so, what is the story?

A woman dressed as Cinderella takes the subway to Comic Con in New York City (US).

LISTENING

A Look at the photo below and read the caption. In the past, how did people explain weather and nature? Who explains these things nowadays?

B Listen to someone telling an ancient story and answer the questions. 🎧56

1. Which part of the world does the story come from?
2. What type of animal were Thunder and Lightning?
3. In the end, where did the king send them?

WORD BANK
myth an old story that often explains nature or tells the history of a people
ram a male sheep
violent using force to hurt someone or damage something

C **Listen for specific information.** Listen again and choose the correct answers. For one question, there is more than one answer. 🎧56

1. At the beginning, where did Thunder and Lightning live?

   a. In the sky   b. In the forest   c. In a town

2. Why was Lightning dangerous?

   a. He killed people.   b. He stole food and money.   c. He burned down buildings.

3. Did Lightning listen to Thunder?

   a. Yes, always.   b. Sometimes.   c. No, never.

4. How many times did the king send them away?

   a. Once   b. Twice   c. Three times

D **Make connections.** Work in groups and discuss the questions.

1. In your country and culture, what are the most famous myths and stories?
2. Do any of them try to explain something like the weather or nature, or do they have some kind of lesson about life that is still true today?

E **PRONUNCIATION: Pausing** Listen to the sentences from the story. Draw lines (I) where the storyteller adds short pauses. How does this make it easier for the listener? 🎧57

1. The son, Lightning, was often angry and violent.
2. His mother ran quickly after him and shouted angrily, "Stop, Lightning! Stop what you are doing!"
3. After a while, the local people complained to their king about Lightning.
4. And often, a few seconds later, you will hear his mother, Thunder, telling him to stop.

F In pairs, practice reading the sentences in **E** aloud with the correct pauses.

In the past, people told myths and stories to explain weather, such as thunder and lightning. In the modern world, scientists help explain nature and the weather.

GRAMMAR

A Read the sentences from the story about Thunder and Lightning. In each sentence, underline the word that describes how the action was done.

His mother ran quickly.   She shouted angrily.   Lightning stopped suddenly.

B Read the Unit 8, Lesson B Grammar Reference in the appendix. Complete the exercises. Then do the exercises below.

ADVERBS OF MANNER	
Cinderella smiled **shyly** at the prince.	Adverbs of manner describe how something is done. Many end in -*ly*, and they often come after a verb.
He opened <u>the door</u> **quietly**. She answered <u>the question</u> **correctly**.	When there is <u>an object</u> (a noun or pronoun) after the verb, the adverb usually comes at the end of the sentence.
He studied **hard** for the exam. They didn't do **well** in school.	Some adverbs of manner don't end in -*ly*. Remember, use *well*, not *good*, as an adverb. ~~They didn't do good in school.~~
She was <u>different</u> from other children. You seem <u>unhappy</u>.	<u>Adjectives</u>, not adverbs, come after stative verbs (*be, have, hear, know, seem*, etc.).

C Circle the correct words to complete the profile. Then take turns reading the story aloud in pairs.

As a child in the UK, Daniel Tammet was (1.) **different / differently** from other children. As a boy, he liked to play alone, and people thought that he acted (2.) **strange / strangely**. In school, he struggled to do (3.) **good / well**. To many of his classmates, Daniel seemed (4.) **unusual / unusually**, and they laughed at him. This hurt Daniel (5.) **deep / deeply**, and he became very (6.) **shy / shyly**.

As a teenager, Daniel discovered he had an incredible ability. He could solve difficult math problems almost (7.) **instant / instantly**. He also discovered another talent: he could learn to speak a language very (8.) **quick / quickly**. Today, he is (9.) **fluent / fluently** in ten languages.

As an adult, Daniel overcame his shyness. He wrote a number of books in which he speaks (10.) **eloquent**[1] / **eloquently** about his life and ideas.

[1]An **eloquent** speaker talks in a clear and powerful way.

D Get into small groups. Add four verbs and two adverbs to the chart below.

E Choose a verb and an adverb. Then act out the combination. Can your group guess what you're doing? Take turns with the people in your group.

66 You're singing nervously!

Verbs		Adverbs	
climb	talk	angrily	quietly
dance	_____	carefully	shyly
laugh	_____	happily	suddenly
run	_____	nervously	_____
sing	_____	quickly	_____

The Black Forest in Germany is the setting for many of Grimm's famous fairy tales.

ACTIVE ENGLISH Try it out!

A Work in pairs. You will each have a different fairy tale picture, one traditional and one modern. Take turns describing what you see. As you describe your picture and listen to your partner, write down any differences between the two pictures. (There are at least seven.) Do not look at your partner's picture!

Student A: Look at the picture on page 211 and describe the traditional fairy tale.

Student B: Look at the picture on page 212 and describe the modern fairy tale.

B Now look at both pictures and check the notes you made about the differences. Did you find them all? Check your answers at the bottom of the page.

C In pairs, discuss the questions.

1. What do you think happens in each fairy tale?

2. How do you think the stories will end?

D **WRITING** Write a short modern fairy tale (100–150 words). You have two options:

Option 1: Think of a traditional fairy tale or myth from your country. Rewrite this story as a modern fairy tale in the 21st century.

Option 2: Write a modern fairy tale based on Student B's picture in the appendix. Use the ideas in the picture and add your own ideas.

In your story, use the simple past and past continuous, and at least three adverbs of manner. Turn to the Unit 8 Writing appendix to see an example.

E When you are ready, exchange stories with a partner. Check the verbs and adverbs in the story, and circle any mistakes.

F Work in groups and take turns telling your stories. When you read your story aloud, remember to add pauses and read with feeling.

" Once upon a time, there was a princess . . .

8B GOALS Now I can . . .

Talk about the meaning of stories _____

Describe how something is done _____

1. Yes, I can.
2. Mostly, yes.
3. Not yet.

1. It's daytime. / It's nighttime. 2. The princess lives in the castle. / The castle is a nightclub. 3. The wolf is guarding the castle and looks evil. / The wolf works at the door of the nightclub (and wears sunglasses). 4. The princess is in the tower, brushing her hair. / The princess is riding a motorcycle to meet the prince. 5. The prince is riding a horse to save the princess. / The prince is in the tower looking at his phone. 6. The characters are wearing fairy-tale clothing. / The characters are wearing modern clothing. 7. The castle is in the country, not near other buildings. / The castle is part of a city.

GLOBAL VOICES

A There is an expression in English: *Every picture tells a story*. Do you have a similar expression in your language? Look at the photo at the bottom of the page. What story do you think it tells?

B Watch interviews with four National Geographic Explorers and photographers. Circle the answers they give to the questions below. There is more than one correct answer for each question.

1. What does every story need?

    a. Surprise and humor

    b. Ancient places

    c. Emotion

    d. Amazing characters

2. How do you tell a story impactfully?

    a. With fairy tales

    b. With photography and video

    c. With beauty and challenges

    d. With good and bad characters

3. What is the story behind an important photo you have taken?

    a. Scientists were releasing red dye into the water.

    b. A scientist was studying volcanoes in Guatemala.

    c. Scientists were studying climate change.

4. How do you think storytelling will change in the next five to ten years?

    a. People will tell fewer stories.

    b. There will be more diversity.

    c. There will be more stories from around the world.

C Read the sentences from the video and guess the missing words. Then watch again and check.

1. "You want to make sure that they look at it and say, 'Wow, I want to _____ more.'"

2. "_____ always need to take you on some kind of journey."

3. ". . . have someone that your audience can feel like they could be _____ with."

4. "There's still going to be a huge need for stories that _____ us."

D In pairs, look through the photos in this book and choose one that you find interesting. Answer the questions about the photo.

1. What story is the photographer telling us?

2. How does the photo tell the story?

Then tell the class about the photo you chose.

National Geographic Explorer Jennifer Adler uses her photos to teach people about Florida's freshwater springs and the animals that live there, like this manatee.

9

WORK

LOOK AT THE PHOTO. ANSWER THE QUESTIONS.

1. What job does this person do?
2. What adjectives describe this job (for example, *interesting*, *dangerous*)? Give reasons for your answers.

WARM-UP VIDEO

A You are going to watch a video about working as a volcanologist. This is a scientist who studies volcanoes. In pairs, say three things you think you will see.

B Watch the video and check your three predictions from **A**.

C Read the sentences from the video and guess the missing words. Then watch the video again and check.

1. "These are n_____ people who stay in their lab."
2. "These are people who really go out and l_____ at things . . ."
3. "This is the b_____ place in the world to camp . . ."
4. ". . . you are o_____, in the outdoors."
5. "The mountain is really d_____."
6. "In most places of the world, it's not a hazard* to the general population; it's a hazard to volcanologists who are going c_____ to the volcano . . ."

*A **hazard** is something that is dangerous.

D What other dangerous jobs do you know? Why are they dangerous? Make a list in pairs.

A scientist, wearing a special suit and helmet to protect against very high temperatures, collects lava samples from the Mount Etna volcano in Italy.

GOALS

Lesson A

/ Discuss skills and qualities for a job

/ Interview for a job

Lesson B

/ Describe a job

/ Talk about your past experience

VOCABULARY

A Read about the job. Do you think you could be a paramedic? Why or why not?

I'm a paramedic. I give medical help in an emergency. You have to be **responsible** to do this job. Each day is different, so you have to be **flexible**, too.

Rahul Singh is a paramedic in Toronto, Canada.

I report to work at 5:30 am. I'm a **punctual** person, so the early start isn't a problem.

Some people work **independently**, but not me. I'm part of a team that includes a driver and another paramedic. The driver knows the most **efficient** ways to get around, and my colleague and I are **knowledgeable** about medical problems.

Our team tries to approach people in a **personable** way, even if they are confused or angry. And when people are injured, we are **cautious** when moving them into the ambulance.

I think I'm pretty **adventurous**, and this job is good for someone who isn't afraid of new experiences. People also say I'm **courageous** to face these difficult situations. I say I'm just doing my job.

B Match the words in blue to the words or phrases with a similar meaning. Use a dictionary.

1. reliable: _____ *responsible* _____

2. brave: _____

3. changes easily: _____

4. by yourself: _____

5. friendly: _____

6. careful: _____

7. knows a lot: _____

8. likes risks: _____

9. on time: _____

10. works quickly / easily: _____

C Look at the graphic. The letters in the word *paramedic* are used to write other words describing skills and qualities needed for that job. In pairs, make a similar graphic about a different job. Then show it to the class.

> **ACADEMIC SKILL**
> **Word forms**
> When you learn a new word, use a dictionary to check its other forms so you can use them correctly; for example,
> *reliable* (adj)
> *reliability* (n)

```
    P u n c t u a l
b r A v e
pe R s o n a b l e
  c A u t i o u s
    M
f l E x i b l e
    D
r e l I a b l e
    C
```

A flight attendant   A travel journalist   An international aid worker

LISTENING

A In pairs, look at the three jobs in the photos above and rank them from 1 (most challenging) to 3 (least challenging). Give reasons for your answers.

B **Listen for key words.** Listen to three people talking about their jobs. Write the correct job for each speaker. Then write the adjectives in blue from the previous page that you hear for each job. 🎧58

Job 1: _____

Adjectives: _____

Job 2: _____

Adjectives: _____

Job 3: _____

Adjectives: _____

C **Make and check predictions.** Read the sentences and circle **T** for *true* or **F** for *false*. Then listen again and check your answers. 🎧58

Job 1:

1. It's a fun and easy job.   T   F

2. You have a good social life.   T   F

3. You have to change your plans easily.   T   F

Job 2:

4. A lot of people apply for this job.   T   F

5. All the work is overseas.   T   F

6. You have to be reliable and brave.   T   F

Job 3:

7. You work by yourself a lot of the time.   T   F

8. You need to find new things to write about.   T   F

D In groups, make a list of the pros (good things) and cons (bad things) for each of the three jobs. Use information from the speakers and your own ideas. Then decide which of the three jobs you would choose.

> One of the good things is that you travel overseas . . .

> Overall, I'd like to be a . . .

> But you don't have a good social life.

SPEAKING

A Read the job advertisement. Then listen to Ines's interview and answer the questions below. 🎧59

Simon: So, Ines, tell me a little about yourself.

Ines: Well, I'm a first-year student at City University, and I'm majoring in journalism.

Simon: And you're working for your school's online newspaper, right?

Ines: Yeah. I write a blog. It focuses on pop culture, fashion, music—stuff like that.

Simon: How long have you worked there?

Ines: For about six months. I post an entry once a week.

Simon: Excellent. But if you work here, you'll need to post every Tuesday and Friday—by noon.

Ines: No problem. I'm very punctual.

Simon: Great. Now, we need someone right away. When can you start?

Ines: On Monday.

Simon: Perfect. Let me talk to my boss, and I'll be in touch with you later this week.

1. How does Ines discuss her abilities and experience? Underline the sentences in the conversation.

2. Is Ines the right person for the job? Why or why not?

STUDENT BLOGGER
ZOOMA MAGAZINE

About the job:

Zooma Magazine needs student bloggers who:
- know a lot about pop culture.
- have good writing skills.
- are punctual and can work independently.

APPLY NOW

B Practice the conversation in **A** with a partner.

C Imagine that you're applying for the blogger job in **A**. With a partner, add two more skills or adjectives to the job ad and role-play a new conversation. Use the Speaking Strategy to help you. Then switch roles and do the role play again.

D Perform your conversation for another pair.

SPEAKING STRATEGY 🎧60
Interviewing for a job

	The interviewer	The applicant
Starting the interview	Thanks for coming in today.	It's great to be here. / My pleasure.
Discussing abilities and experience	Tell me a little about yourself.	I'm a student at . . . I'm majoring in . . .
	Can you (work independently)?	Yes, I can. For example, . . .
	Are you (punctual)?	Yes, I am. For example, . . .
	Do you have any experience (writing a blog)?	Yes, I write one for my school newspaper now.
Ending the interview	Do you have any questions?	Yes, I do. / No, I don't think so.
	When can you start?	Right away. / On Monday. / Next week.
	I'll be in touch.	I look forward to hearing from you.

GRAMMAR

A Read the Unit 9, Lesson A Grammar Reference in the appendix. Complete the exercises. Then do the exercises below.

THE PRESENT PERFECT	
Question	Response
How long **have** you **worked** there?	(I've **worked** there) <u>for</u> two years.
How long **has** she **worked** there?	(She's **worked** there) <u>since</u> 2012.
You can use the present perfect (*have / has* + past participle) to talk about events that started in the past and continue into the present. Note that many past participles are irregular. Use *for* + a length of time (*for ten minutes, for the summer, for two years, for a while*). Use *since* + a point in time (*since 2014, since last September, since I was a child*).	

B **PRONUNCIATION: Reduced *for* in time expressions** Say the first question and answer in the grammar chart above. Then listen and repeat. 🎧61

C **PRONUNCIATION: Reduced *for* in time expressions** Listen and complete the sentences with a time expression. Then practice saying the sentences with a partner. 🎧62

1. I've lived in the same city for _____.

2. He hasn't been in class for _____.

3. I haven't eaten for _____.

D Use the phrases below to write questions in the present perfect with *how long*.

1. go to this school   *How long have you gone to this school?* _____

2. study English   _____

3. know your best friend   _____

4. have the same hairstyle   _____

5. live in your current home   _____

E Use the questions in **D** to interview three of your classmates. Write their answers in the chart using *for* or *since*. Who has done each thing the longest? Share your results with the class.

Name	Question 1	Question 2	Question 3	Question 4	Question 5

Ian Simpson has worked as a boat builder for over 25 years.

A camp counselor plays a game with children at a summer camp in Washington State (US).

ACTIVE ENGLISH Try it out!

A Read the qualities, abilities, and experience below. In your notebook, list the qualities, abilities, and experience needed for these jobs: video-game tester, camp counselor, lifeguard, dog walker. You can use the ideas in the box more than once. Add your own ideas, too.

Qualities	Abilities / Experience	
• a personable and energetic person who loves the outdoors • an efficient person who is knowledgeable about computers • flexible, patient, and kind to animals • an adventurous and responsible person	**be able to . . .** • swim well • work flexible hours • walk long distances • work independently • speak English well	**have experience . . .** • caring for animals • working with children • playing video games • doing first aid

B Choose a job in **A** to apply for. Tell a partner your choice. Then:

• Complete the questions according to the job that your partner is applying for. Add your own idea at the end. Use the questions to interview your partner. Take turns.

• Decide if your partner is good for the job. Why or why not?

❝ Thanks for coming in today. So, tell me . . . what do you do now?

Interview questions

Name: _____

Job he or she is applying for: _____

1. What do you do now? How long have you done it?

2. Are you _____? Give me an example.
   (quality)

3. Can you _____? Please explain.
   (ability)

4. Do you have any experience _____?
   (doing something)

5. Your question: _____?

9A GOALS   Now I can . . .

Discuss skills and qualities for a job _____

Interview for a job _____

1. Yes I can.
2. Mostly, yes.
3. Not yet.

VOCABULARY

A Read the article and answer the questions in pairs.

In 2008, Emily Ashe traveled with her family on a National Geographic cruise to Mexico. On the ship, she met Dr. Tierney Thys, a famous marine biologist. Emily says, "I remember listening to her talk about ocean sunfish and then seeing a picture of her swimming next to one and thinking, 'Wow, I could do that one day.'"

Being a marine biologist might sound like a glamorous job, but it's also very demanding and sometimes hazardous under the ocean. You spend long, exhausting periods of time observing and studying sea life, and the work isn't always well paid. But marine biologists like Tierney often love their jobs; they usually educate people about the ocean, which can be very rewarding.

Now, after meeting Tierney over a decade ago, Emily has graduated from Eckerd College in St. Petersburg, Florida with a major in marine science. She hopes to follow in Tierney's footsteps,[1] and teach kids and the public about marine ecosystems.[2]

[1] To **follow in someone's footsteps** means to do the same thing as someone else.
[2] An **ecosystem** is the plants, animals, and environment in a particular area.

1. Why did Emily want to become a marine biologist?
2. What do marine biologists do?
3. How does Emily hope to "follow in Tierney's footsteps"?

B Match the words in blue to the word or phrase with the opposite meaning.

1. easy ⟷ _demanding_   4. relaxing ⟷ _____
2. _____ ⟷ badly paid   5. _____ ⟷ unsatisfying
3. _____ ⟷ dull   6. safe ⟷ _____

> **WORD BANK**
> exhausting tiring
> hazardous dangerous
> glamorous exciting and attractive

C For each answer in **B**, think of a different job; for example, being a nurse is a demanding job. Which job would you like to do? Which would you never do? Tell a partner.

Dr. Tierney Thys is a marine biologist. She studies ocean sunfish.

This piece of art by Asher Jay is titled "Where Do We Draw the Line?" It shows that many animal habitats are disappearing as cities grow and protected areas decrease.

ASHER JAY:
CREATIVE
CONSERVATIONIST

A *conservationist* is a person who works to protect the environment.

1. Can your passion[1] also be your profession? For "creative conservationist" Asher Jay, the answer is yes. She is an artist, writer, and activist. She uses her art to tell people about issues that affect animals around the world, like the illegal ivory trade and habitat loss.

2. Asher was born in India in 1985 and was raised around the world to be a global citizen. She now lives in New York. She has been passionate[2] about wildlife since she was a child. As a girl, she often found sick animals and brought them home to care for them. Her mother taught her that all life has a right to exist.

3. Now, working as an artist, everything Asher does in her creative work is to help conservation. For example, she spent two months traveling in Africa, and she collected garbage on her travels. She took the garbage back to New York and used it to create artwork about how the growth of human cities is affecting wildlife. As well as paintings, she has created animated films about pollution[3] in the oceans.

4. Asher loves what she does, but working with nature can still result in unexpected and hazardous experiences. One night, while she was in Africa for work, she woke up and heard lions walking around her tent. Asher was scared, but the experience was still rewarding. "Nature is a . . . tutor," she says, "and the learning never stops."

5. On a typical day, Asher spends a lot of time working on her art, which includes paintings, billboards, films, and sculptures. But anything can happen, and each day is unpredictable, so Asher has to be flexible. "I never know what's next for me," she explains.

6. Asher Jay has turned her love for art and animals into a career. She says there are many ways to turn what you care about into a job. So, what are you passionate about? 🎧63

[1] A **passion** (n) is something you love or feel strongly about.
[2] If you are **passionate** (adj) about something, you care about it a lot.
[3] **Pollution** is something that makes land, air, or water dirty and unsafe.

A Find these words in your dictionary: *job, career, profession*. How are they similar? How is a *career* or *profession* different from a *job*? Tell a partner.

B **Make predictions.** Read the title of the article and look at the image. Guess: What does a creative conservationist do? Tell a partner. Then read the first paragraph to check your ideas.

C **Identify main ideas.** Read the rest of the article. In which paragraph can you find the answer to each question below? Write the paragraph number next to the question.

_____ a. Is Asher's job ever dangerous?

_____ b. When did Asher first become interested in animals?

_____ c. What's a normal day like for Asher?

_____ d. What are some examples of Asher's work to help conservation?

D Check your answers in **C** with a partner. Then take turns asking and answering the four questions.

E **Scan for details; infer information.** What personal qualities does Asher Jay have that make her good at her job? Underline ideas in the reading. Then think of two words not in the reading.

F Answer the question at the end of the last paragraph. Share your answer with a partner, and he or she will suggest one possible job that matches your interests.

❝ I love to play the guitar. I also like to play video games.

Maybe you could write music for video games. ❞

LISTENING

A **Make predictions.** Look at the photo below. Gino is a storyboard artist. What do you think he does? Tell a partner.

B **Check predictions.** Listen and circle the correct answer. 🎧64

    a. Gino illustrates comic books.

    b. He draws pictures for children's books.

    c. He creates pictures of events in a movie.

    d. He takes photos of famous actors.

C **Listen for details.** Read the sentences. Then listen and circle **T** for *true* or **F** for *false*. Correct the false sentences in your notebook. 🎧65

    Gino says . . .

1. the best part of his job is meeting famous people.	**T**	**F**
2. his job is dull sometimes.	**T**	**F**
3. working with a director is usually pretty easy.	**T**	**F**
4. it's common to work long hours in his job.	**T**	**F**

D **Take notes.** Gino gives people advice about becoming a storyboard artist. What advice does he give? Listen for key words and take notes. Then choose the correct answers below. 🎧66

> **i** Notice how Gino uses the words *first*, *second*, and *finally* to list his points.

    a. Be knowledgeable about making movies.

    b. Be able to work independently.

    c. Be a good artist.

    d. Be a hard worker.

E Does Gino's job sound interesting to you? Why or why not? Tell a partner.

Some storyboard artists use pencil and paper, while others draw on the computer.

GRAMMAR

A Compare the underlined verbs in the sentences. What are the two verb forms called?

1. Asher Jay <u>became</u> a National Geographic Emerging Explorer in 2014.

2. She <u>has been</u> passionate about wildlife since she was a child.

B Read the Unit 9, Lesson B Grammar Reference in the appendix. Complete the exercises. Then do the exercises below.

THE SIMPLE PAST AND THE PRESENT PERFECT	
Use **the simple past** to talk about completed actions and situations at a specific time in the past.	Asher Jay **was born** in India <u>in 1985</u>. (at a specific time) She **spent** <u>two months</u> in Africa. (action finished)
Use **the present perfect** to talk about . . . 1. actions that began in the past and continue now. 2. past actions when the time that they happened is unknown or not important.	1. Asher Jay **has turned** her love for art and animals into a career. (continues now) 2. She**'s visited** Africa many times. (exact time is not important)
We often use the present perfect to ask about experiences in life (things you have done / haven't done before): *Have you ever **been** to Japan? Yes, I **have**. / No, I **haven't**.*	

C Complete the conversation. Write the simple past or present perfect form of the verbs.

A: How long (1. work) _____ you _____ for this company?

B: For three months. I (2. start) _____ in June.

A: What (3. do) _____ you _____ before that?

B: I (4. study) _____ business in college.

A: (5. enjoy) _____ you _____ it?

B: Yes, I did. For one term, I studied in Toronto, Canada.
(6. be) _____ you ever _____ there?

A: Yes, I have. I (7. go) _____ there for vacation last summer with a friend. We (8. have) _____ a great time!

> **i** It is common to start a conversation with a question in the present perfect and then ask questions in the simple past to get more information.

D Work in pairs and start a conversation about each topic (1–6) with *Have you ever . . .?*
If your partner answers, *Yes, I have*, then ask for more information and write it down.
Ask two of your own questions in 7 and 8.

Start the conversation: *Have you ever . . . ?*	Yes / No	Ask for more information: *Where? When? What? Who with? How?*
1. have a job interview		
2. win a competition		
3. travel overseas		
4. meet a famous person		
5. do yoga		
6. go on vacation with friends		
7.		
8.		

❝ Have you ever had a job interview?
                    Yes, I have. ❞
❝ What was the job?

ACTIVE ENGLISH Try it out!

A Work in pairs and imagine you are looking for a new job. Make a list of what you need to know about the job (for example, type of work, hours).

B Read the job advertisement and answer the questions with a partner.

   1. Does it have all the information you listed in **A**? If not, what is missing?

   2. What are the pros and cons of this type of job?

   3. What sort of person is it good for?

C In pairs, imagine you are the manager of a business. Choose the type of business and think of a job title. Design and write a short job ad.

> ## WANTED
> ### PART-TIME CHEFS AND SERVERS
>
> This summer, our Italian restaurant needs part-time chefs and servers to work evenings and weekends. We are looking for personable and flexible people to join our fun team. The work is demanding but rewarding. Experience is helpful but not required. Full training is provided. Email your resume to Mr. Wright at **themanager@thepastaplace.com**.
>
> **APPLY NOW**

D As a class, put your ads from **C** around the classroom, walk around, and read them all. Then choose a job that you would like to apply for.

E Compare the two emails to the manager in response to the ad in **B**. Which is better? Why?

To: themanager@thepastaplace.com
Subject: Part-Time Server Position

Dear Mr. Wright,

I am writing to apply for the position of part-time server at your restaurant. I have worked as a server in a restaurant before, and I was a friendly and efficient member of the staff. Currently, I am a first-year college student, and I am able to work evenings and weekends. I have attached my resume and a letter of recommendation from a past employer.

I look forward to hearing from you.

Sincerely,

Jake Stephenson

Send

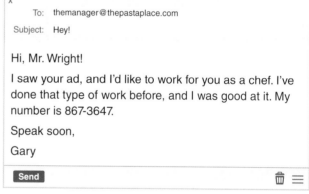

To: themanager@thepastaplace.com
Subject: Hey!

Hi, Mr. Wright!

I saw your ad, and I'd like to work for you as a chef. I've done that type of work before, and I was good at it. My number is 867-3647.

Speak soon,

Gary

Send

F **WRITING** Look at the job ad you chose in **D** and write a formal email to the manager. Describe your past experience and use the Useful Expressions to help you.

USEFUL EXPRESSIONS
Dear Sir or Madam, / Dear Mr. / Ms. _____,
I am writing to apply for . . .
I have worked . . .
Currently, I am . . .
I am able to work . . .
I have attached . . .
I look forward to hearing from you.
Sincerely, / Best regards,

9B **GOALS** Now I can . . .

Describe a job _____

Talk about my past experience _____

1. Yes, I can.
2. Mostly, yes.
3. Not yet.

GLOBAL VOICES

A Look at the people in the photo below. What do you think their job is? How would you describe it?

B Watch a video about fisherman and National Geographic photographer Corey Arnold. Number the questions (1–4) in the order they are answered.

_____ a. Why is being a fisherman so dangerous?

_____ b. What kinds of things did Corey take photos of at first?

_____ c. What type of people go to Alaska to be fishermen?

_____ d. How did Corey photograph the "Selfie Generation"?

C Guess the answers to the questions. Then watch the video again and check your answers.

1. What type of person is usually interested in fishing in Alaska?

   a. adventurous   b. punctual   c. knowledgeable

2. What kind of environment does the weather create on the boat?

   a. rainy   b. hazardous   c. exciting

3. Over time, how did Corey feel about photographing people?

   a. shy   b. nervous   c. comfortable

4. For his story "Unplugging the Selfie Generation," how did Corey contact millennials?

   a. through social media   b. with an ad   c. by visiting universities

5. What did Corey learn about this generation while doing the story?

   a. They aren't visiting national parks.   c. They are passionate about nature.

   b. They are on their phones all the time.

D Imagine you are an interviewer. Write five questions for Corey based on the information he gives in the video.

E Work in pairs and role-play an interview with Corey. Take turns being the interviewer (asking your questions from **D**) and being Corey (answering with information from the video).

Men working on a crab fishing boat in the Bering Sea. Photo by Corey Arnold.

REAL WORLD LINK GIVE AN ELEVATOR PITCH

Alan Alford, a student at the University of South Florida, gives his elevator pitch as part of a competition for business students.

A Have you ever heard of an *elevator pitch*? What do you think it might be? Read the first paragraph of the article and check if your ideas are correct.

Be Ready with Your Elevator Pitch

An *elevator pitch* is given when you have a short amount of time with someone and want to sell them your new idea. Imagine you work for a company and you have a great idea, but you are never in the room with the executives who make the decisions. Should that stop you? No! Always be ready to present your idea clearly and quickly—you might not be in the right meetings, but you never know when you will step into an elevator with the CEO and will have his or her complete attention for thirty seconds.

This is also true for job interviews. When the interviewer says, "Tell me about yourself," you need to have your elevator pitch ready to sell yourself. In other words, convince the interviewer you are the best person for the job in a short amount of time. A good elevator pitch quickly shows your qualities and skills to an employer. Make sure your pitch says who you are, what you do, and what you want by taking the following steps.

• Introduce yourself; say your name with a smile.
• Tell your story; say what you do now and what you have done in the past.
• Explain what you want; ask for a chance to show what you can do.

Finally, avoid some common mistakes. Speak clearly and confidently—but not too quickly. If you feel nervous, try to slow down. Don't use big, complicated words; make it easy to understand. And remember: a good elevator pitch should be no more than a minute or two.

B Read the rest of the article and circle **T** for *true* or **F** for *false*.

1. You need to sell your skills and qualities in a job interview.   **T**   **F**

2. You should only talk about what you are doing now, not about the past.   **T**   **F**

3. At the end of your pitch, you should say, "I'd like the opportunity to show you . . ."   **T**   **F**

4. You should speak faster so you sound more confident.   **T**   **F**

5. If you have a lot of experience, you should speak for longer than a minute or two.   **T**   **F**

C Listen to elevator pitches from two different people in job interviews. Check (✓) the best column in the feedback form for each item and decide who is best for the job. 🎧67

Did Speaker 1 . . .	☹	☺	😊	😊😊
introduce herself?				
tell her story?				
explain what she wants?				
speak clearly and confidently?				
speak for one minute or less?				

Did Speaker 2 . . .				
introduce himself?				
tell his story?				
explain what he wants?				
speak clearly and confidently?				
speak for one minute or less?				

D In pairs, compare your feedback about the two elevator pitches in **C**. Do you agree? Which speaker do you think is better for the job? Why?

> " I think the first person told her story well.
>
> So do I, and I think the second person didn't introduce himself well. "

E Follow the steps to prepare an elevator pitch.

1. Think of a job you would like to do in the future and write a short job description.

2. Write an elevator pitch to respond to "Tell me about yourself" during an interview for this job. Use the advice in the article. After writing, practice saying your pitch and memorize it.

F **You Choose** Choose one of the options for giving your elevator pitch.

Option 1: Work in pairs and role-play a job interview. Take turns saying, "Tell me about yourself," and giving your pitch.

Option 2: Stand up in front of the class and present your elevator pitch. As you are watching others' pitches, try to guess the type of job the person is looking for.

Option 3: Make a video recording of your elevator pitch that you can send to employers. Play the video for the class.

G As you watch an elevator pitch by another student, take notes on the feedback items in **C**. Then meet with the speaker and give your feedback. Do they agree with you?

10

STAY IN TOUCH

LOOK AT THE PHOTO. ANSWER THE QUESTIONS.

1. Would you like to be part of an online event like this? Why or why not?
2. How do you normally stay in touch with family and friends? By texting? Video calls?

WARM-UP VIDEO

A When you want to find out new facts and information, where do you look?

B Watch the video and answer the questions.

1. Where can you call to find out information?
2. Who will answer the phone?
3. Why does Rosa think people often call them?

C Watch the video again and write the missing numbers.

1. The telephone number is _____.
2. There are _____ librarians on the team.
3. The helpline began in _____.
4. They receive around _____ calls per year.
5. A great white shark has around _____ teeth.

D Would you prefer to use the internet to find the answer to a question or to call the New York Public Library and ask a librarian? Why?

E If you called the New York Public Library, what question would you like to ask? Tell a partner and try to find out the answer before the next class.

A group of singers performs as part of an online event to raise money for a non-profit organization.

GOALS

Lesson A
/ Talk about ways to stay in touch
/ Make formal and polite calls

Lesson B
/ Discuss how you use the phone
/ Communicate informally

VOCABULARY

A Read the article. Then answer the questions below.

> **Phone Data**
>
> In a survey of teenagers (ages 13–17) with phones, nearly 100% said their phone is their favorite way to pass time and to stay in touch with other people. They love it so much that over three quarters of them check their messages as soon as they wake up. A different survey found that, for adults, phones are important for work, with around half of them making video calls and attending virtual meetings on their phones. Both teens and adults said they feel anxious when their phones are on silent—or worse still—when they don't have a signal!

1. What three things do most teenagers use their phones for?

2. What do adults also use their phones for?

3. What makes teens and adults feel anxious?

B Does any of the information surprise you? Why or why not?

C Complete each phrase in the Word Bank with the missing verb or noun. The answers are in the article.

D Ask and answer the questions in pairs.

1. What are the three most important things you use your phone for?

2. When you wake up, what is the first thing you look at on your phone?

3. Do you normally stay in touch by texting, calling, or making video calls? What does it depend on?

4. How do you feel when your phone is on silent or you don't have a signal?

WORD BANK

spend time / 1. _____ time

get in touch / 2. _____ in touch (or contact)

check your phone / check your 3. _____ / check your email

call someone / 4. _____ a call / return a call

go to a meeting / 5. _____ a meeting

get a text / get a message

The phone 6. _____ on silent. / on mute.

can't get a / don't have a 7. _____

People check their phones and use social media in a cafe in Borama, Somalia.

A family photo taken during a video call in Singapore

LISTENING

A Listen to six conversations. Which are phone calls? Which are video calls? Write **P** for *phone* or **V** for *video*. 🎧68

1. _____   2. _____   3. _____   4. _____   5. _____   6. _____

B **Infer information; make predictions.** Read the sentences below. Then listen again to the six conversations and decide which sentence could come next in each one. 🎧68

1. a. OK, I'll check my messages.
   b. No, thanks. I'll call back later.
   c. Yes, I left a message.

2. a. Sorry, I always forget to click it.
   b. Sorry, I'm making a call.
   c. I'll put you on mute.

3. a. May I ask who's calling?
   b. Would you like to leave a message?
   c. Please leave me a message, and I'll call you back.

4. a. Maybe her laptop is turned off.
   b. I'll ask her to leave and try again.
   c. Try checking your messages.

5. a. Can I take a message?
   b. Is your phone on silent?
   c. Do you mind if I call you again later?

6. a. Check your text messages.
   b. Sorry, I don't have a signal.
   c. OK, and what's your phone number?

C **Check predictions.** Listen and check your answers in **B**. 🎧69

D **PRONUNCIATION: Stress with clarification** Listen to the conversation. Why does Speaker B stress the underlined number? 🎧70

A: My number is 555-6749.   **B:** 555-6749?   **A:** Yes. 6-7-4-9.

E **PRONUNCIATION: Stress with clarification** Listen and complete the conversations. 🎧71

1. **A:** My username is nancy_p12.
   B: Did you say _____?
   A: No, p12. That's p as in *Paul*.

2. **A:** My username is @photoguy.
   B: _____?
   A: That's correct.

3. **A:** My email address is joym@sf.edu.
   B: Was that _____ at sf.edu?
   A: No, it's joy m as in *Mary*.

F Practice the conversations in **E** with a partner. Then use new information and practice again.

SPEAKING

A Celia and Lisa are chatting when their phone call is interrupted. Listen to the conversations. Then answer the questions. 🎧72

Lisa: Hello?

Celia: Lisa? Hi. It's Celia.

Lisa: Oh, hey, Celia. How're you doing?

Celia: Pretty good. So, are you ready for the big test tomorrow?

Lisa: Almost, but I have one question . . . (phone beeps) Oh, Celia, can you hang on? I've got another call coming in.

Celia: Yeah, no problem.

Lisa: Hello?

Prof. Larson: Yes, hello. May I speak to Lisa Sanchez, please?

Lisa: Speaking.

Prof. Larson: Lisa, this is Professor Larson. You left me a message earlier today. You had a question about tomorrow's exam.

Lisa: Oh, right. Professor Larson, could you hold for a moment?

Prof. Larson: Of course.

Lisa: Hello, Celia? Can I call you back? I have to take the other call.

Celia: Sure. Talk to you later.

1. Why is Lisa and Celia's conversation interrupted?

2. Which conversation is more formal? Underline the phrases in the conversation that help you decide.

B Practice the conversation in **A** with two classmates. Use your own names in the conversation.

C Make the conversation below more formal by changing the underlined words. Use the Speaking Strategy to help you. Then practice it with a partner.

Hana: Hello?

Martin: Hi. Is Kurt there?

_____

Hana: Who's calling?

_____

Martin: This is Martin.

Hana: OK, hang on.

_____

Martin: Sure.

Hana: Sorry, he's not in. Can I take a message?

_____

Martin: No, thanks. I'll call back later.

D Role-play a new phone conversation between Hana and Martin from **C**. This time Kurt is home. Before you begin, decide if the conversation will be formal or informal.

E Perform your new conversation from **D** for another pair. Can they tell if the call is formal or informal?

SPEAKING STRATEGY 🎧73
Using the phone

Asking for someone and responding	Hi, Lisa? / Hi. Is Lisa there? / Can I speak to Lisa, please? Hello. May / Could I speak to Lisa, please? [formal] This is Lisa. / Speaking.
Asking for identification of caller	Who's calling? May I ask who's calling? [formal]
Asking someone to wait	Hang on. / Can you hang on (for a moment / second)? Would / Could you hold (for a moment / second)? [formal]
Taking a message	Can I take a message? May I take a message? Would you like to leave a message? [formal]

GRAMMAR

A Read the Unit 10, Lesson A Grammar Reference in the appendix. Complete the exercises. Then do the exercises below.

ASKING FOR PERMISSION						RESPONSES
Would	it be OK	if	I	called	back later?	Certainly. / Of course. / Sure, no problem. (I'm) sorry, but . . .
	you mind					No, not at all. / No, go ahead. (I'm) sorry, but . . .
Do	you mind	if	I	call	back later?	No, not at all. / No, go ahead. (I'm) sorry, but . . .
May / Could / Can			I	call	back later?	Certainly. / Of course. / Sure, no problem. (I'm) sorry, but . . .

B Look at the photo below. A passenger is asking a flight attendant for permission. Use the words in parentheses to complete the questions.

1. (move to another seat)

   Would you _____?

2. (have a vegetarian meal)

   May _____?

3. (use the restroom now)

   Would it _____?

4. (turn on my laptop now)

   Can _____?

C Read each situation. Use the verbs in parentheses to ask permission.

1. Your friend is doing his or her homework. You have finished your homework, and you want to watch TV. Ask permission informally. (turn on)

   _____

2. You're invited to a party on Saturday night. You want your friend to go, too. Ask the host's permission a little formally. (bring)

   _____

3. You were sick yesterday and missed an important test in class. You want to take it this Friday. Ask your teacher's permission formally. (take)

   _____

4. Your teacher doesn't allow phones in class. You need to keep your phone on silent, but you are waiting for an important text. Ask your teacher's permission formally. (check)

   _____

D With a partner, take turns asking and answering the questions in **C**. Refuse (say *no* to) at least one request and give a reason.

A flight attendant and passengers on a flight from Iceland to Greenland

ACTIVE ENGLISH Try it out!

A Read the article with advice about customer service over the phone. Is the article for customers or for customer service representatives?

What Drives Customers Crazy on the Phone?

When people call customer service, they often get angry with the representative. Here are the top five reasons why customers get angry and how you can keep them happy.

1. **Waiting for someone to pick up**
   Customers hate waiting. Answer the call quickly and avoid putting them on hold.

2. **When no one knows the answer**
   Avoid saying you don't know the answer to a customer's question or transferring them to someone else. Have a positive attitude and find out the answer.

3. **No apology[1]**
   If the company has made a mistake, apologize. Customers want to feel that their problem is your problem.

4. **Repeating information**
   Customers hate it when they have to repeat information. Listen and get it right the first time.

5. **Rude or unfriendly service**
   Even if you feel tired, greet the caller politely and offer help in a friendly way.

[1]An **apology** (n) is when someone says they are sorry. To **apologize** (v) means to say sorry.

B Listen to a phone call. What does the customer service representative do wrong? Use the five items from the article in **A** to help you. 🎧74

C Listen to a call with a different customer service representative. What does she do well? Use the five items from the article in **A** to help you. 🎧75

D Imagine that you are going to make a call to a customer service representative about a late product. In your notebook, write down:

- the name of the product
- when you ordered it
- the order number
- your contact number

E In pairs, role-play a phone conversation. Then switch roles and repeat.

Student A: You are the customer. Use your information from **D**.

Student B: You are the customer service representative. You need to ask for and write down the customer's information. Decide if you are going to be polite and helpful (and solve the problem) or rude and unfriendly!

10A GOALS   Now I can . . .

Talk about ways to stay in touch _____

Make formal and polite calls _____

1. Yes, I can.
2. Mostly, yes.
3. Not yet.

VOCABULARY

A Read the quiz below and match the words in blue to their opposites.

1. polite _____

2. respond _____

3. turn up _____

4. ban _____

5. be distracted by _____

6. post _____

> **WORD BANK**
>
> A **device** is a piece of electronic equipment used for a special purpose; for example, a smartphone or tablet.
>
> If you are **addicted to** something, you can't stop doing or using it.

Phone Etiquette: How Polite Are You?

1. You're on a date. You get a text from a friend. What do you do?

   a. Check it and **respond** right away.

   b. **Ignore** the message. Answering it now would be **rude**.

   c. My idea: _____

2. A man on the bus is listening to loud music. What do you do?

   a. Ask him to **turn down** the music.

   b. Put on your headphones and **turn up** your music loud, too.

   c. My idea: _____

3. I think we should . . .

   a. **ban** phones in crowded places like subways and airplanes.

   b. **allow** phones everywhere at any time.

   c. My idea: _____

4. You are talking to your boss, but she **is distracted by** her phone. What do you do?

   a. Stop talking and ask why she is **addicted to** her phone.

   b. Keep talking and hope she starts to **pay attention to** you.

   c. My idea: _____

5. You want to post some funny photos of your friend online. What do you do?

   a. Show your friend the photos first and ask if it's OK.

   b. **Post** them and, if he doesn't like them, **delete** them.

   c. My idea: _____

B Take the quiz. Complete with your own ideas and circle your answers. Then compare your answers in groups of three.

A woman pauses in the street to check her phone in Hong Kong, China. Is this a good idea?

HAVE SMARTPHONES
CHANGED OUR LIVES
FOR **BETTER** OR FOR **WORSE**?

1. _____

Smartphones have changed the way we live. Billions of people around the world are using their phones to make calls, send texts, and check email. <u>Many of them</u> are also booking car rides, comparing product reviews, following the news, and posting on social media. Some people prefer to do their banking on their phones, and others want to check how many steps they are taking each day in order to stay healthy.

2. _____

These benefits, however, come at a high cost to our mental[1] and social lives. We keep checking our phones more and more throughout the day, and <u>this</u> is making us increasingly distracted. As we become addicted to our phones, we spend less time in the "real" world and more time in the virtual[2] world. We often don't pay attention to what is happening right in front of us.

3. _____

Researchers are familiar[3] with this trend. They are studying smartphone use and our ability to complete tasks.[4] In one study, <u>they</u> asked three groups of participants to complete a math problem and some other tasks. The first group agreed to keep their phones in another room. The second group put their phones in their pockets. The researchers allowed the third group to place their phones on their desks. The participants did not use their phones during the study. At the end of the exercise, the first group did better than <u>the others</u>.

4. _____

In a second study, participants ate a meal with friends or family at a restaurant. One group left their phones on the table during the dinner. Another group put their phones away. At the end of the meal, the first group reported that they felt distracted by their phones and enjoyed eating their meal less.

5. _____

One result of <u>all this</u> is that more and more people are choosing to turn off their phones for long periods of time. For example, some are taking "digital-free weekends" and going two days with no phone or internet. They prefer spending more of their free time with friends and family or doing exercise outside, rather than staring at a screen. People who do this report feeling calmer, with less stress in their lives. Why not try <u>it</u> this weekend and see what happens? 🎧76

[1]**Mental** means related to the mind or thinking.
[2]If something is **virtual**, it's happening online or through a computer, not in real life.
[3]If something is **familiar**, you know about it because of previous experience.
[4]A **task** is an activity or piece of work you have to do.

A In pairs, read the title of the article and answer the questions.

1. How do you think the article will answer the question in the title?

2. How would you answer the question? Why?

B **Read for main ideas.** Read the article and match each question to a paragraph (1–5).

a. How do smartphones affect us socially?

b. Is it time to take a break from your phone?

c. What are the different ways we use smartphones?

d. What are the disadvantages of smartphone use?

e. How do smartphones affect us mentally?

C Read the article again and make a list of the ways in which smartphones have changed our lives . . .

• for better.

• for worse.

Overall, what do you think the writer's opinion about smartphones is?

D Find these words underlined in the article and write what they refer to in your notebook.

1. Many of them (paragraph 1) *the billions of people with smartphones*

2. this (paragraph 2)

3. they (paragraph 3)

4. the others (paragraph 3)

5. all this (paragraph 5)

6. it (paragraph 5)

E Find these adjectives in the reading. What prepositions follow them? Do you know any other adjective + preposition combinations?

1. addicted _____   3. distracted _____

2. familiar _____

ACADEMIC SKILL

Collocations

When learning a new word, it is important to also study the collocations the word is part of. A collocation is two or more words that usually go together; for example, *pay attention to* and *take a break from*.

F **Think critically.** Work with a partner and complete steps 1–3.

1. Describe the studies in paragraphs 3 and 4 with your books closed. Can you remember what happened?

Student A: Describe the study in paragraph 3.

Student B: Describe the study in paragraph 4.

2. How can you explain the results of the studies?

3. Do you think a "digital-free weekend" is a good idea? Why or why not?

People attending a silent disco at the Open'er Music Festival in Gdynia, Poland take a break from their phones and dance to music they only hear through headphones.

LISTENING

A **Listen for gist.** Read the sentences below. Then listen to three different conversations and choose the best answer for each sentence. 🎧77

WORD BANK
If a person does something **at the last minute**, he or she does it at the latest time possible.

Conversation 1

1. The speakers are in a _____.

   a. classroom   b. restaurant   c. movie theater

Conversation 2

2. The speakers are _____ a party.

   a. taking photos at   b. posting pictures from   c. looking at photos from

Conversation 3

3. The speakers are waiting for their friend Manny. Manny is _____.

   a. late for a party   b. still at school   c. talking on his phone

B **Listen for details; infer information.** Listen again and choose the best answer. 🎧77

Conversation 1

1. The man is asking the girl to _____.

   a. turn off her phone   b. speak more quietly   c. turn down her music

2. The girl _____.

   a. apologizes and agrees   b. ignores the man   c. gets angry with the man

Conversation 2

3. The woman thinks the photo of her is _____.

   a. fun   b. silly   c. terrible

4. The woman decides to _____.

   a. ignore people's   b. tell Connor to   c. both a and b
      comments   delete the photos

Conversation 3

5. The man texts Manny, and Manny _____.

   a. responds right away   b. ignores the text   c. calls him back

6. The woman thinks Manny is _____.

   a. polite   b. angry   c. rude

C Answer the questions with a partner.

1. In each conversation, what happened? Use your answers in **A** and **B** to help you explain.

2. Have you ever been in any of these situations? If so, what happened?

66 | In the first conversation, the
     girl was . . . and the man
     asked her to . . .

GRAMMAR

A Study the underlined verbs in the sentences from the reading. In each sentence, what verb form comes after the first verb? What do you notice about the verb *prefer*?

1. Others <u>want to check</u> how many steps they are taking each day.

2. We <u>keep checking</u> our phones more and more throughout the day.

3. Some people <u>prefer to do</u> their banking on their phones.

4. They <u>prefer spending</u> more of their free time with friends and family.

B Read the Unit 10, Lesson B Grammar Reference in the appendix. Complete the exercises. Then do the exercises below.

VERB + INFINITIVE VS. VERB + GERUND	
I **need** <u>to buy</u> a new phone.	Certain verbs can be followed by an <u>infinitive</u>: *agree, decide, hope, learn, need, plan, seem, want, would like*
I **avoid** <u>talking</u> on the phone when I'm driving.	Certain verbs can be followed by a <u>gerund</u> (verb + *-ing*): *appreciate, avoid, dislike, enjoy, feel like, keep, (not) mind*
I **tried** <u>to call</u> you earlier. I **tried** <u>calling</u> you earlier.	Certain verbs can be followed by an infinitive or a gerund: *begin, can't stand, hate, like, love, prefer, start, try*

C How do you feel about the activities below? Write sentences in your notebook using the verbs in the box.

avoid	can't stand	enjoy	hate	(not) like	(not) mind	need	prefer

I hate talking on the phone. I prefer to text people.

1. talk on the phone
2. receive texts late at night
3. get the news online
4. take selfies in public
5. make calls while I'm eating
6. spend time on my own
7. play games on my phone
8. post on social media

D Work in small groups. Compare your answers from **C**.

“ I can't stand taking selfies in public. It's embarrassing!

Really? I think it's fun. ”

A woman takes a selfie in front of the Eiffel Tower in Paris, France.

ACTIVE ENGLISH Try it out!

A Work in pairs. Turn to the Unit 10 Writing appendix and read the messages. Which of the messages (a–f) . . .

1. are emails?
2. is an advertisement?
3. has an emoji?
4. are replies to earlier messages?

B Complete the guidelines for writing informal messages by circling the correct answers. Find examples of each rule in the messages in the Writing appendix.

1. You **can** / **can't** use informal language.
2. **Do** / **Don't** include extra, unnecessary information.
3. **Avoid** / **Don't avoid** using all capital letters (for example, HELLO!).
4. You **can** / **can't** use well-known abbreviations.
5. With very informal messages, you **can** / **can't** leave out small words such as pronouns (*I*, *you*, *he*, *she*) and articles (*a*, *an*, *the*).
6. Writing informal messages is **similar to** / **not similar to** speaking.

C WRITING In pairs, you are going to write six informal messages using the Useful Expressions and the prompts below.

Student A: Write message 1 at the top of a piece of paper and then pass the paper to Student B.

Student B: Respond below with message 2 and pass the paper back to Student A.

Student A: Respond with message 3 and so on.

Message 1: You are having a party. Invite your partner. Tell him / her why, when, and where.

Message 2: Say you would like to come to the party.

Message 3: Ask your partner what he / she likes doing at parties; for example, does he / she enjoy dancing or playing games?

Message 4: Reply and ask permission to bring a friend.

Message 5: Respond to your partner's request, saying yes or no.

Message 6: Reply with a final message and an emoji.

> **USEFUL EXPRESSIONS**
> Hi! / Hello, / Hey _____,
> Are you free . . .?
> Want to come to my . . .?
> Sounds great. / Good idea! /
> I'd love to.
> Do you like / enjoy . . .?
> Can I . . .? / Is it ok if . . .?
> Sure, no problem. / Sorry, but . . .
> Looking forward to it!
> See you soon!

D With your partner, read the six messages on your paper from **C** and decide if they follow the guidelines in **B**.

10B GOALS Now I can . . .

Discuss how I use the phone _____

Communicate informally _____

1. Yes, I can.
2. Mostly, yes.
3. Not yet.

GLOBAL VOICES

A You are going to watch a video titled, "Talking Tech." Try to guess the missing words in the questions from the video. Then watch the video and check your answers.

1. What type of t_____ do you use most often?

2. What do you l_____ about it?

3. What drives you c_____ about smartphones?

4. How do you usually c_____ with people?

5. What b_____ you about communication these days?

B Work in pairs and watch the video again. Student A will answer questions 1–5; Student B will answer 6–10.

Student A	Student B
1. What does Maite use her phone and laptop for? _____	6. What does Maite like about her devices? _____
2. What does Marcel like about his phone? _____	7. What does Pedro use his phone for? _____
3. What drives Pedro crazy about smartphones? _____	8. What drives Maite crazy about her smartphone? _____
4. How does Maite prefer to communicate? _____	9. How does Pedro prefer to communicate with his friends? _____
5. What bothers Maite about communication these days? _____	10. What bothers Pedro about communication these days? _____

C Ask your partner his or her set of questions and write the answers in your notebook. Then watch the video again and check them.

D Interview your partner with the questions from **A**.

People use devices as they commute to work on a boat from Vallejo to San Francisco in California (US).

11

TECHNOLOGY

LOOK AT THE PHOTO. ANSWER THE QUESTIONS.

1. What old technology is in the picture?
2. What did people use it for in the past? What can it be used for now?

WARM-UP VIDEO

A Can you remember or imagine an old computer? Describe it to a partner. How have computers changed since then? Think of one or two ways.

B Look up any words below you don't know. Then watch the video. Check (✓) the items you see.

- ☐ a keyboard
- ☐ a monitor
- ☐ a mouse
- ☐ a screen
- ☐ an error message
- ☐ a printer

C Read the statements below and guess the answers. Then watch the video again and check your answers.

| button | internet | programs |
| desk | nothing | televisions |

1. Jayka: "If you don't have a _____, where do you put this?"
2. Tyler: "Kind of like those old _____ that are, like, very boxy."
3. Brooke-Monaé: "Apps! Games! Websites! Everything. But this thing right here has _____!"
4. Host: "You can't do anything, or even type, until you hit a reset _____ . . ."
5. Dylan: "Are there any _____ on it?"
6. Host: "How do you go on the _____?"

D How did the kids feel about the old computer? Would you like to use it? Why or why not?

A woman makes a call from a telephone booth in the Scottish Highlands. Some of these old booths are now hotspots where you can access the internet.

e-mail + text + phone

GOALS

Lesson A
/ Talk about devices
/ Describe how things used to be

Lesson B
/ Explain how technology works
/ Compare similar items

VOCABULARY

A Look at the photo of an athlete wearing a fitness tracker. What can this type of technology do? Then read the ad.

The new **BeFit Alpha** is the most advanced fitness tracker at an affordable price.

- It's made with durable materials and comes with a rechargeable battery.
- The user-friendly screen means it's practical to use, even on the longest workouts.
- The customizable straps come in a variety of fashionable colors.

BeFit. The most reliable name in wearable technology.

B Study the words in blue from **A**. Then circle **T** for *true* or **F** for *false*.

If something is . . .

1. *advanced*, it's very modern.	T	F
2. *affordable*, it's expensive.	T	F
3. *durable*, it's strong.	T	F
4. *rechargeable*, you need to change the battery.	T	F
5. *user-friendly*, it's difficult to use.	T	F
6. *practical*, it's useful and logical.	T	F
7. *customizable*, you can change it.	T	F
8. *fashionable*, it looks old.	T	F
9. *reliable*, you can trust it.	T	F
10. *wearable*, you can wear it on your body.	T	F

ℹ The suffixes *-able* / *-ible* / *-ble* mean *capable of* or *can*. If something is *affordable*, you can afford it (it is not too expensive).

C Check your answers in **B** with a partner. For the false statements, write correct definitions.

D Think of a device you use (for example, a phone, a tablet) and choose three words from **A** to describe it. Then write a short ad (two to three sentences) for the device using your own words. Read your ad to a partner.

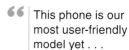 This phone is our most user-friendly model yet . . .

LISTENING

A Look at the words in the Word Bank. What technology is *indispensable* in your life now? What technology from the past was a *fad* or a *flash in the pan*?

B **Listen for the main idea.** Listen to a lecture and choose the best word to complete the title. 🎧78

Guessing the Future: Predictions about technology that were

_____.

a. reliable   c. wrong

b. creative   d. confusing

C **Listen for details; take notes.** Listen again. Complete the missing information in the chart. 🎧78

Year	Technology	Prediction (then)	Number	Description (now)
_1876_	telephone	"The Americans have need of the telephone, but ___*we do not*___."	about _5_ billion smartphones	_indispensable_
_____	automobile	"The horse is here to stay, but the automobile _____."	more than _____ billion cars	_____ _____ _____
_____	television	"Television won't last. It's just a _____."	more than _____ billion TVs	_____
_____	internet	"The internet will _____."	over _____ billion users	_____

D Choose one piece of technology from **C** and predict how it will be different 20 years from now and 50 years from now. Tell a partner. Do you agree with his or her predictions? Why or why not?

- **General Electric made this TV in 1948.**
- **The screen was 9.5 inches (24 cm) by 7.5 inches (19 cm).**
- **The picture was in black and white.**
- **In the US, there were only four major TV channels.**

SPEAKING

A Listen to Alan and Kim's conversation. Then answer the questions with a partner. 🎧79

Alan: Hey, Kim. I saw your sister on social media the other day. She's really changed a lot.

Kim: Yeah? Why do you say that? She still looks the same.

Alan: Yeah, but now she's got all these friends, and she's really funny. She used to be so different—you know, kind of shy.

Kim: A lot of people say that about my sister. They think that she's this quiet person, but, actually, she's very outgoing.

Alan: Really?

Kim: Yep. Once she feels comfortable with you, she's really friendly, and she talks a lot.

Alan: Wow, I had no idea!

1. How do most people describe Kim's sister?

2. What is Kim's sister really like?

B Practice the conversation with a partner. Do you know anyone like Kim's sister?

C Read the statements below and check (✓) the ones you agree with.

☐ 1. Learning English is easy.

☐ 2. Everybody should get married.

☐ 3. Fitness trackers are affordable.

☐ 4. Wearing black is always fashionable.

☐ 5. Modern technology is always reliable.

☐ 6. The apps on your phone should be practical.

SPEAKING STRATEGY 🎧80
Offering a counterargument

Stating what other people think	A lot of people say (that) . . . Some people think (that) . . .	she's shy.
Explaining what you think	(But,) actually, . . . (But,) in fact, / in reality, . . . (But,) the truth / fact / reality is . . .	she's very outgoing.

D With a partner, compare your opinions about the statements in **C**. Talk about the statements you <u>don't</u> agree with. Use the Speaking Strategy to help you.

E Tell a partner something surprising about you or your country.

❝ A lot of people think it's warm in Mexico all year, but, in reality, Mexico City can be cold in the winter.

❝ Some people say learning English is easy, but, actually, it's hard.

Why do you say that? ❞

❝ Well, the grammar is difficult and . . .

GRAMMAR

A Read the sentences. Are the underlined verb forms talking about the past or present? How is the spelling different in the affirmative and negative forms?

1. In the 1800s, people <u>used to ride</u> horses; they <u>didn't use to have</u> cars.

2. My sister <u>used to be</u> shy, but now she's very outgoing.

B Read the Unit 11, Lesson A Grammar Reference in the appendix. Complete the exercises. Then do the exercises below.

USED TO			
Subject	(not) use(d) to	Verb	
I	**used to**	wear	glasses.
She	**didn't use to**	own	a computer.

Did	Subject	use to	Verb		Responses
Did	you	**use to**	wear	glasses?	Yes, I did. / No, I didn't.
	she		own	a computer?	Yes, she did. / No, she didn't.
Remember, don't write ~~didn't used to~~ or ~~Did you used to~~.					

C Complete the sentences with *used* or *use*.

1. People _____ to write more letters.

2. I didn't _____ to shop online.

3. Did you _____ to be shy?

4. Phones _____ to be more reliable.

5. I didn't _____ to eat meat.

D **PRONUNCIATION:** *used to / use to* Listen to the sentences in **C** and follow the steps.

1. Notice how the pronunciation of *used to* and *use to* sound the same. In spoken English, the /d/ in *used* usually disappears.

2. Listen again and repeat the sentences.

E Follow the steps below.

1. Write down three true statements about things you used to do on three pieces of paper.

2. Give the papers to your teacher.

3. Your teacher will give you three pieces of paper with statements from your classmates.

4. Walk around the class and ask questions to find out who the papers belong to.

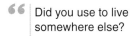

> Did you use to live somewhere else?
>
> No, I didn't. I've always lived in this city.
>
> Yes, I did. I used to live in Tokyo.

In the early 1900s, New York City taxis used to be horses and carriages.

Jenny Tough, running in the mountains on the Isle of Skye, Scotland

ACTIVE ENGLISH Try it out!

A Look at the photo of adventurer Jenny Tough. Which device do you think she takes on every trip? Why? Listen and check your prediction. 🎧82

    a. a fitness tracker   b. a laptop   c. a camera

B Listen again and take notes about Jenny's life in the past and now. 🎧82

	In the Past	Now
Home	As a child, she used to live in Canada.	
School / Work		
Travel		

C Take notes about your life five years ago and now. Try to write down things that are different, if possible.

Five Years Ago
Home: _____
Family: _____
Friends: _____
Work / School: _____
Favorite activities: _____
Favorite TV shows / movies: _____
Other: _____

Now
Home: _____
Family: _____
Friends: _____
Work / School: _____
Favorite activities: _____
Favorite TV shows / movies: _____
Other: _____

D Tell a partner how your life has changed in the past five years. Whose life has changed more?

    ❝ My older brother used to live at home, but now he's away at college.

11A GOALS   Now I can . . .

Talk about devices _____

Describe how things used to be _____

1. Yes, I can.
2. Mostly, yes.
3. Not yet.

VOCABULARY

A Rank the household appliances and devices from 1 to 7 (1 = very important, 7 = not important).

_____ a. alarm clock   _____ d. remote control   _____ f. vacuum cleaner

_____ b. laptop   _____ e. smart TV   _____ g. washing machine

_____ c. phone

B Match the sentences below to items a–g in **A**.

_b_ **1.** **Log in** with your username and password.

_____ **2.** Where is it? I hate having to **stand up** to change the channel!

_____ **3.** My battery's **run out**. Where can I **charge** it?

_____ **4.** I **plugged** it **in** in the living room, but it won't reach the stairs.

_____ **5.** We need to get up early, so I've set it to **go off** at 6 am.

_____ **6.** You can **look up** the show you want under *search*, or you can **scroll down** to see what's popular now.

_____ **7.** Can you **load** it and **switch** it **on**? I need clean clothes for my interview.

> ℹ️ A phrasal verb is a verb with two or more words: the main verb and a smaller word (like *up*, *at*, *on*).
>
> Some phrasal verbs can be separated without a change in meaning: *Look up* phrasal verbs in your dictionary. / *Look* phrasal verbs *up* in your dictionary.

C Match the verbs in **blue** to the definitions.

1. put electricity into a device: _____*charge*_____

2. move down on a screen: _____

3. get up from sitting: _____

4. put things into a machine: _____

5. start making a noise: _____

6. turn on an electrical device: _____

7. connect a device to electricity: _____

8. connect to a computer or website using personal information: _____

9. search for a piece of information: _____

10. use up all of something: _____

D Work in pairs and take turns choosing a verb from **C**. Act out the verb and have your partner guess the action.

> 66 Are you loading clothes into a washing machine?
>
> I know! You're plugging something in. 99

How many devices do you see in the photo? What do you think the family members are doing on their devices?

READING

HOW SMART IS YOUR HOME?

In the past, people used to buy household appliances to make their lives easier. For example, it used to take a long time to clean floors and carpets, but then the vacuum cleaner made it easier and faster. This is still true today, but now, many household objects are also "smart." (1.) _____ For example, when you switch on a smart TV, it often knows what you are watching and when. Or, if you have a device that turns on your music or looks up the weather for you, then it's probably collecting some of your personal information. Two technology reporters, Kashmir Hill and Surya Mattu, decided to find out what living in a smart home is really like.

Kashmir's Story

Kashmir turned her one-bedroom apartment in San Francisco, US into a smart home. She connected lots of appliances to the internet, including her lights, coffee maker, baby monitor, vacuum cleaner, TV, toothbrush, and even her bed. (2.) _____ Kashmir could watch her house when she wasn't there. Her toothbrush sent her messages if she forgot to brush her teeth. If she was cold at night, her bed turned up the heat. And she could use her smartphone to switch on her robot vacuum cleaner. (3.) _____ Not everything was user-friendly. When she asked her coffee machine to make a cup of coffee, sometimes it didn't understand her instructions. When

Kashmir got a bad night's sleep, her bed told her she slept poorly, which was very annoying! And to control everything, she had to log in to thirteen different apps.

Surya's Story

Meanwhile, Kashmir's coworker Surya plugged a router[1] into all of Kashmir's devices so he could see the information coming from her smart home. He could see every time a device was talking to servers[2] outside the home and sending out personal information about Kashmir's life. (4.) _____ He knew when she got up, when she brushed her teeth, and which TV shows she liked. All the smart objects in her home sent this kind of information back to the companies that produced them. In other words, Kashmir's smart home had the power to tell other people a lot of information about her private life. (5.) _____

[1] A **router** is a device that receives and sends information between computer networks.
[2] A **server** is the main computer that stores information from other computers.

A Make predictions. Look at the title of the article. What do you think a *smart home* is?

B Identify missing information. Read the article and match the sentences (a–e) to the spaces.

a. However, there were also disadvantages.

b. As a result, Kashmir and Surya started to wonder how "smart" it really was to live in a smart home!

c. In other words, they are connected to the internet and can report on your life.

d. What were the advantages?

e. He could tell when the lights were switched on and off.

C Answer the questions about the article.

1. What is the same about buying household appliances in the past and today?

A dog catches a ride on a smart robotic vacuum cleaner.

ACADEMIC SKILL

Discourse markers

Discourse markers, such as *however* and *as a result*, can connect information and ideas in an article. Try to use discourse markers in your own writing.

2. What is different?

3. What helpful things did Kashmir's smart toothbrush and bed do?

4. Why did her coffee maker and bed annoy her?

5. What information about Kashmir did Surya learn from the router?

6. Where did the smart devices send Kashmir's personal information?

D Read the Academic Skill box above **E**. Then underline the discourse markers in the text (including the sentences in **B**) that . . .

1. introduce an example.

2. explain something in another way.

3. contrast something.

4. show the result of something.

E Circle your feelings about the article. Then compare with a partner.

1. I **am** / **am not** surprised by some of the information in the article.

2. I **already knew** / **didn't know** this about smart homes and smart products.

3. I **think** / **don't think** there is a problem with giving my personal information to companies.

LISTENING

A Complete the sentences with the words *blind*, *sight*, and *vision*. Use your dictionary to help you.

1. _____ or _____ is the ability to see things.

2. If you are _____, you can't see.

B Listen and choose the best answer to complete each sentence. 🎧84

1. Doctor Spenser and the scientists _____ a new tool.

    a. will develop   b. are working on   c. have completed

2. The glasses have a small _____ inside.

    a. brain   b. pen   c. camera

3. The tool _____.

    a. stops blindness from happening   b. gives blind people some vision back   c. gives blind people perfect vision

C **Listen for the order of events.** How does the tool work? Read the sentences below. Listen again and number the steps (1–5) in the order your hear them. 🎧84

_____ a. The person can see the pen.

_____ b. The blind person puts on special glasses and looks at an object, such as a pen.

_____ c. The picture is sent to the device in the person's brain.

_____ d. Doctors put a small device in a blind person's brain.

_____ e. The glasses take a picture of the pen.

D Use your answers in **B** and **C** to explain how this new technology works. What do you think of this tool? Tell a partner.

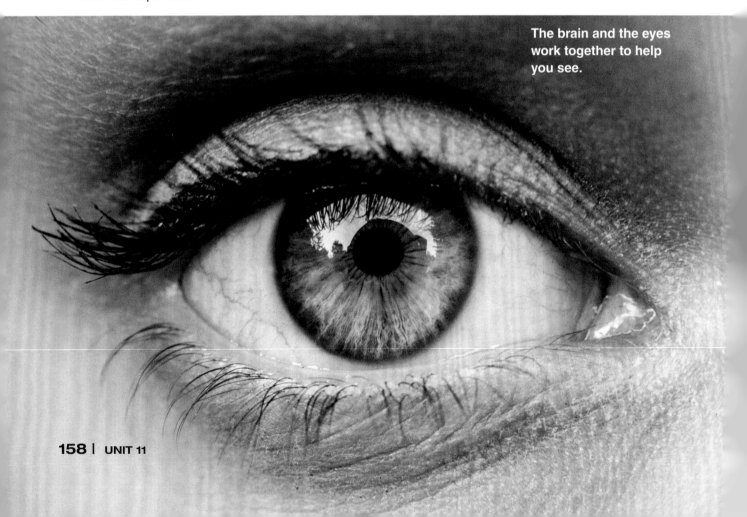

The brain and the eyes work together to help you see.

Both the Chevrolet Bolt and the Tesla Model S are electric cars.

GRAMMAR

A Read the Unit 11, Lesson B Grammar Reference in the appendix. Complete the exercises. Then do the exercises below.

COMPARISONS WITH *AS . . . AS*	
Affirmative	**Negative**
Phone A is **as** <u>big</u> **as** phone B. (Phone A is 15 cm. Phone B is 15 cm.)	Camera A is**n't as** <u>affordable</u> **as** Camera B. (Camera A costs $200. Camera B costs $150.)
Phone A costs **as** <u>much</u> **as** phone B. (Phone A costs $200. Phone B costs $200.)	Maria did**n't** do **as** <u>well</u> **as** Carlos on the test. (Carlos scored 95%. Maria scored 70%.)

B Read about the two cars. Then with a partner, make sentences using *(not) as . . . as* about them. Which car do you think is better?

	Car 1: Chevrolet Bolt	Car 2: Tesla Model S
price	$35,000+	$100,000+
durability	lasts 5+ years	lasts 5+ years
popularity	popular	only popular with the rich

❝ They're both electric cars, but the Model S isn't as affordable as the Bolt.

C With your partner, complete the chart with two electronic devices (for example, two different phones, two different tablets). In your opinion, which product is better? Explain with sentences using *(not) as . . . as*.

	1: _____	2: _____
price		
size		
durability		
popularity		

ACTIVE ENGLISH Try it out!

A Read about a robot. What problems does Paro help solve?

Being around pets and animals can help people with stress and older people with dementia. However, in hospitals and nursing homes, it isn't practical to have real animals. In other words, bringing real animals to these places would be difficult and problematic. One solution is Paro the robot, an advanced piece of technology that moves and sounds like a baby seal and helps people feel calm. For example, if a patient is very nervous, holding Paro can be as relaxing as holding a real animal. Paro costs around $6,000, which is expensive, but using Paro is easier than using real animals. As a result, Paro has helped people all around the world.

Paro the robotic seal

B You are going to solve a problem with a new type of robot. In pairs, choose one of the topics and think of a typical problem people have with it.

- doing chores around the house
- learning a new language
- building things (for example, a new house)
- doing exercise and getting in shape

" Let's choose *doing chores around the house.*

One problem is cleaning the windows if you live in a tall building . . . "

C With your partner, design a robot that will solve your problem from **B**. Discuss the following:

1. What is the name of the robot?
2. What exactly will the robot do?
3. What will the robot look like? Draw a simple picture of it.
4. Why is the robot as good as (or better than) a human?
5. How much will the robot cost to buy?

D **WRITING** In the same pairs, write a short paragraph about your robot, similar to the paragraph in **A** about Paro. Use the Useful Expressions.

E Work with another pair and use your writing from **D** to present your new robot.

Presenters: Present your robot. You can look at your writing, but don't read it all. Try to remember the ideas. You can also show your picture from **C**.

Listeners: As you listen, answers questions 1–5 in **C**. At the end of the presentation, ask two new questions about the robot.

11B GOALS Now I can . . .

Explain how technology works _____

Compare similar items _____

1. Yes, I can.
2. Mostly, yes.
3. Not yet.

GLOBAL VOICES

A In pairs, try to remember information from the article *How Smart Is Your Home?*

1. What was it about?

2. What did the two people do?

3. What did they find out?

B Watch a video with National Geographic Explorer Amber Case. Check (✓) the smart devices she mentions.

☐ bed   ☐ phone   ☐ toothbrush   ☐ vacuum cleaner

☐ coffee maker   ☐ refrigerator   ☐ television   ☐ watch

C Watch the video again and choose the correct answers.

1. Amber is a cyborg anthropologist. She studies how . . .

   a. humans interact with technology.   c. technology works.

   b. humans make technology.

2. A smart refrigerator can . . .

   a. tell us what food is affordable.   c. make a grocery list and send it to a phone.

   b. cook a meal.

3. Amber thinks that a lot of modern smart technology . . .

   a. calms us.   c. is very noisy.

   b. distracts us.

4. She thinks the Roomba is a good example of calm technology because it . . .

   a. sends notifications to your phone.   c. plays a lot of different music.

   b. works in the background.

5. In the future, Amber thinks designers should focus more on . . .

   a. what technology is good at doing.   c. combining the best of both **a** and **b**.

   b. what humans are good at doing.

WORD BANK

If you **interact with** someone or something, you act together and have an effect on each other.

D In groups, discuss the questions.

1. What do you like about modern technology (for example, smartphones, the internet)?

2. What makes you angry about technology?

3. Can you think of any examples of calm technology that make your life easier and more relaxing?

Amber Case is a National Geographic Explorer, speaker, author, and researcher.

TRAVEL

LOOK AT THE PHOTO. ANSWER THE QUESTIONS.

1. Where are these people? What are they doing?

2. Name a place you want to travel to. Why do you want to go there?

WARM-UP VIDEO

A When you travel a long distance (for example, for vacation or to visit family), what type of transportation do you normally take? Why?

B Watch a video about twenty-four hours at Changi Airport in Singapore. What times of day do you see on the airport clocks (for example, 7:00 am)?

C Watch the video again. Number the actions (1–8) in the order you see them.

_____ a. A plane takes off.

_____ b. People serve lunch around noon.

_____ c. Someone checks a bag.

_____ d. In the evening, people wait (and sleep) near their gate.

_____ e. A man buys a cup of coffee.

_____ f. A woman walks through shops with her luggage.

_____ g. Workers load luggage onto the plane.

_____ h. Engineers work near the runway.

D In pairs, choose a place you travel from (for example, airport, train / bus station). List all the steps a traveler takes from arriving to leaving this place. For example, (1.) arrive, (2.) check in, etc.

E Present your list from **D** to the class. Who wrote the most steps?

The V-Train is a sightseeing train that takes tourists through the Baekdudaegan mountains in South Korea.

GOALS

Lesson A
/ Explain how to prepare for a trip
/ Say that something is necessary

Lesson B
/ Describe travel experiences
/ Ask questions about travel

12A BEFORE YOU GO

VOCABULARY

A Imagine your friend is preparing to go on a long trip. Write down one piece of advice for your friend before he or she goes. Then share your advice with the class and take notes on other people's advice.

B Read the article. Is any of the advice from **A** in it?

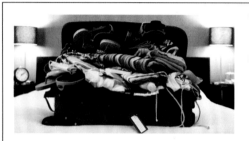

You've **booked** your **tickets**. Now comes one of the most stressful parts of travel: preparing to leave!

• Start by asking: Do I have a **valid** passport? Do I need to **apply for a visa**?

• **Download a weather app** so you know the temperature where you're going and can decide what clothes you'll need.
• Avoid taking a big suitcase. Leave the hair dryer and electric shaver at home, but make sure you **pack a travel adapter** to charge your phone if you're leaving the country.
• If you **get travel insurance**, it should include medical bills and any expensive items like cameras or laptops.
• Before you leave for the airport, **check in online**, and if you want foreign currency, **exchange some money** before you get to the airport—it'll be more expensive there!
• Don't forget to **lock the front door** and ask a friend or neighbor to **water the plants**.

> **WORD BANK**
>
> **travel** (v) to go to places that are usually far away: *We traveled across the country by train.*
>
> **journey** (n) going a long distance from one place to another: *The journey took three days.*
>
> **trip** (n) going for a short time to another place and back again: *I'm going on a business trip to Lima.*

C Cover the article in **B** and match the words to complete the phrases. Then check your answers.

_e_ **1.** get		a. a travel adapter
___ **2.** apply for		b. a weather app
___ **3.** download		c. the plants
___ **4.** pack		d. online
___ **5.** book		e. travel insurance
___ **6.** check in		f. a visa
___ **7.** exchange		g. the door
___ **8.** lock		h. money (into foreign currency)
___ **9.** water		i. tickets

D With a partner, talk about your past travel experiences. How did you prepare? What tasks did you do?

LISTENING

A **Listen for gist.** Listen to a conversation about a trip and answer the questions. 🎧85

1. Paula is in New York. What season is it? _____

2. Where is Paula going? _____

3. What is it going to feel like there? _____

4. Who is she traveling with? _____

5. Why is Paula calling Lewis? _____

B **Listen for details.** Listen again. Who has to do each task? Write **P** for *Paula*, **L** for *Lewis*, or **X** if the task is not mentioned. 🎧85

1. pack a suitcase _____
2. apply for a visa _____
3. check the weather _____
4. clean the house _____
5. check in online _____
6. buy an adapter _____
7. water the plants _____
8. pick up a package _____

C **PRONUNCIATION: Reduced *have to* and *has to*** Listen to the sentences. Notice the pronunciation of *have to* and *has to*. Then listen again and repeat. 🎧86

1. He has to lock the front door.
2. She has to get a new passport.
3. We have to check in online.
4. They don't have to pack a travel adapter.

D In pairs, look back at your answers in **B**. Take turns saying the answers using sentences with *have to* and *has to*. Pay attention to the pronunciation.

66 | Paula has to pack her suitcase.
She doesn't have to apply for a visa. | 99

E Do you ever ask your friends or neighbors for help? If so, what do you ask them to do? If not, why not?

When visiting Hawaii, you have to pack sunscreen and a swimsuit.

SPEAKING

A Esther and Mina are preparing to leave on a trip. Listen to their conversation. What is the problem? 🎧87

Esther: We have to leave in thirty minutes. Have you finished packing?

Mina: Yes, I have . . .

Esther: You look worried. What's wrong?

Mina: I can't remember where I put my passport.

Esther: Oh, no!

Mina: It's here somewhere.

Esther: When did you last have it?

Mina: About ten minutes ago. Let me think . . . Oh, there it is. I put it on the dresser.

Esther: What a relief!

B Practice the conversation with a partner.

C Talk about a time when you lost something or forgot something important. What did you do? Tell a partner.

D Study the Speaking Strategy. Practice saying the sentences in the chart.

SPEAKING STRATEGY 🎧88
Saying you've forgotten something

I forgot + noun	I forgot my bus pass.
I forgot + infinitive	I forgot to empty the trash.
I don't remember + gerund	I don't remember turning off the lights.
I can't remember where + clause	I can't remember where I put my car keys.

E You are going to perform a short conversation with a partner about forgetting something. Follow the steps below.

Step 1: Choose a location.

    ☐ the airport   ☐ the office

    ☐ school   ☐ other: _____

Step 2: Choose something you forgot to take or do.

    ☐ ticket   ☐ pack your toothbrush

    ☐ report   ☐ lock the door

    ☐ textbook   ☐ other: _____

Step 3: Write and practice a short conversation. Remember to switch roles. Then perform your conversation for the class.

    ❝ OK, it's time to get on the plane.

    ❝ Oh, no! Can you call a friend for help?

Wait a minute! I think I forgot to lock my front door!

GRAMMAR

A Read the Unit 12, Lesson A Grammar Reference in the appendix. Complete the exercises. Then do the exercises below.

MODAL VERBS OF NECESSITY		
	Present forms	**Past forms**
Affirmative	You **must** show your ID to get on the plane. I **have to** buy a backpack for my trip. We**'ve got to** pack a travel adapter.	I **had to** wait for an hour.
Negative	I **don't have to** check any luggage.	I **didn't have to** wait long.
Use *must*, *have to*, and *have got to* to say that something is necessary.		

B Look at the trip preparation to-do list. The tasks that are checked (✓) are finished. In your notebook, use the words in parentheses to write eight sentences with *has / have to* or *doesn't / don't have to*. Check your answers with a partner.

People hike in the Cordillera Blanca mountain range in Peru.

To-Do List
1. buy a backpack (I)
✓ 2. prepare a first-aid kit (she)
3. get a shot (he)
✓ 4. renew passports (they)
5. check in online (we)
6. pack (she)
✓ 7. check the weather (he)
✓ 8. get travel insurance (you)

66 She doesn't have to prepare a first-aid kit. She's already done it.

C Complete each item with something that is true for you.

1. When I was younger, I had to . . .
2. Before I get on a plane, I must . . .
3. Before I leave home every day, I've got to . . .
4. I'm good at . . ., so I don't have to study it much.
5. The last time I took a trip, I didn't have to . . .
6. In order to pass this class, I have to . . .

D Share your ideas from **C** with a partner.

66 When I was younger, I always had to be home early.

Really? What time did you have to be home? 99

66 I had to be home by 8:00 every night.

ACTIVE ENGLISH Try it out!

a tent

A Imagine you and a partner are going on a camping trip for three days. You will be in the forest, far away from any towns or cities. You already have a tent. With your partner, look at the fourteen items below and . . .

* circle the items that are necessary for your trip.

* check (✓) the items that you would like to bring but that are not necessary.

* cross out the items that are not necessary at all.

backpack   cans of food   ice cream   phone
bottles of water guitar   money   plastic plates and cups

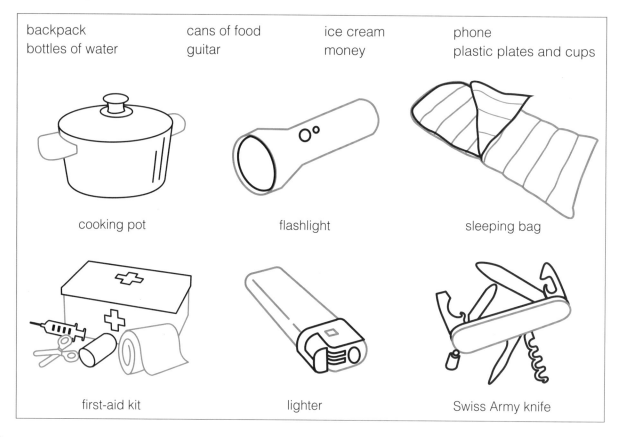

cooking pot   flashlight   sleeping bag

first-aid kit   lighter   Swiss Army knife

B Join another pair. Together, you must decide what to take on your trip. You can only take six items. Choose from the items in **A** and think of your own ideas. Consider these things:

* food   * shelter
* safety   * water

“ We've got to take bottles of water.

I like ice cream, but we don't have to bring any. ”

C Tell the class the items your group has decided to take and explain your reasons.

12A GOALS   Now I can . . .

Explain how to prepare for a trip _____

Say that something is necessary _____

1. Yes, I can.
2. Mostly, yes.
3. Not yet.

VOCABULARY

A Read the email between two friends. What two types of transportation are they using?

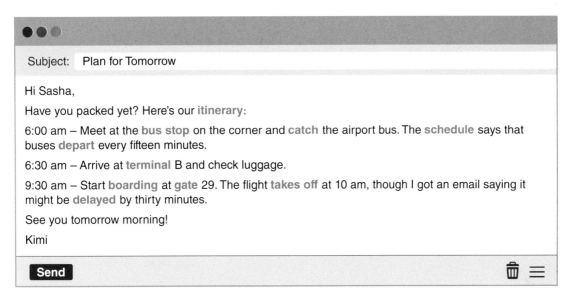

Subject: Plan for Tomorrow

Hi Sasha,

Have you packed yet? Here's our **itinerary**:

6:00 am – Meet at the **bus stop** on the corner and **catch** the airport bus. The **schedule** says that buses **depart** every fifteen minutes.

6:30 am – Arrive at **terminal** B and check luggage.

9:30 am – Start **boarding** at **gate** 29. The flight **takes off** at 10 am, though I got an email saying it might be **delayed** by thirty minutes.

See you tomorrow morning!

Kimi

Send

B Complete the word web with the words in **blue** from the email. Then add two of your own travel words to the word web and compare with a partner.

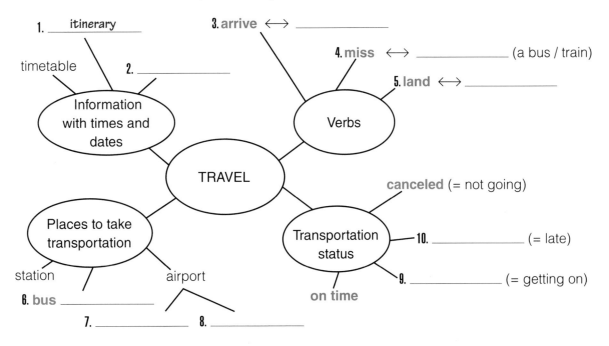

1. _itinerary_

timetable

2. _____

Information with times and dates

3. arrive ⟷ _____

4. miss ⟷ _____ (a bus / train)

5. land ⟷ _____

Verbs

TRAVEL

Places to take transportation

station

6. bus _____

7. _____

8. _____

airport

Transportation status

on time

canceled (= not going)

10. _____ (= late)

9. _____ (= getting on)

C You are going to travel for a few days with some friends. In pairs, plan your travel itinerary. Decide:
- where you are traveling to.
- which type(s) of transportation (train, bus, or plane) you are taking.
- what times you need to arrive and leave.

D With your partner, write a short email describing your itinerary from **C**. Then exchange emails with another pair. Which pair has the most exciting itinerary?

GOING SOLO
IS THE WAY TO GO!

How do you usually travel? Do you normally go somewhere with your family, a close friend, or a group of friends? Do you like joining a tour group where someone else makes the schedule?

Have you ever thought about "going solo"? In recent years, more and more people have started striking out on their own. A recent travel report found that a quarter of all travelers are planning a solo trip this year, and interestingly, 84% of solo travelers are women.

You may think that traveling alone would be scary or boring, but according to people who do it, that's not exactly true. Though solo travelers have to plan their own itineraries and deal with travel requirements like applying for visas alone, they often have positive experiences and make new friends. Many enjoy booking the flights and hotels of their choosing, and when planning and packing for the journey, they only need to worry about their own wants and needs.

There are many different things you can do on a vacation alone. Some solo travelers use the time to learn or practice an outdoor activity, such as golf, mountain climbing, or scuba diving. You can even go and stay on a ranch and learn how to ride a horse. Why not pretend to be a cowboy or cowgirl for a day?

You may not believe this, but some travelers like to study on their vacations. They even go to "vacation college" at a university or join a research team as a volunteer worker. This allows them to "play scientist" for a week or two while helping someone with his or her project. It can be hard work, but it's also very satisfying.

For solo travelers of different ages and genders, there are many travel options. There are tours for women only and for people over the age of sixty. And, of course, there are trips for singles who are looking to meet someone special. One company offers trips that focus on fine dining—there is time for sightseeing during the day and for sharing delicious meals with new friends at night.

So, for your next vacation, if you haven't considered going solo, think about it.

Bon voyage!

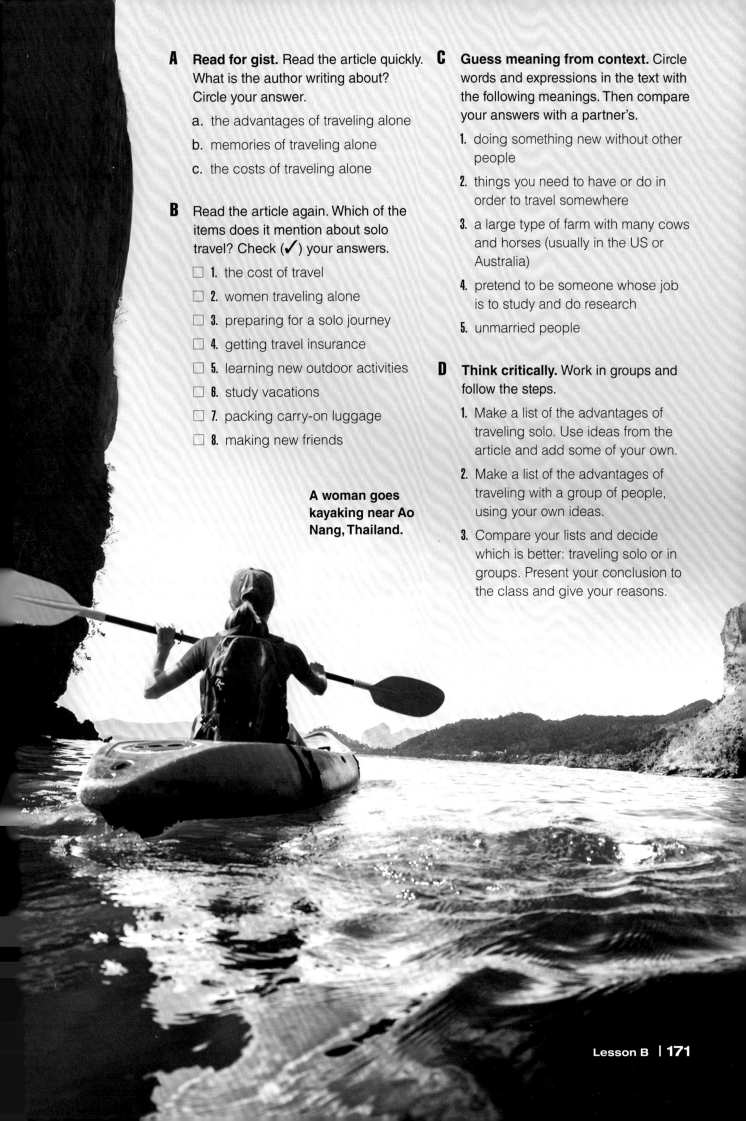

A **Read for gist.** Read the article quickly. What is the author writing about? Circle your answer.

a. the advantages of traveling alone

b. memories of traveling alone

c. the costs of traveling alone

B Read the article again. Which of the items does it mention about solo travel? Check (✓) your answers.

☐ 1. the cost of travel

☐ 2. women traveling alone

☐ 3. preparing for a solo journey

☐ 4. getting travel insurance

☐ 5. learning new outdoor activities

☐ 6. study vacations

☐ 7. packing carry-on luggage

☐ 8. making new friends

A woman goes kayaking near Ao Nang, Thailand.

C **Guess meaning from context.** Circle words and expressions in the text with the following meanings. Then compare your answers with a partner's.

1. doing something new without other people

2. things you need to have or do in order to travel somewhere

3. a large type of farm with many cows and horses (usually in the US or Australia)

4. pretend to be someone whose job is to study and do research

5. unmarried people

D **Think critically.** Work in groups and follow the steps.

1. Make a list of the advantages of traveling solo. Use ideas from the article and add some of your own.

2. Make a list of the advantages of traveling with a group of people, using your own ideas.

3. Compare your lists and decide which is better: traveling solo or in groups. Present your conclusion to the class and give your reasons.

LISTENING

A **Make predictions.** In pairs, look at the photo of National Geographic Explorer Andrés Ruzo. You are going to hear him answer the five questions. How do you think he will answer them?

    a. Are you planning a trip at the moment? __3__

    b. Do you travel a lot? _____

    c. Have you ever had a journey where things went wrong? _____

    d. Why do you like traveling? _____

    e. How do you normally prepare for trips? _____

B **Listen for gist.** Listen to Andrés answering the five questions. Match the questions in **A** (a–e) with his answers (1–5). 🎧90

C **Listen for details.** Read the sentences and guess the missing words. Then listen to the whole interview and check your predictions. 🎧91

    1. Members of Andrés's family lived in Peru, Nicaragua, and the _____ .

    2. His parents used to say, "Travel is the best _____ ."

    3. Andrés thinks traveling is like stepping into the pages of a _____ or walking onto the _____ of a documentary.

    4. Andrés says, "Almost 8 billion people across the planet are living and experiencing their loves, fears, hopes, and dreams—just like _____ are."

    5. Many of his trips are for work. Others are to visit family or for his own personal _____ .

    6. His advice is to prepare for _____ and then just go with the flow.

    7. In Miami, they often had hurricanes and bad weather, so his flights were often delayed, rerouted, or _____ .

    8. According to Andrés, even bad travel situations become part of the adventure story that you can tell your family and friends when you come _____ .

D Work in pairs and role-play the interview with Andrés Ruzo.

    • **Student A:** Ask the five questions in **A**.

    • **Student B:** Answer the questions using some of Andrés's words.

E Switch roles and repeat the interview role play from **D**.

WORD BANK

When you **go with the flow**, you are relaxed about a situation and don't try to change it.

A person's **perspective** is their personal point of view.

When an airplane is **rerouted**, it is sent a different way.

National Geographic Explorer Andrés Ruzo has traveled to many amazing places, including the Momotombo Volcano in Nicaragua, as seen here.

GRAMMAR

A Complete the grammar chart with the missing questions.

a. Did you have to get a visa?

b. Are you planning a trip now?

c. How long will you be away for?

d. Can you show me your passport?

e. Where do you usually go?

f. How many times have you been there?

QUESTION FORM REVIEW		
	Yes / No questions	**Wh- questions**
Simple present	Do you travel a lot?	1. _____
Present continuous	2. _____	Where are you thinking of going next?
Present perfect	Have you ever been to Rome?	3. _____
Simple past	4. _____	When did you apply for it?
Future with *will*	Will you ever go there again?	5. _____
Modal verbs (*can, should*, etc.)	6. _____	How can I change my seat?

B Read the Unit 12, Lesson B Grammar Reference in the appendix, complete the exercises, and check your answers in **A**. Then do the exercises below.

C Work in pairs and write questions about travel to match the answers.

1. No, I haven't.

2. By plane.

3. Yes, they do.

4. Yes, you can.

5. Last summer.

D Join another pair. Ask your questions from **C** and have them guess the matching answers. Then switch roles.

E Ask your classmates if they have ever done the seven activities below. When someone answers *yes*, ask a follow-up question. Write the person's name and the extra information. Try to be the first person to complete 1–7.

Have you ever . . .?	Name	Extra information
1. visit / a big city		
2. be / on a train		
3. talk / to a flight attendant		
4. forget / something on a trip		
5. lose / your luggage		
6. get / sick while traveling		
7. miss / a flight, train, or bus		

66 Have you ever visited a big city?

66 Which city did you visit?

Yes, I have. 99

ACTIVE ENGLISH Try it out!

How was your check-in experience today?

Heathrow

HAPPY@NOT

Heathrow

A Look at the photo of a customer survey machine at Heathrow Airport in London, UK. What other types of places, services, or products ask people to rate them? Do you ever rate products or answer customer surveys? Tell the class.

B Work in pairs and read the questions from different customer surveys. Match each place or service in the box to two questions. Write **H** for *hotel*, **A** for *airline*, etc.

| airline (A)   bus (B)   hotel (H)   restaurant (R)   tour group (T) |

1. Have you flown with us before? __A__

2. How did you hear about our sightseeing trips? _____

3. Did you take off and land on time today? _____

4. Was your driver welcoming and friendly? _____

5. What was the reason for your stay? _____

6. How polite was your server today? _____

7. Will you recommend our meals to others in the future? _____

8. How would you rate your guide today? _____

9. Do you normally book your room on our website? _____

10. What feedback can you give on your journey to the airport today? _____

C Read the Academic Skill and categorize the questions in **B** as closed questions or open questions.

D **WRITING** In pairs, choose one of the places or services in **B** and imagine you work at the company that owns it. Follow the steps:

1. Make a list of things you want to know about your customers and their experiences.

2. Write a customer satisfaction survey. You can use the questions from **B** and also write seven or eight new questions. Include both open and closed questions.

E After you have written your survey, exchange with another pair and answer the questions below about their survey.

1. Are the questions written correctly?

2. Is the survey easy to follow?

3. Are there both closed questions and open questions?

ACADEMIC SKILL

Closed and open questions

When you want to find out information and do research, ask both closed questions and open questions. Closed questions have *yes / no* answers and are good for getting results (for example, *Will you fly with us again in the future?*). Open questions are good for finding out more information because they need longer answers (for example, *How did you find out about our services?*).

USEFUL EXPRESSIONS

Have you ever . . .?
Do / Did you . . .?
Was your . . . excellent / good / poor?
How would you rate . . .? ☺ ☺ ☹
Can you give us feedback on . . .?
What was the reason . . .?
How comfortable / polite / friendly was your . . .?
Will / Would you recommend us to . . .?

12B GOALS   Now I can . . .

Describe travel experiences _____

Ask questions about travel _____

1. Yes, I can.

2. Mostly, yes.

3. Not yet.

GLOBAL VOICES

A Discuss the questions as a class.

1. Do you enjoy traveling to new places or other countries? Why or why not?

2. Have you ever been away from home for a long time? Did you feel homesick? What did you miss?

B Watch a video. Number the topics (1–4) in the order they are discussed.

_____ a. Countries the students have traveled to   _____ c. Reasons they enjoy traveling

_____ b. Differences between their countries   _____ d. Homesickness and missing home
and the US

C Watch the video again. For each question, check (✓) the answers you hear.

1. What do the students in the video like about traveling?

☐ experiencing new things   ☐ making new friends   ☐ trying new food

☐ going shopping   ☐ meeting new people   ☐ visiting new places

☐ learning about new cultures   ☐ staying in hotels

2. Which countries have they visited?

☐ Argentina   ☐ Greece   ☐ Italy   ☐ Mexico

☐ Colombia   ☐ India   ☐ Jamaica   ☐ Peru

3. What differences did they notice between their home country and the US?

☐ the cars   ☐ the coffee size   ☐ the language

☐ the clothes   ☐ the landscape   ☐ the weather

4. What do they miss about home?

☐ family and friends   ☐ food   ☐ holidays   ☐ sports   ☐ TV   ☐ weather

D Prepare a two-minute presentation for visitors to your country. Your presentation should include information and advice on . . .

- daily life in your country and differences visitors might notice.

- ways to meet people and things to do when you feel homesick.

You can use images in your presentation.

USEFUL EXPRESSIONS

Today, I'd like to talk about . . .

First of all, . . .

Take a look at this picture. It shows . . .

One difference is that . . .

Next, I'm going to talk about . . .

Thanks for listening. Are there any questions?

The view from City Palace
in Udaipur, India

REAL WORLD LINK MAKE A TRAVEL AD

This photo, taken in a Japanese-style garden in Almaty, Kazakhstan, is part of a social media trend called "Follow Me To," in which the person in the photo seems to lead the photographer to an amazing travel destination.

A Where do you often see advertisements? Compare the places for advertising and rank them from 1 to 7 (1 = most effective, 7 = least effective). Then discuss with a partner.

_____ in a newspaper _____ on the radio _____ in the street _____ on a website
_____ on public transportation _____ on social media _____ on TV

" I think advertising on social media isn't as effective as advertising on TV.

Really? I think advertising on social media is more effective. "

B Read the blog post. Where does the writer think modern travel companies should advertise? Why?

TRAVEL ADVERTISING IN THE 21ST CENTURY

In the past, travel companies used to advertise destinations in newspapers and magazines, or on TV. They used to put a photo of a beautiful beach on the page or show people having fun by the pool on the screen. But nowadays, if you want tourists to come, social media is indispensable and much more effective than traditional forms of advertising. Here are five tips to make your company go viral.[1]

1. **Keep posting**

   Give customers a reason to look up your travel company by being the local expert. Provide free information about things to do, how to get around, and the best places to shop and eat. If tourists find it useful, they will share your posts with friends.

2. **The power of the image**

On social media, everyone is addicted to images, so you have to use a high-quality camera to take beautiful photos of destinations for your posts. People also enjoy taking virtual tours, which allow them to "visit" a place through a series of photos or videos.

3. **Reviews are key**

Include customer reviews in your advertising and invite people to write their own reviews. If someone gives you a negative review, don't ignore them! You must get in touch and show that you can solve their problem.

4. **Contests and prizes**

Competitions are as popular as ever, and people love winning prizes! Post questions about a destination to test people's knowledge, or hold a travel photo contest. Offering a big prize to the winner, like a free flight or hotel room, will get a lot of people interested.

5. **Influencers**

Spend time following other people on social media who influence tourism and travel. "Like" their posts and encourage them to like and follow you. You could even offer them a free trip with your company so they can review and post about your services.

[1]*If something **goes viral** (slang), it quickly becomes popular or well known on the internet.*

C In pairs, read the blog post again and answer the questions.

1. Where did travel companies use to advertise?

2. According to the article, what must travel companies give for free?

3. What does the article say you have to use for taking photos?

4. When is it very important to get in touch with customers?

5. Why are competitions still a good way to advertise?

6. How can influencers help travel companies?

D Work in groups and discuss how you could advertise your city, town, or local region to tourists. Follow the steps:

1. Describe the type of tourist who might come (for example, young, likes hiking).

2. Make a list of sightseeing places and things to do for the type of tourist from step 1.

3. Make a list of other reasons to stay in your city or town, such as hotels, local food, shopping, and transportation.

E **You Choose** In your groups, choose one of the options to plan and make an advertisement about your travel destination from **D**.

Option 1: Make a five-minute presentation with photos and information for tourists.

Option 2: Create a two-minute video advertisement for social media. Show interesting places and record some narration.

Option 3: Take photos of the destination to post on social media. Then write some information about the place(s) in the photos to go with the post.

F Work with another group. Watch their presentation or video advertisement, or look at their social media post. Would you like to travel to their destination? Why or why not?

LANGUAGE SUMMARIES

UNIT 1: MY LIFE

LESSON A	LESSON B
Vocabulary	**Vocabulary**
be going out <u>friends</u> **classmate** good ~ **coworker** / **colleague** close ~ **friend** best ~ **get along well** old ~ **girlfriend** / **boyfriend** next-door neighbors (not) **know** (someone) (very) **well** **neighbor** **spend time together** **work together**	**fail** fail (v) ↔ succeed (v) **get** (good / bad) **grades** failure (n) ↔ success (n) <u>have</u> successful (adj) ~ **free time**, ~ **fun** give up (quit) (v) ↔ <u>meet</u> keep trying (v) ~ **friends**, **classes** ~ **pass** **prepare for exams** <u>take</u> ~ **classes**, ~ **exams**, ~ **tests**, ~ (music / tennis) **lessons**
Speaking Strategy **Introducing a person to someone else** Mr. Otani, I'd like to introduce you to Andre. Mr. Otani, I'd like you to meet Andre. Junko, this is Ricardo. Junko, meet Ricardo. Junko, Ricardo.	**Responding to introductions** It's (very) nice to meet you. (It's) nice / good to meet you, too. Nice / Good to meet you. You, too. **Asking for someone's name again** I'm sorry, I'm terrible with names. I'm sorry, I've forgotten your name.

UNIT 2: LET'S EAT!

LESSON A	LESSON B
Vocabulary	**Vocabulary**
awful too + (adjective)	diet on the go
baked	(healthy / unhealthy) **habits** takeout
cooked	health benefits
delicious	increase
fried	lifestyle
frozen	plenty
juicy ↔ dry	prevent
oily	reduce
salty	
spicy ↔ mild	
sweet ↔ sour	
tasty	
terrible	
yummy	

Speaking Strategy	
Making suggestions	**Responding to suggestions**
Statements	Good / Great idea!
Let's have Thai food.	(That) sounds good (to me).
Questions	(That's) fine with me.
Why don't we have Thai food?	I don't really want to.
How about having Thai food?	I don't really feel like it.

When rejecting a suggestion, it's common to give an explanation: *I don't really feel like it. I'm too tired.*

UNIT 3: MYSTERIES

LESSON A	LESSON B
Vocabulary	**Vocabulary**
(bring) **good luck** ↔ intuition	data affect
(avoid) **bad luck** on the other hand	do research behavior
increase (your)	explanation pesticide
chances	figure out
(more / less) **likely**	investigate artifact
(to) ↔ **unlikely** (to)	make sense excavate
lucky ↔ **unlucky**	proof site
on purpose ↔ **by**	have ~, need ~, wonder
chance	there's (no) ~
take a chance	solve
	(have a) **theory**

Speaking Strategy	
Saying something is likely	**Saying something is *not* likely**
I bet (that) Marco plays the drums.	I doubt (that) Marco plays the drums.
Marco probably plays the drums.	
Maybe / Perhaps Marco plays the drums.	

You can use *Are you sure?* to ask if a person is certain about something.

UNIT 4: TRENDS

LESSON A	LESSON B

Vocabulary
 about /
   approximately
 almost / nearly
 exactly
 increase ↔
   decrease
 trend
 	
 a lot (**more / less**)
 much (**more / less**)
 	
 billion
 million
 thousand
 1.46 million = one
   point four six million
 	
 a couple of
 groceries
	Vocabulary
	 be in style
	 brand
	 casual
	 expensive ↔ **inexpensive**
	 influencer
	 (someone) **looks good /**
	   great / terrible in (clothing)
	 (clothing) **looks good / great /**
	   terrible on (someone)
	 style (n)
	 stylish (adj)
	 (not) **suit** (someone)
	 unique
	
	 accessory
	 get dressed up

Speaking Strategy

Polite disagreement I know what you're saying, but . . . I see / know what you mean, but . . . I'm not sure about that. That's not a bad idea, but . . .	**More direct disagreement** I'm afraid I disagree. Sorry, but I disagree. I totally / completely disagree.

You can use more direct expressions with people you know well (friends, family, etc.).

UNIT 5: MY NEIGHBORHOOD

LESSON A	LESSON B

Vocabulary
 do laundry
 do the dishes
 drop off
 go grocery
   shopping
 make a reservation
 make a(n) (doctor's)
   appointment
 make dinner
 pick up
 sweep
 vacuum
 	
 do household
   chores
 run errands
	Vocabulary
	 bike lanes
	 cyclists
	 get around
	 get to
	 on foot
	 pedestrians
	 sidewalks
	 traffic
	 walkable
	
	 by
	 ~ bike (ride my) bike
	 ~ bus / subway take the bus / subway
	 ~ car drive
	 ~ taxi take a taxi
	 ~ train take / catch a train
	   walk
	
	 bohemian
	 magical

Speaking Strategy

Making appointments

I'm calling to / I'd like to . . . make an appointment with a counselor / Dr. Smith / the dentist.
I'm calling to / I'd like to . . . make a doctor's / hair appointment.
I'm calling to / I'd like to . . . reschedule my appointment / our meeting.

Scheduling the time
Can you come in / Could we meet / How's tomorrow at 2:00?
That's perfect. / That works for me.
No, that (time / day) doesn't work for me.

UNIT 6: GOALS

LESSON A	LESSON B

Vocabulary
apply (to) (v) / **application** (n) environmental
arrange (v) /   mission
  arrangement (n)
choose (v) / **choice** (n)
consider (doing) (v) /
  consideration (n)
decide (to do) (v) / **decision** (n)
intend (to do) (v) / **intention** (n)
plan (to do) (v) / **plan** (n)
recommend (doing
  something) (v) /
  recommendation (n)
	Vocabulary
	at some point after graduation
	be my own boss in a month
	create a resume next year
	do an internship this summer
	eventually
	go back to school paid position
	in a few days / weeks terms
	in the near future achieve your dreams
	opportunity face challenges
	someday financial support
	soon overcome
	take time off

Speaking Strategy	
Responding to bad news (I'm) sorry to hear that. That's too bad. How disappointing. You must be disappointed.	**Offering to help** If you want to talk, (just) call me. If there's anything I can do, (just) let me know.

UNIT 7: CELEBRATIONS

LESSON A	LESSON B
Vocabulary **celebrate** fans **decorate** inspiration **get together** live **guests** **have a good time** **invite** **occasion** a party **attend / go to** ~ **have** ~ , **host** ~, **organize** ~, **plan** ~, **throw** ~	**Vocabulary** **compete** (v) charm **competition** (n) / shrine **competitor** (n) wish / **gather** make a wish **participate** (v) **participation** (n) / **participant** (n) **perform** (v) **performance** (n) / **performer** (n) **prize** **race** **take place** **tradition**

Speaking Strategy	
Inviting someone to do something Do you want to go with me? Would you like to go with me? How'd you like to go with me? **Accepting an invitation** Sure, I'd love to. That sounds great.	**Refusing an invitation** I'm sorry, but I can't. I have plans. Unfortunately, I can't. I have to work. I'd love to, but I'm busy (then / that day).
When refusing an invitation, it's polite to give a simple explanation.	

UNIT 8: ONCE UPON A TIME

LESSON A	LESSON B
Vocabulary **based on** contribute **best-selling** **(main) character** **director** **easy to follow** ↔ **hard to follow** **fiction** **predictable** ↔ **unpredictable** **realistic** ↔ **unrealistic** **take place** **The story is about . . . / It tells the story of . . .**	**Vocabulary** **ancient** myth **brave** ram **clever** violent **discover** **evil** diversity **incredible** impactful (adj) / **magic** impactfully (adv) **succeed** **traditional**
Speaking Strategy **Telling a story** I just heard an amazing / interesting / unbelievable story. It's a story about . . . One day . . . Later, . . . / After that, . . . As it turns out, . . . In the end, . . .	**Showing interest and finding out what happened** What's it about? Oh, no! / Really? So what did he / she do? What happened next? Are you serious? / Wow!

UNIT 9: WORK

LESSON A	LESSON B
Vocabulary **adventurous** **cautious** **courageous** **efficient** **flexible** **independently** **knowledgeable** **personable** **punctual** **responsible**	**Vocabulary** **demanding** **exhausting** **glamorous** **hazardous** **rewarding** **well paid**
Speaking Strategy **Interviewing for a job** *Starting the interview* Thanks for coming in today. It's great to be here. / My pleasure. *Discussing abilities and experience* Tell me a little about yourself. I'm a student at . . . I'm majoring in . . . Can you (work independently)? Yes, I can. For example, . . .	Are you (punctual)? Yes, I am. For example, . . . Do you have any experience (writing a blog)? Yes, I write one for my school newspaper now. *Ending the interview* Do you have any questions? Yes, I do. / No, I don't think so. When can you start? Right away. / On Monday. / Next week. I'll be in touch. I look forward to hearing from you.

UNIT 10: STAY IN TOUCH

LESSON A	LESSON B
Vocabulary	**Vocabulary**
can't get a / don't have a signal	(be) **addicted to** at the last minute
get in touch / stay in touch (or contact)	(something)
go to / attend a meeting	**ban ↔ allow**
on silent / on mute	**be distracted by ↔**
spend time / pass (the) **time**	**pay attention to**
	device
<u>call</u> <u>get</u>	**polite ↔ rude**
~ **someone** ~ **a call**	**post ↔ delete**
make a ~ ~ **a message**	**respond ↔ ignore**
return a ~ ~ **a text**	**turn up ↔ turn down**
<u>check</u>	
~ **your email**	
~ **your messages**	
~ **your phone**	

Speaking Strategy	
Using the phone	*Asking someone to wait*
Asking for someone and responding	Hang on. / Can you hang on (for a moment /
Hi, Lisa? / Hi. Is Lisa there? / Can I speak to Lisa,	second)?
please?	Would / Could you hold (for a moment /
Hello. May / Could I speak to Lisa, please? [formal]	second)? [formal]
This is Lisa. / Speaking.	
	Taking a message
Asking for identification of caller	Can I take a message?
Who's calling?	May I take a message?
May I ask who's calling? [formal]	Would you like to leave a message? [formal]

UNIT 11: TECHNOLOGY

LESSON A	LESSON B
Vocabulary	**Vocabulary**
advanced a fad	**charge** calm
affordable a flash in the pan	**go off** dementia
customizable indispensable	**load**
durable	**log in** interact with
fashionable	**look up**
practical	**plug in**
rechargeable	**run out**
reliable	**scroll down**
user-friendly	**stand up**
wearable	**switch on**

Speaking Strategy	
Offering a counterargument	*Explaining what you think*
Stating what other people think	(But,) actually, she's very outgoing.
A lot of people say (that) she's shy.	(But,) in fact, / in reality, she's very outgoing.
Some people think (that) she's shy.	(But,) the truth / fact / reality is she's very outgoing.

UNIT 12: TRAVEL

LESSON A	LESSON B
Vocabulary	**Vocabulary**
apply for a visa journey	**boarding** go with the flow
book tickets travel	**bus stop** perspective
check in online trip	**canceled** rerouted
download a weather app	**catch** ↔ **miss** (a bus / train)
exchange some money	**delayed**
get travel insurance	**depart** ↔ **arrive**
lock the front door	**gate**
pack a travel adapter	**itinerary**
valid	**on time**
water the plants	**schedule**
	take off ↔ **land**
	terminal

Speaking Strategy
Saying you've forgotten something
I forgot + noun: I forgot my bus pass.
I forgot + infinitive: I forgot to empty the trash.
I don't remember + gerund: I don't remember turning off the lights.
I can't remember where + clause: I can't remember where I put my car keys.

 MY LIFE

LESSON A

THE SIMPLE PRESENT VS. THE PRESENT CONTINUOUS	
Simple present	**Present continuous**
Use the simple present to talk about habits, schedules, and facts.	Use the present continuous to talk about actions that are happening right now. Also, use the present continuous to talk about actions happening in the extended present (nowadays). Notice the <u>time expressions</u>.
I <u>always</u> **take** a shower in the morning. The express train **arrives** at 9:03 am. They **don't speak** Italian. They **speak** French.	She**'s taking** a shower. Can she call you back? Hurry up! The train **is leaving**! How many classes **are** you **taking** <u>this term</u>? She **is working** at a cafe <u>these days</u>.
Sometimes, the simple present and the present continuous have similar meanings, but use of the present continuous can show a situation is more temporary.	
I **live** in Tokyo. **A:** Every summer, my family goes to the beach. **B:** Nice! **Do** you **stay** in a hotel?	<u>At the moment</u>, I**'m living** in Tokyo. **A:** Let's have lunch at my hotel. **B:** Sounds good. Where **are** you **staying**?
With the simple present, we often use adverbs of frequency, such as *always*, *sometimes*, and *never*. With the present continuous, we often use time expressions such as *at the moment*, *right now*, and *currently*.	

A Veronique Lesarg is a doctor. Use the simple present or present continuous to complete her profile.

My name (1. be) _____ Veronique Lesarg. I (2. live) _____ in

Montreal. I (3. be) _____ a pediatrician, a doctor for children. I usually

(4. work) _____ in a hospital, but these days, I (5. volunteer) _____

for an organization called Doctors Without Borders. They (6. send) _____ staff to

other countries. This year, I (7. work) _____ in Ethiopia. At the moment,

I (8. write) _____ to you from a small village. There's no hospital here, so right now

we (9. build) _____ one.

B Write two simple present and two present continuous questions about Veronique Lesarg. Then answer them in your notebook.

1. _____   3. _____

2. _____   4. _____

LESSON B

REVIEW OF THE SIMPLE PAST				
Subject	**Verb**		**Time expression**	
I You He / She We They	**missed** **didn't miss** **had** **didn't have**	a tennis lesson	yesterday. two days / weeks ago. last week / month.	The simple past ending for regular verbs is -ed. For irregular verbs, see the list below.

	Yes / No questions	Answers
With *be*	**Were** you in class today?	Yes, I **was**. / No, I **wasn't**.
With other verbs	**Did** you **pass** the test?	Yes, I **did**. / No, I **didn't**.
	Wh- questions	Answers
With *be*	Where **were** you last night?	(I **was**) at my friend's house.
With other verbs	When **did** you **meet** your girlfriend?	(We **met**) last year.

REGULAR SIMPLE PAST VERBS				IRREGULAR SIMPLE PAST VERBS			
Base form	**Simple past**	**Base form**	**Simple past**	**Base form**	**Simple past**	**Base form**	**Simple past**
change	changed	pass	passed	be	was / were	know	knew
die	died	play	played	come	came	make	made
enter	entered	practice	practiced	do	did	meet	met
finish	finished	prepare	prepared	eat	ate	read	read
graduate	graduated	study	studied	get	got	run	ran
help	helped	talk	talked	give	gave	take	took
live	lived	travel	traveled	go	went	think	thought
marry	married	use	used	have	had	win	won
move	moved	work	worked	keep	kept	write	wrote

A Read about Diego's experience. Complete the sentences with the correct simple past form of the verbs in parentheses.

In high school, I (1. study) _____ a lot and got good grades. But the first time

I (2. take) _____ the university entrance exam, I (3. fail) _____. That

(4. be) _____ hard. To prepare for the next exam, I (5. go) _____ to a test prep

center. Two good things (6. happen) _____ after I went there: I (7. meet) _____

my girlfriend in the class, and the next time I (8. take) _____ the entrance exam,

I (9. pass) _____ it!

B Write simple past questions about Diego. Then answer them in your notebook.

1. Was Diego a good student in high school? _____   4. _____

2. _____   5. _____

3. _____   6. _____

C Write sentences about things you *did* or *didn't do* yesterday. Use the verb phrases provided.

1. go to school   *I didn't go to school yesterday. I was sick.*

2. study for a test   _____

3. do homework   _____

4. practice English   _____

D Ask a partner *Yes / No* questions to learn his or her answers from **C**. Then ask a follow-up *Wh-* question.

> " Did you go to school yesterday?
> No, I didn't. "

> " Why not? What did you do?
> I stayed home. I was sick. "

2 LET'S EAT!

LESSON A

THE COMPARATIVE FORM OF ADJECTIVES	
This restaurant is **bigger than** that one.	Use the comparative form of an adjective to compare two things.
Your cooking is **better than** my mom's. My cold is **worse** today **than** it was yesterday.	The comparative of *good* is *better*. The comparative of *bad* is *worse*.
I'm tall, but Milo is **taller**.	Sometimes, you can use the comparative form without *than*.

One syllable	sweet → sweet**er**	Add *-er* to many one-syllable adjectives.
	large → larg**er**	Add *-r* if the adjective ends in *-e*.
	big → big**ger**	Double the final consonant and add *-er* if the adjective ends in consonant + vowel + consonant.
Two syllables	simple → simpl**er** quiet → quiet**er**	Add *-r* or *-er* to some two-syllable adjectives.
	spicy → spic**ier**	Change the final *-y* to *-ier* if the adjective ends in *-y*.
	crowded → **more** crowded famous → **more** famous	Add *more* to other two-syllable adjectives, especially those ending in *-ing*, *-ed*, *-ous*, or *-ful*.
Three or more syllables	relaxing → **more** relaxing comfortable → **more** comfortable	Add *more* to all adjectives with three or more syllables.

A Write the comparative form of the adjectives.

1. mild _____
2. tasty _____
3. popular _____
4. hungry _____
5. bad _____

6. thin _____
7. good _____
8. important _____
9. nice _____
10. expensive _____

B Read the statements. Then make a sentence using the comparative form of the adjective in parentheses followed by *than*.

A can of soda has 44 grams of sugar.

A glass of iced tea has 0 grams of sugar.

1. (sweet) _____

Some people like baked chicken.

Everyone loves grilled chicken.

2. (popular) _____

Korean dishes are very spicy.

English dishes are not so spicy.

3. (spicy) _____

The streets in the village are empty.

There are a lot of cars on the streets in the city.

4. (busy) _____

It costs $30 to eat at the French restaurant.

It costs $10 to eat at the coffee shop.

5. (expensive) _____

i Use *than* after the comparative when the two things being compared are mentioned in the same sentence: *The popcorn is saltier than the pretzels.*

LESSON B

THE SUPERLATIVE FORM OF ADJECTIVES	
It's **the oldest** restaurant in Paris. (The other restaurants are not as old.)	Use the superlative form of an adjective to compare something to an entire group.
It's **one of the oldest** restaurants in Paris. (It's one of many old restaurants in Paris.)	Use *one of . . .* to show that something or someone is part of a group.
Mario's has **the best** pizza in the city. It was **the worst** movie of the year.	The superlative of *good* is *the best*. The superlative of *bad* is *the worst*.

One syllable	sweet → **the** sweet**est** large → **the** larg**est**	Add *the* and *-est* or *-st* to many one-syllable adjectives.
	big → **the** big**gest**	Double the final consonant and add *-est* if the adjective ends in consonant + vowel + consonant.
Two syllables	quiet → **the** quiet**est** simple → **the** simpl**est**	Add *the* and *-est* or *-st* to some two-syllable adjectives.
	spicy → **the** spic**iest**	Add *the* and change the final *-y* to *-iest* if the adjective ends in *-y*.
	crowded → **the most** crowded famous → **the most** famous	Add *the most* to other two-syllable adjectives, especially those ending in *-ing*, *-ed*, *-ous*, or *-ful*.
Three or more syllables	relaxing → **the most** relaxing comfortable → **the most** comfortable	Add *the most* to all adjectives with three or more syllables.

A Write the superlative form of the adjectives.

1. cheap _____
2. healthy _____
3. nervous _____
4. friendly _____
5. bad _____

6. unusual _____
7. good _____
8. helpful _____
9. tasty _____
10. expensive _____

B Make questions with the words below and the superlative form of the adjectives.

1. Who / the / healthy / person in your class? _____

2. Who is / good / cook in your family? _____

3. Who / popular / celebrity on TV? _____

4. What / bad / tasting food or drink? _____

5. What / famous / building in your city? _____

6. Where / cool / cafe to meet friends? _____

C Take turns asking and answering the questions in **B** with a partner.

③ MYSTERIES

LESSON A

STATIVE VERBS				
Thinking verbs	**Having verbs**	**Feeling verbs**	**Sensing verbs**	**Other verbs**
appear believe doubt know remember think	belong have own	dislike hate like love mind prefer	feel hear look see taste	agree mean need seem want

Stative verbs describe states, thoughts, and feelings, not actions. We normally use these verbs in the simple present, not the present continuous.

*He **seems** like a nice guy. He **is seeming** like a nice guy.*

Some stative verbs, however, can be used in the present continuous. When used this way, their meaning changes.

*Do you **think** he's lucky?* (think = believe) *He **looks** happy.* (look = appear) *She **has** a lucky object.* (have = own; possess) *I **see** a big dog over there.* (see = view) *I **see** what you mean.* (see = understand)	*I'm **thinking** about it.* (think = consider) *Who **is looking** in the window?* (look = direct eyes toward) *Are you **having** a good time?* (have = experience) *Sorry, I can't make it. I'm **seeing** a friend tomorrow.* (see = meet)

When you ask about how someone feels, you can use either form with no change in meaning.

*How **do you feel**?*

*How **are you feeling**?*

A Circle the correct word(s) to complete each sentence. In one item, both answers are possible.

1. I bet that lucky people **have / are having** more friends.

2. **Do you think / Are you thinking** some people are just luckier in life?

3. Lucky charms **seem / are seeming** to really work.

4. **Do you know / Are you knowing** the answer to question four?

5. **I doubt / I'm doubting** it's a fact.

6. **I hear / I'm hearing** that Professor Wiseman is a well-known psychologist.

7. It **looks / is looking** like Amy called me at 2:00.

8. **A: Do you belong / Are you belonging** to the International Student Club?

   B: No, but **I think / I'm thinking** of joining.

9. **A: How do you feel? / How are you feeling?**

   B: Not great. **I have / I'm having** a cold.

10. **I see / I'm seeing** the doctor soon. Can I call you back later?

LESSON B

MODALS OF PRESENT POSSIBILITY			
Subject	**Modal**	**Main verb**	
Bigfoot	**may / might / could**	live	in North America.
The Loch Ness Monster	**can't**	be	real. There are no sea monsters.

You can use *may*, *might*, or *could* to say something is possible in the simple present.
Use *can't* to say something is impossible.
You can use *may* or *might* with *not*: He **might not** / **may not** speak French.
Do not use *could* with *not* for present possibility.

Questions and short answers		
With *be*	Is the Loch Ness Monster real?	It **may / might / could** be. No, it **can't** be.
With other verbs	Does Bigfoot live in North America?	It **may / might / could**. No, it **can't**.

A Complete the conversations with a modal, and a verb if needed.

1. **A:** How old is Karen?

   B: I don't know. She _____ 35.

   C: She _____ 35. She graduated from high school in 1994.

2. **A:** Do ghosts exist?

   B: They _____. No one knows for sure.

3. **A:** Where's Lauren?

   B: I'm not sure. She _____ with Lin. They always hang out together after school.

   A: She _____ with Lin. Lin is on vacation this week.

4. **A:** Are the Nazca Lines a type of calendar?

   B: They _____. It's one possible explanation.

B In your notebook, write a sentence about each mysterious image using different modals of present possibility. Then compare your ideas with a partner.

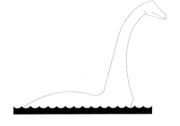

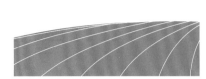

1. Bigfoot

2. The Loch Ness Monster

3. Aliens

C Match the questions to the answers.

_____ 1. Is the Loch Ness Monster real?

_____ 2. Do aliens live on the moon?

_____ 3. Does Rose live near here?

_____ 4. Are these footprints from a giant human?

_____ 5. Does Bigfoot live in North America?

_____ 6. Is your mother at home?

a. She may be.

b. They may.

c. They might be.

d. It might.

e. She might.

f. It could be.

 **TRENDS**

LESSON A

QUANTITY EXPRESSIONS WITH SPECIFIC NOUNS				
Quantity	*of*	**Noun phrase**	**Verb**	
All **Most** **A lot** **Half** **Some** **None**	**of**	my friends them	like	online shopping.

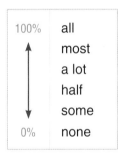

100%	all
↑	most
	a lot
	half
↓	some
0%	none

We can use these quantity expressions to talk about amounts with specific nouns.
Most of *the students are from Japan.*
A lot of *them are from Tokyo.*
Half of *my homework is finished.*
Some of *the building is under construction.*
The word *of* is optional after *all* when it is followed by a specific noun phrase, but *of* must be used with a pronoun (*it, them, you,* etc.).
All (of) *my friends live at home.* ***All of*** *them live at home.* ~~**All** them live at home.~~

QUANTITY EXPRESSIONS WITH GENERAL NOUNS

Quantity	Plural count noun	
All **Most** **A lot of** **Some**	students	study hard.

Use *all*, *most*, *a lot of*, and *some* followed by a plural noun to make more general statements.
*These days, **most** stores have websites.*
***Some** people hate online shopping.*
These expressions can also be used with noncount nouns.
***A lot of** traffic comes from road accidents.*

A Circle the correct word(s) to complete each sentence. In one item, both answers are possible.

1. **Some** / **Some of** people want to be happy in life.

2. **Most** / **Most of** my friends speak English, but **none** / **none of** them speak it at home.

3. **Some** / **Some of** students live with their families because it's cheaper.

4. **Half** / **Half of** our neighbors have children, but **none** / **none of** them have pets.

5. **All** / **All of** parents want their children to do well in school.

6. **All** / **All of** the instructors at my school are really strict.

B Do you agree with the sentences in **A**? If not, rewrite them by changing the quantity.

LESSON B

ADVICE WITH *COULD, SHOULD, OUGHT TO,* AND *HAD BETTER*

You	**could**		it online (or at a store).
He	**should / ought to**		it online. It's cheaper.
She	**shouldn't**	buy	it at a store. It's more expensive.
We	**'d better**		it now. Tomorrow, the price increases.
They	**'d better not**		it now. It's too expensive.

Use *could*, *should / shouldn't*, *ought to*, and *had better* (*not*) to make suggestions and give advice in the present or near future.
These words come before the base form of a verb and are the same for all persons.
Use *could* to make a suggestion. It is often used to offer two or more choices.
Use *should* or *ought to* to give advice. Both are stronger than *could*.
In the negative, use *shouldn't* (*should not*).
Use *had better* (*not*) to give strong advice. It sounds like a warning or an order.
In speaking, use the contracted form (*You'd better . . . / We'd better not . . .*).

A Complete the conversations with the expressions in the boxes. Use each expression only once.

| could | ought to | shouldn't |

A: I don't know what to wear to the party tonight.

B: You (1.) _____ wear black pants or your new skinny jeans.

A: It's a formal dinner party.

B: Oh, then you (2.) _____ wear jeans. They're too casual. You definitely
(3.) _____ wear the black pants.

could	'd better	'd better not

A: I still don't understand this grammar.

B: You (4.) _____ get some help. The test is on Thursday.

C: Maybe you (5.) _____ take the test on Friday. That would give you extra time.

B: Either way, you (6.) _____ wait to talk to the teacher. There's not much time!

⬡5 MY NEIGHBORHOOD

LESSON A

<table>
<tr><td colspan="5" align="center">REQUESTS WITH MODAL VERBS AND MIND</td></tr>
<tr><td colspan="3" align="center">Making requests</td><td colspan="2" align="center">Responding to requests</td></tr>
<tr>
<td>Informal
↕
Formal</td>
<td>Can / Will you
Could / Would you</td>
<td>help</td>
<td rowspan="2">me, please?</td>
<td>Sure, no problem. / I'd be glad to. /
Of course. / Sure thing.
Sorry, / I'd like to, but I can't.</td>
</tr>
<tr>
<td>Would you mind</td>
<td>helping</td>
<td>No, not at all. / No, I'd be glad to.
Sorry, / I'd like to, but I can't.</td>
</tr>
</table>

Use *Can you, Will you, Could you,* or *Would you* + verb to make requests.

To make a more formal request, use *Would you mind* + verb + *-ing*. Note: When responding to a *Would you mind . . .* request, you should say, *No, not at all.* or *No, I'd be glad to.* if you can do what the person asked.

To make a request more polite, add *please.*

A You need help preparing for a birthday party. Read each sentence. Then use the words in parentheses to write a request.

1. There are a lot of dirty dishes in the sink. (could / do)
   Could you do the dishes, please?
   _____

2. You need something at the grocery store. (would / mind / go)
   _____

3. The rugs are dirty. (can / vacuum)
   _____

4. You don't have enough snacks. (would / make)
   _____

5. You need some flowers. (will / buy)
   _____

6. Someone needs to watch the soup on the stove. (would / mind / watch)
   _____

7. The birthday cake is still at the pastry shop. (could / pick up)

_____

8. You need to blow up the birthday balloons. (would / mind / blow up)

_____

B In your notebook, write a different response to each request.

LESSON B

SUBJECT RELATIVE CLAUSES WITH *THAT*		
El Alto is <u>a city</u>		is next to La Paz.
Hongdae is <u>a neighborhood</u>	**that**	has a lot of stores and restaurants.
Telecommuters are <u>people</u>		work from home using a computer.

Relative clauses follow nouns. They describe or define the noun.
La Paz is <u>a city</u> ***that is nearly 12,000 feet (3,650 m) above sea level.***

Relative clauses with *that* can describe or define an object (something) or a person (someone).
Jane is <u>the woman</u> ***that lives next door to me.***

When *that* is followed by a verb, we call it a subject relative clause.
El Alto is a city. It is next to La Paz. El Alto is <u>a city</u> ***that is next to La Paz.***

The verb in the clause agrees with the noun it describes / defines.
A telecommuter is ***a person*** *that* ***works*** *from home.*
Telecommuters are ***people*** *that* ***work*** *from home.*

A Match the two halves of the sentences.

1. I live in a small town _____
2. Central Park is a relaxing place _____
3. Pedestrians are people _____
4. Bike lanes are parts of the street _____
5. A cable car is a type of transportation _____

a. that's in the middle of New York City.
b. that carries people in the air.
c. that is very quiet and has a lot of parks.
d. that walk on the sidewalk.
e. that only cyclists can use.

B Join the two sentences with a subject relative clause.

1. Melbourne is a very walkable city. It's in Australia.
   Melbourne is a very walkable city that is in Australia.

2. Soho is a neighborhood in New York. It's trendy and fashionable.

   _____

3. Selma Hayek is a Mexican actress. She works in Hollywood.

   _____

4. Tokyo has a subway system. It's one of the busiest in the world.

   _____

5. Fernando Botero is a Colombian artist. He's from the city of Medellin.

   _____

6. In Europe, there are a lot of very old cities. They have many interesting places to visit.

   _____

 **GOALS**

LESSON A

PLANS AND DECISIONS WITH *BE GOING TO* AND *WILL*	
Plans	I'm going to study science in college. I'm not going to apply to school next year.
Decisions	**A:** Oh, no, I forgot my wallet! **B:** Don't worry! I'll pay for lunch. **A:** We're having a surprise party for Mark. **B:** OK, I won't say anything to him!

We often use *be going to* to talk about future plans.
I'm going to attend Harvard University in the fall.

We often use *will* to talk about decisions we make at the moment of speaking.
A: *I'm going for a walk.* **B:** *I'll come with you.*

Question forms with *be going to*		
Yes / No questions	**Are you going to** study science?	Yes, I am. / Maybe. No, I'm not.
Wh- questions	**What are you going to** do after graduation?	I'm going to take a gap year.

Contractions (*is / are*)
you're not = you aren't
she's not = she isn't

Contractions (*will*)
I'll / you'll / he'll / she'll / we'll / they'll
will not = won't

A Complete the statements and questions with the correct form of *be going to*. Some items have more than one answer.

1. (I / not) _____ learn English in another country.

2. (you) _____ join a club on campus?

3. (I) _____ apply to college soon.

4. (we / not) _____ study for the test.

5. (she) _____ travel next year?

6. (we) _____ live in a dorm room.

7. (he / not) _____ attend a private school.

8. (you) _____ finish your homework?

B Complete the sentences with the correct form of *be going to* or *will*.

1. I _____ attend college in the fall. I want to major in biology.

2. I'm bored and don't know what to do. Wait, I know . . . I _____ call my friend.

3. **A:** What would you like today?

   B: Let's see . . . I _____ have the chicken and rice, please.

4. I bought my ticket last month. I _____ visit Paris from July 1 to July 14.

5. **A:** This box is too heavy!

   B: Wait! I _____ help you.

6. I _____ apply to three schools.

PREDICTIONS WITH *BE GOING TO* AND *WILL*	
She**'s going to** / **will** be very successful. Some students **aren't going to** / **won't** pass the exam.	You can use *be going to* and *will* to make predictions (guesses) about the future.
He**'ll** <u>definitely</u> / <u>probably</u> study business in college. <u>Maybe</u> he**'ll** study business in college. He <u>definitely</u> / <u>probably</u> **won't** study history.	You can use *definitely*, *probably*, or *maybe* to say how certain you are about a prediction. Notice the placement of these words in the sentences with *will* and *be going to*.
She**'s** <u>definitely</u> / <u>probably</u> **going to** attend college in the fall. <u>Maybe</u> she**'s going to** be a teacher after graduation. She <u>definitely</u> / <u>probably</u> **isn't going to** go to college. / She**'s** <u>definitely</u> / <u>probably</u> **not going to** go to college.	*Definitely*: You are 100% certain of something. *Probably*: You are fairly certain of something. *Maybe*: You think something is possible.
A: Is she **going to** go to graduate school? **B:** <u>Maybe</u>. I'm not sure. **A: Will** she go to graduate school? **B:** <u>Probably not</u>. I think she wants to get a job.	You can ask a *Yes* / *No* prediction question with *be going to* or *will*. It's common to answer these questions with only *definitely*, *probably*, or *maybe*. To express the negative, add *not* after *definitely*, *probably*, or *maybe*.

A Answer each question with the words in parentheses and be *going to* or *will*. Each item has more than one possible answer.

1. **A:** What are Mario's plans for next year?

   B: I'm not sure. (he / go back to school / maybe) _____.

2. **A:** Are Clara and Tony going to get married?

   B: Yeah, (they / get married / definitely / someday) _____.

3. **A:** Is Rob going to go to the school party tonight?

   B: (not / go / probably / he) _____. He's sick.

4. **A:** Jun applied to Seoul National University. It's hard to get accepted there.

   B: I know, but (get accepted / definitely / he) _____. He's smart.

5. **A:** Where's the bus? It's late.

   B: (probably / not / be / it) _____ here for a while. Traffic is bad.

6. **A:** Is it going to rain today?

   B: Yeah, (rain / it / probably) _____ tomorrow, too.

B Read the text about a college student and think of questions to ask about her future. Write the questions below. Then take turns asking and answering your questions with a partner.

Naomi is a very good student at a top university. She wants to be a doctor someday. Last summer, she did an internship at a hospital in Sydney, Australia. She loved it there. In Sydney, she dated a guy named Alex, but after she returned home, they broke up. Recently, she applied to Stanford Medical School in the US. She hopes she will be accepted.

1. Education: <u>**Will Naomi be accepted into Stanford Medical School?**</u>

2. Job: _____

3. Finances (money): _____

4. Love life: _____

5. Travel experience: _____

> 66 Will Naomi be accepted into Stanford Medical School?
>
> Yeah, probably. She's a very good student. 99

7 CELEBRATIONS

LESSON A

AGREEING WITH OTHER PEOPLE'S STATEMENTS: *SO, TOO, NEITHER,* AND *EITHER*				
	Statements	*So / Neither*	*be / do*	**Subject**
Affirmative	*With* be*:* I'm going to Emi's party.	**So**	am	I.
			is	he / she.
			are	we / you / they.
	With other verbs: I have a costume.	**So**	do	I / we / you / they.
			does	he / she.
Negative	*With* be*:* I'm not going to Emi's party.	**Neither**	am	I.
			is	he / she.
			are	we / you / they.
	With other verbs: I don't have a costume.	**Neither**	do	I / we / you / they.
			does	he / she.

Responses like *So am I* or *Neither do we* can be used to agree with other people's statements. Use *so* in your response when agreeing with an affirmative statement. Use *neither* when agreeing with a negative one.

These responses are most common in the first person singular (*So do I*) and the first person plural (*So are we*). When used with other subjects (*he, she, you, they*), these responses are used to show a similarity.

I like parties, and **so** *does Ali.* (Both the speaker and Ali like parties.)

The verb form in the response should match the verb form used in the statement.

A: *I* <u>bought</u> *my costume for the party.*   ***B:* So** <u>did</u> *I.*

In casual conversation, you can use *Me, too* (with affirmative statements) or *Me neither* (with negative statements). They can be used as responses to statements with *be* as well as other verbs.

A: *I'm going to Emi's party. I have my costume ready.*   ***B:*** *Me,* **too***.*
A: *I don't have my costume, but I'm not worried about it.*   ***B:*** *Me* **neither***.*

	Statements		Subject	be / do	too / either
Affirmative	*With be:* I'm going to Emi's party.		I	am,	**too.**
			He / She	is,	
			We / You / They	are,	
	With other verbs: I have a costume.		I / We / You / They	do,	**too.**
			He / She	does,	
Negative	*With be:* I'm not going to Emi's party.		I	'm not	**either.**
			He / She	's not	
			We / You / They	're not	
	With other verbs: I don't have a costume.		I / We / You / They	don't	**either.**
			He / She	doesn't	

Like the expressions with *so* and *neither*, you can use responses with *too* and *not . . . either* to agree with other people's statements. Use *too* in your response when agreeing with an affirmative statement. Use *not . . . either* when agreeing with a negative one.

These responses are most common in the first person singular (*I am, too*) and first person plural (*We do, too*). With other subjects (*he, she, you, they*), these responses are used to show a similarity.

I like parties, and Ali does, **too**. (Both the speaker and Ali like parties.)

The verb form in the response should match the verb form used in the statement.

A: I bought *my costume for the party.*   *B: I* did, **too**.

A Agree with each statement in at least two ways.

1. I like to host parties.

_____

2. I'm never late to class.

_____

3. I don't speak Italian.

_____

4. I'm planning to study abroad next year.

_____

5. I did well on the exam.

_____

B Combine the sentences using the words in parentheses.

1. I'm having a good time. They're having a good time. (so)
   I'm having a good time, and so are they.

2. I throw a lot of parties. She throws a lot of parties. (so)

_____

3. I don't watch the Super Bowl. He doesn't watch the Super Bowl. (either)

_____

4. I'm inviting a lot of friends. They're inviting a lot of friends. (too)

_____

5. You don't celebrate the lunar New Year. We don't celebrate the lunar New Year. (neither)

_____

LESSON B

TIME CLAUSES WITH *BEFORE, AFTER, WHEN*	
Time clause	**Main clause**
❶ **Before** the festival starts,	Violetta speaks.
❷ **After** the party ended,	we went home.
❸ **When** you throw powder in the air,	you say, "Holi Hai!"
Main clause	**Time clause**
❶ Violetta speaks	**before** the festival starts.
❷ We went home	**after** the party ended.
❸ You say, "Holi Hai!"	**when** you throw powder in the air.

A time clause can show the order of two or more events.
In ❶: Violetta speaks. Then the festival starts.
In ❷: The party ended. Then we went home.
In ❸: The two events (You say, "Holi Hai!" You throw powder in the air.) happen at almost the same time, or one happens immediately after the other.

When the time clause comes first, put a comma before the main clause.

A Combine the two sentences into one sentence using *after*, *before*, or *when*. Use commas if necessary. Each item has more than one possible answer.

1. I brush my teeth. I eat breakfast.

   _____

2. My friends and I get together. We have a good time.

   _____

3. I get a present. I send a thank-you message.

   _____

4. Guests come to our house. We clean up.

   _____

5. Students take the college entrance exam. They study very hard.

   _____

6. A person turns 20 years old. He or she throws a big party.

   _____

B Check your answers in **A** with a partner. Are the sentences in **A** true for you or for people in your country?

“ Before I eat breakfast, I brush my teeth. This is true for me.

Really? I always brush my teeth after I eat! ”

8 ONCE UPON A TIME

LESSON A

THE PAST CONTINUOUS: STATEMENTS				
Subject	*was / were (not)*	**Verb + -ing**		
I / He / She	**was / wasn't**	**studying**	English	at four o'clock. last summer. after lunch.
You / We / They	**were / weren't**			

Use the past continuous to talk about an action in progress in the past. The action can happen at a specific point in time or over a period of time.

*I **was working** until 8 pm last night.*

We don't usually use the past continuous with stative verbs (*hear*, *need*, *know*, etc.).

~~*I **was needing** some new boots last winter.*~~

You can use the past continuous with the simple past to show that one action was in progress when another action happened. Notice the use of *when*.

I <u>was taking</u> a shower when the phone <u>rang</u>.

THE PAST CONTINUOUS: QUESTIONS						
	Wh- word	*was / were*	Subject	Verb + -ing		**Answers**
Yes / No questions		**Were**	you	**reading**	a story?	Yes, I **was**. / No, I **wasn't**.
			they			Yes, they **were**. / No, they **weren't**.
		Was	he / she			Yes, he / she **was**. / No, he / she **wasn't**.
Wh- questions	What	**were**	you	**reading**?		(I **was reading**) a story.
			they			(They **were reading**)
		was	he / she			(He / She **was reading**) a story.

A Complete the story by writing the verbs in the past continuous.

Last summer, I (1. eat) _____ dinner in a restaurant with two friends. We
(2. talk) _____ when a woman walked in. She (3. wear) _____ a big hat,
so we couldn't see her face. The restaurant was nearly empty, but she sat next to our table.

Later, my friend wanted to pay the bill, but he couldn't find his wallet. We looked on the floor,
but it wasn't there. Then I noticed the woman in the hat (4. not / sit) _____ at the
table anymore. The restaurant called the police. The police knew the woman, and they
(5. look) _____ for her. But they never found her, and my friend never got his
money back.

B Complete each sentence with the past continuous or simple past form of the verbs.

1. They (talk) _____ loudly when the phone (ring) _____.

2. The woman (look) _____ at me when I (turn) _____ around.

3. When we (arrive) _____, she (stand) _____ outside her house.

4. It (rain) _____ when we (reach) _____ the top of the mountain.

5. When there (be) _____ a fire at the office, Gill (not / work) _____.

6. Sorry, I (not / listen) _____. What (say) _____ you _____ ?

LESSON B

ADVERBS OF MANNER	
Cinderella smiled **shyly** at the prince.	Adverbs of manner describe how something is done. Many end in -*ly*, and they often come after a verb.
He opened <u>the door</u> **quietly**. She answered <u>the question</u> **correctly**.	When there is <u>an object</u> (a noun or pronoun) after the verb, the adverb usually comes at the end of the sentence. *He opened* **quietly** *the door.*
She drives **fast**. He studied **hard** for the exam. They didn't do **well** in school.	Some common adverbs of manner don't end in -*ly*. Some examples are *fast*, *hard*, and *well*. Remember: Use *well*, not *good*, as an adverb. *They didn't do* **good** *in school.*
She was <u>different</u> from other children. You seem <u>unhappy</u>.	<u>Adjectives</u>, not adverbs, come after stative verbs (for example, *be*, *have*, *hear*, *need*, *know*, *seem*).

A Rewrite each sentence using the adverb form of the word in parentheses. Use a different verb if necessary.

1. He is fluent in three languages. (fluent)

   <u>He speaks three languages fluently.</u>

2. In the story of Lightning and Thunder, Thunder shouted and was angry when Lightning acted in a violent way. (angry, violent)

   _____

3. In the *Star Wars* movies, Luke Skywalker is a brave fighter. (brave)

   _____

4. When she left the party, Cinderella lost a shoe. (accidental)

   _____

5. In the story, the man disappears in a mysterious way. (mysterious)

   _____

6. The girl is only six, but she is a very good singer. (good)

   _____

B In five minutes, how many sentences can you make with the words below? Time yourself. You can use present or past forms of the verbs. Compare your answers with a partner's.

boy	fight	beautifully
dragon	run	bravely
girl	sing	fast / quickly
song	struggle with	slowly

❝ The boy and girl fought the dragon bravely.

 # WORK

LESSON A

THE PRESENT PERFECT: STATEMENTS

Subject	*have / has (not)*	Past participle		
I / You / We / They	**have** **haven't**	**worked**	here	for six months.
He / She	**has** **hasn't**			

You can use the present perfect to talk about events that started in the past and continue into the present.

Contractions

I have = I've
she has = she's
we have = we've

have not = haven't
has not = hasn't

BASE, SIMPLE PAST, AND PAST PARTICIPLE FORMS

Regular verbs			Irregular verbs					
Base	Simple past	Past participle	Base	Simple past	Past participle	Base	Simple past	Past participle
call	called	called	be	was / were	been	leave	left	left
change	changed	changed	become	became	become	make	made	made
live	lived	lived	begin	began	begun	put	put	put
look	looked	looked	come	came	come	read	read	read
move	moved	moved	do	did	done	say	said	said
study	studied	studied	drink	drank	drunk	see	saw	seen
talk	talked	talked	find	found	found	sleep	slept	slept
try	tried	tried	get	got	gotten	speak	spoke	spoken
use	used	used	give	gave	given	take	took	taken
want	wanted	wanted	go	went	gone	tell	told	told
work	worked	worked	have	had	had	think	thought	thought
			know	knew	known	write	wrote	written

Use the past participle after *have / has (not)* to form the present perfect.
Verbs that are regular in the simple past take the same *-ed* ending for the past participle:
talk / talked / talked.
Verbs that are irregular in the simple past have irregular past participle forms: *speak / spoke / spoken*.

THE PRESENT PERFECT: *WH-* QUESTIONS

Wh- word	*have / has*	Subject	Past participle		Answers
How long	**have**	you	**worked**	there?	(I**'ve worked** there) for two years.
	has	she			(She**'s worked** there) since 2012.

Use *for* + a length of time (*for two years, for a long time, for the entire summer, for my whole life*).
Use *since* + a point in time (*since 2014, since last September, since Friday, since I was a child*).

A In your notebook, use the words to make as many sentences in the present perfect as you can.

They He We	has have	been worked	a flight attendant friends at that company	for since	elementary school. a long time.

B Complete the quotes. Use the present perfect form of the verbs in parentheses and *for* or *since*.

Ronaldo: "I (1. live) _____ in the United States (2.) _____ August.

I (3. study) _____ English (4.) _____ I was in high school. I'm studying

for an exam right now. I (5. not / sleep) _____ well (6.) _____ two days.

I (7. drink) _____ three cups of coffee (8.) _____ 9:00."

Anita: "My son (1. be) _____ in college (2.) _____ three years.

He (3. not / come) _____ home (4.) _____ a year. I miss him. He

(5. have) _____ a part-time job (6.) _____ March. We

(7. not / talk) _____ on the phone (8.) _____ a month."

LESSON B

THE SIMPLE PAST AND THE PRESENT PERFECT		
	Simple past	**Present perfect**
	Use the simple past to talk about completed actions and situations at a specific time in the past.	Use the present perfect to talk about actions that began in the past and continue now, or that happened at a past time that is unknown or not important.
Statements	I **worked** there from 2017 to 2019. I **didn't go out** last weekend.	I**'ve worked** here for three years. I**'ve visited** New York three times.
Questions and answers	When **did** you **work** there? From 2017 to 2019.	How long **have** you **worked** there? For three years. How many times **have** you **visited**? Three times.

ever / never
We often use the present perfect with *ever* or *never* to ask about experiences in life (things you have done / haven't done before).
*Have you **ever** been to Paris? (ever = in your life) Yes, I have. / No, I haven't.*
*I've **never** read this book. (never = not in my whole life)*

already / yet
We often use *yet* (in questions and negatives) and *already* (in affirmative sentences) with the present perfect.
*Have you finished your work **yet**?*
*No, I haven't finished it **yet**. / Yes, I've **already** finished it.*

A Circle the correct form of the verb.

1. I **moved** / **have moved** to Vietnam with my family in 1998.

2. We **ate** / **have eaten** at this restaurant many times.

3. Dave **graduated** / **has graduated** from Harvard University three years ago.

4. Alice **didn't fly** / **hasn't flown** on a plane before. It's her first time.

5. I live in Mexico City, but I **wasn't born** / **haven't been born** here.

6. **Did he call / Has he called** you last night?

7. I **lived / have lived** in Seoul since last summer.

8. **Did you ever meet / Have you ever met** my manager? Let me introduce you to him.

B Complete the conversations with the simple past or present perfect form of the verbs.

| be | go | have |

A: (1.) _____ you ever _____ to Argentina?

B: Yes, I have. I (2.) _____ to Buenos Aires last year.

A: (3.) _____ you _____ a good time?

B: Yes, it's an amazing city!

| apply | not / receive | send |

A: Did you (4.) _____ for the job?

B: Yes, I did. But I (5.) _____ a reply yet.

A: When (6.) _____ you _____ your application?

B: Last Monday.

| live | move | never / be |

A: That's my old house.

B: When (7.) _____ you _____ there?

A: When I was a child. My family (8.) _____ to a new house in 2005. I (9.) _____ back to it.

10 STAY IN TOUCH

LESSON A

	ASKING FOR PERMISSION						RESPONSES
❶	Would	it be OK	if	I	called	back later?	Certainly. / Of course. / Sure, no problem. (I'm) sorry, but…
❷	Would	you mind					No, not at all. / No, go ahead. (I'm) sorry, but . . .
❸	Do	you mind	if	I	call	back later?	No, not at all. / No, go ahead. (I'm) sorry, but . . .
❹	May / Could / Can			I	call	back later?	Certainly. / Of course. / Sure, no problem. (I'm) sorry, but . . .

❶ & ❷ The use of the simple past verb (*called*) makes requests with *Would* sound slightly more polite or formal.
❷ & ❸ When responding to a request made with *Would you mind / Do you mind*, answer with *no* to give your permission (For example, *No, I don't mind. You can call back later.*).
❹ *May I* and *Could I* are more formal than *Can I*.

A Unscramble the words to make questions.

1. I / make / can / quick call / a

   _____

2. him / a / leave / could / message / I

   _____

3. OK / turned / it / phone / be / on / would / I / my / if

   _____

4. you / a photo / would / took / if I / of you / mind

   _____

B Complete the conversations. Then practice them with a partner.

1. **A:** _____ _____ mind if I opened the window?

   B: _____, not _____ _____. It's really hot in here.

2. **A:** May _____ _____ here?

   B: _____ _____, but my friend is sitting there.

3. **A:** _____ _____ mind if I turn up the volume a bit? It's hard to hear.

   B: _____, _____ ahead.

4. **A:** _____ _____ _____ OK if I didn't turn in my homework today?

   B: _____, no _____. Just turn it in tomorrow.

C In your notebook, write the opposite response to each question in **B**.

LESSON B

VERB + INFINITIVE VS. VERB + GERUND	
I **need** <u>to buy</u> a new phone.	Certain verbs can be followed by an <u>infinitive</u> (*to* + verb).
I **avoid** <u>talking</u> on the phone when I'm driving.	Other verbs can be followed by a <u>gerund</u> (verb + *-ing*).
I **tried** <u>to call</u> you earlier. I **tried** <u>calling</u> you earlier.	Some verbs can be followed by an infinitive or a gerund.

Verbs followed by an infinitive		Verbs followed by a gerund		Verbs followed by an infinitive or a gerund	
agree	need	appreciate	finish	begin	love
choose	plan	avoid	imagine	can't stand	prefer
decide	seem	dislike	keep	hate	start
hope	want	enjoy	(not) mind	like	try
learn	would like	feel like	suggest		

A Underline the gerund or the infinitive in each sentence. Then check (✓) the correct sentences. Change the incorrect sentences.

1. ☐ I learned to speak Spanish in high school.

2. ☐ I avoid to call people on the phone.

3. ☐ I began to raise my voice.

4. ☐ I enjoy to play games on my phone.

5. ☐ I agreed turning down the television.

6. ☐ I prefer to respond to texts quickly.

7. ☐ I finished to do my homework and then I called a friend.

8. ☐ I tried texting you twice, but you didn't reply.

B Complete each question with the infinitive or gerund form of the verb in parentheses. Sometimes both forms are possible.

1. What do you need (do) _____*to do*_____ this weekend?

2. Who's someone you'd like (meet) _____?

3. What's something you can't stand (do) _____?

4. When did you start (learn) _____ English?

5. What TV shows do you enjoy (watch) _____?

C Answer the questions in **B**. Use complete sentences.

1. *I need to clean my house because some friends are coming over for dinner.*

2. _____

3. _____

4. _____

5. _____

11 TECHNOLOGY

LESSON A

USED TO			
Subject	**(not) use(d) to**	**Verb**	
I / You / He / She / We / They	**used to**	wear	glasses.
	didn't use to	own	a computer.

Use *used to* to describe habits and actions that happened during a period of time in the past but that no longer happen.

*People **used to** ride horses for transportation.*

Use time expressions like *now*, *today*, or *these days* to make a contrast between the present and the past. *We **didn't use to** own a computer, but <u>now</u> we have three of them at home.*

Notice the spelling of *use to* in negative statements. ~~I **didn't used to** own a computer.~~

Question	Subject	*use to*	Verb		Responses
Did	you	**use to**	own	a printer?	Yes, I did. / No, I didn't.
Where did			go	on vacation?	I used to go to Canada.

Notice the spelling of *use to* in questions. ~~Did you **used to** wear glasses?~~

A Circle the correct answer to complete each sentence about *used to*.

1. Use *used to* to talk about the   a. present.   b. past.

2. *Used to* is followed by   a. the base form of a verb.   b. a gerund (*-ing* form).

3. Use *use to* in negative statements and   a. responses.   b. questions.

B Write sentences to compare life today with life 100 years ago. Use the time expressions given. Follow the model.

1. People had bigger families. (nowadays)
    People used to have bigger families. Nowadays, families are smaller.

2. Not many people owned a television. (today)

3. Not many women worked outside of the home. (now)

4. Telephones weren't portable. (these days)

5. Technology wasn't affordable. (now)

6. People read books instead of watching TV. (today)

LESSON B

COMPARISONS WITH *AS . . . AS*	
Phone A is **as** <u>big</u> **as** phone B. (Phone A is 15 cm. Phone B is 15 cm.) Phone A costs **as** <u>much</u> **as** phone B. (Phone A costs $200. Phone B costs $200.)	Use *as* + adjective / adverb + *as* to show that two things are equal.
Camera A is**n't as** <u>affordable</u> **as** Camera B. (Camera A costs $200. Camera B costs $150.) Maria did**n't** do **as** <u>well</u> **as** Carlos on the test. (Carlos scored 95%. Maria scored 70%.)	You can use *not as . . . as* to show that things are not equal.
My phone works **as** well **as** <u>your phone</u>. My phone works **as** well **as** <u>yours</u>. I like this phone **as** much **as** that <u>phone</u>. I like this phone **as** much **as** that <u>one</u>. She studies **as** hard **as** <u>he studies</u>. (not common) She studies **as** hard **as** <u>he does</u>. (common) She studies **as** hard **as** <u>him</u>.	Sometimes after *as . . . as*, you can end a sentence with a pronoun. In spoken and written English, it's common not to repeat the main verb after *as . . . as*, but to use the verb *do* or a pronoun.

A Unscramble the sentences. Some have more than one possible answer.

1. speaks / she / as / you / English / do / well / as

2. us / don't / as / have / many / you / classes / as

3. computer / heavy / as / this / is / as / one / that

4. my / durable / as / tablet / as / isn't / yours

5. jacket / as / that / isn't / this / one / as / fashionable

B Compare the two vacuum cleaners in the chart by completing the sentences with *(not) as … as*. There may be more than one possible correct answer.

	The Vacuum Star	**The Vacuum Pro**
weight	6 kilos	6 kilos
price	$450	$150
durability	lasts 5–10 years	lasts 4–5 years
popularity	☆☆☆	☆☆☆☆☆
convenience	Robotic; cleans everywhere by itself	Robotic; cleans everywhere by itself

1. weight

   The Vacuum Star _____ is as heavy as _____ the Vacuum Pro.

2. price

   The Vacuum Pro _____ the Vacuum Star.

3. durability

   The Vacuum Pro _____ the Vacuum Star.

4. popularity

   The Vacuum Star _____ the Vacuum Pro.

5. convenience

   The Vacuum Star _____ the Vacuum Pro.

 **TRAVEL**

LESSON A

<table>
<tr><td colspan="3" align="center">MODAL VERBS OF NECESSITY</td></tr>
<tr><td></td><td align="center">Present forms</td><td align="center">Past forms</td></tr>
<tr><td>Affirmative</td><td>You must <u>show</u> your ID to get on the plane.
I have to <u>buy</u> a backpack for my trip.
He has to <u>pack</u> an adapter.
We've got to <u>exchange</u> some money.
She's got to <u>check in</u> online.</td><td>I / You / He / She / We / They had to <u>wait</u> at the airport for an hour.</td></tr>
<tr><td>Negative</td><td>I don't have to <u>check</u> any luggage.
She doesn't have to <u>show</u> her passport.</td><td>I / You / He / She / We / They didn't have to <u>wait</u> long.</td></tr>
</table>

Use *must*, *have / has to*, and *have / has got to* + <u>the base form of a verb</u> to say that something is necessary.

In spoken and written English, *have / has to* is most common.

Must is often used to talk about rules or laws. *Must* is stronger than *have (got) to*.

Only *have to* can be used in the negative.

Use *had to / didn't have to* to talk about things that were necessary / not necessary in the past.

A Correct the error in each sentence.

1. She doesn't has to pack her suitcase. _____

2. They have to leave yesterday. _____

3. I haven't to water the plants. _____

4. All passengers must to board the flight now. _____

5. We didn't had to pay in cash. _____

6. You got to check in before your flight. _____

7. He had give his house keys to a friend. _____

LESSON B

QUESTION FORM REVIEW		
	Yes / No questions	**Wh- questions**
Simple present	Do you travel a lot? Yes, I do. / No, I don't.	Where do you usually go? I often go to Canada.
Present continuous	Are you planning a trip now? Yes, I am. / No, I'm not.	Where are you thinking of going next? I'm thinking of visiting Peru.
Present perfect	Have you ever been to Rome? Yes, I have. / No, I haven't.	How many times have you been there? I've been twice before.
Simple past	Did you have to get a visa? Yes, I did. / No, I didn't.	When did you apply for it? I applied about six months before I left.
Future with *will*	Will you ever go there again? Yes, I will. / No, I won't.	How long will you be away for? I'll be away for about a year.
Modal verbs (*can*, *should*, etc.)	Can you show me your passport? Yes, certainly. / No, sorry. I don't have one.	How can I change my seat? You can call the airline.

Subject and object questions	
In subject questions, the question word is the subject of the verb. *Who* **traveled** with you? *My best friend* (traveled with me). *What* **is** in the car? *Your suitcase* (is in the car). The word order is the same as an affirmative sentence.	In object questions, the question word is NOT the subject of the verb. *Where* **did** you **go** on vacation? (We went) *to Hawaii* (on vacation). *What* **did** you **pack**? (I packed) *too many clothes!* You need an auxiliary verb (*do*, *be*) in object questions.

A Unscramble the questions.

1. planning / she / trips / like / does

_____?

2. does / it / how / on the subway / long / take

_____?

3. train / are / they / why / the / taking

_____?

4. ever / your / an / lost / luggage / has / airline

_____?

5. have / plans / you / made / what / for the summer

_____?

6. where / did / year / you / go / last

_____?

7. you / to join / our / would / tour group / like

_____?

8. will / how / many / in the group / people / be

_____?

9. books / who / flights / normally / your

_____?

10. your / what / with / happened / flight

_____?

B Match the answers below to the questions in **A**.

_____ a. No, never. I've been really lucky.

_____ b. My assistant usually does.

_____ c. Yes, she does.

_____ d. About half an hour.

_____ e. I haven't made any yet. What about you?

_____ f. We didn't go anywhere. We stayed at home.

_____ g. It was canceled!

_____ h. Thanks, but I like traveling solo.

_____ i. About six. It's quite small.

_____ j. They're afraid of flying.

INFORMATION GAP ACTIVITIES

UNIT 1: LESSON B, READING

D

Student A: BLACK

1. He's a successful entertainer.

2. In school, he was quiet and shy and wasn't good at sports. Other boys bullied him.

3. He worked hard to learn yo-yo tricks and became a world champion. He performs all over the world.

Student B: Lindsey Stirling

1. She's a musician (a violinist).

2. As a child, her parents couldn't afford to pay for many music lessons. She didn't win the TV talent show she was on.

3. She made an album, won an award, and has a very popular channel online.

UNIT 8: LESSON B, ACTIVE ENGLISH

A

Student A: Look at the picture of a traditional fairy fale below. Take turns describing your picture to a partner and listening to him / her describe his / her picture. Write down any differences between the two pictures. (There are at least seven differences.) Do not look at your partner's picture!

UNIT 8: LESSON B, ACTIVE ENGLISH

A

Student B: Look at the picture of a modern fairy tale above. Take turns describing your picture to a partner and listening to him / her describe his / her picture. Write down any differences between the two pictures. (There are at least seven differences.) Do not look at your partner's picture!

WRITING MODELS

UNIT 1

Start by explaining what you couldn't do and why you wanted to learn.

When I was fourteen, I couldn't swim. As a child, I was afraid of the water, so I never learned. Usually, this wasn't a problem, but in the summer, things were different. All of my friends went to the public pool on hot days. I went, too, but I had to watch them have fun. Finally, I decided to take swimming lessons at a place near my house. The class met twice a week. At first, I was very nervous, but I didn't give up. I practiced, and by the end, I was a good swimmer.

Use *at first* to talk about what happened at the beginning of a process, before things changed.

UNIT 3

Use verbs like *believe*, *say*, and *think* to introduce opinions.

The Yonaguni Monument
The Yonaguni Monument is a group of large underwater rocks about 25 meters (82 feet) high in the Pacific Ocean, near Japan. The mysterious objects look like the pyramids in Egypt and the Americas. Some scientists believe they may be from an ancient underwater city, but there is no proof. We need to do more research to solve this mystery.

The Marfa Lights
The Marfa Lights often appear in the night sky near the desert town of Marfa, Texas (US). The lights are about the size of a basketball, and there are often two or three of them. Some people say they could be lights from cars or planes, but in fact, the Marfa Lights first appeared in 1883—before there were such vehicles. The lights sometimes seem to fly close to houses, so some people think they might be aliens from space.

Use *in fact* when introducing evidence or stating something true that is different from what people said or thought.

UNIT 4

My Style Profile

1. For school or work, I usually get dressed up.
2. It's important for clothes to be comfortable, stylish, and inexpensive.
3. My two favorite clothing items are my gray sweater and black skirt. They suit me.
4. I look good in these colors: black, white, red, gray, dark blue.
5. My favorite brands or clothing stores are Mango and UNIQLO.
6. I walk to and from my office Monday through Friday, so I wear casual sneakers for the commute and then change into high heels at the office. I need to dress formally for work, so I often wear skirts, nice pants, or sometimes a suit. Also, my office is always cold, so I really need some warm sweaters, long sleeve blouses, and stylish jackets. On the weekends, I like to wear very casual clothes, such as jeans, sweatshirts, and sweatpants.

Remember to use the simple present to describe habits and routines.

Use *also* to add more information.

UNIT 6

My name is Miguel Sanz. I am a student at the Universidad Nacional Autónoma de México (UNAM) in Mexico City. This May, I am going to graduate with a degree in journalism. In my third year at UNAM, I did an internship at El Universal, one of Mexico's largest media companies. There, I helped senior reporters with different news stories by doing research. I also helped manage the company's social media accounts. In my free time, I enjoy playing sports, and at UNAM, I am on the chess and swim teams. I also like learning languages, and in addition to Spanish, I speak English and some Portuguese. After graduation, I'm going to travel around Europe during the summer. Then I'm going to do an internship with a media company in Spain because I definitely intend to work as a journalist in the future.

Use the simple past to describe your previous work experiences.

End your profile by describing your future goals. Use *be going to* or *will*.

UNIT 7

In Korea, we have a holiday called Chuseok. It usually takes place in September or early October. It is a holiday for giving thanks and remembering our ancestors. Many people travel to their hometowns to spend Chuseok with their families.

Ancestors are people who were in your family many, many years ago.

Every family celebrates Chuseok a little differently. In my family, we prepare traditional foods a day or two before Chuseok. On Chuseok morning, my family does a special ceremony to remember our ancestors. After that, we have a big meal, and we give each other small gifts. In the evening, we have a nice dinner. After the meal, we play games or watch TV. There are lots of fun TV shows on during Chuseok!

Time expressions, such as *on Chuseok morning*, can come at the beginning of the sentence, followed by a comma (,).

Time expressions like *during Chuseok* can also come at the end of a sentence and no comma is needed.

UNIT 8

Many fairy tales begin with the phrase *Once upon a time*.

A Modern Little Red Riding Hood
Once upon a time, there was a young girl who always wore a red sweatshirt with a hood. One night, the girl's grandmother called to say she was sick, so the girl left quickly to bring some soup to her grandmother. The girl got directions to her grandmother's house on her phone. Everything was working fine until suddenly her phone's battery died. She was lost!

Use an adverb of manner to describe how an action was done.

Use past continuous and simple past verbs.

It was very cold and dark outside. The young girl ran nervously through the streets until she found a store that was open. Fortunately, the owner of the store was friendly and let the girl charge her phone there. Soon, her phone was working again, so she got the directions she needed and found her grandmother's house. Her grandmother ate the soup, felt better, and they lived happily ever after.

Many fairy tales end with the sentence *They lived happily ever after*.

a.

From: Katya Petrova
Subject: Project meeting

Hi,

I've received some possible designs, so let's meet. Are you free today at noon? It's important to choose the best design ASAP.

– K

ASAP is an abbreviation that means *as soon as possible*.

b.

SAVE! SAVE! SAVE!
25% discount on **ALL** orders today only!
You **MUST** click here **NOW** for more details!

c.

Jez

Hi! Lunch today @ 12? New place on the corner?

In English, @ can be used as an abbreviation for *at*.

d.

Sounds great but have meeting about project @ 12. Sorry 😟 How about tomorrow?

It's OK to use emojis in informal messages, but don't use more than one or two.

e.

From: Sandra Chung
Subject: Party for Kelvin

Hi everyone,

Kelvin is leaving next week, so we're having a small party. I can get a present. Does anyone like making cakes? Or maybe we could buy him a nice one?

See you in the conference room next Friday at 1 pm!

Best,
Sandra

f.

To: Sandra@email.com
Subject: RE: Party for Kelvin

Good idea! I can make it. Chocolate?

Send

CREDITS

Illustrations ©Cengage Learning

Cover Keng Po Leung/Alamy Stock Photo; **2–3** (spread) Susan Seubert/National Geographic Image Collection; **4** © John Stanmeyer; **5** (cl) AJ_Watt/iStock/Getty Images Plus/Getty images, (c) Lucky Business/Shutterstock.com, (cr) JGI/Jamie Grill/Getty Images; **6** Jonathan Erasmus/iStock/Getty Images; **7** Sorrorwoot Chaiyawong/Alamy Stock Photo; **8** Logan Werlinger/Barcroft Media/Getty Images; **9** Dina Litovsky/Redux; **10–11** (spread) © Giordano Ciampini; **12** SK/Alamy Stock Photo; **13** Hamza Khan/Alamy Stock Photo; **16–17** (spread) Foxys Forest Manufacture/Shutterstock.com; **18** TinasDreamworld/Alamy Stock Photo; **19** LauriPatterson/E+/Getty Images; **20** Tei Sinthip/Shutterstock.com; **21** Alastair Miller/Bloomberg/Getty Images; **22** Nikreates/Alamy Stock Photo; **23** Frank Bienewald/LightRocket/Getty Images; **24** © News Life Media/StockFood; **26** © Ami Vitale; **27** Jonathan Nackstrand/AFP/Getty Images; **29** Woman's Value/Camera Press/Redux; **30–31** (spread) © Josselin Cornou; **32** AGE Fotostock/Alamy Stock Photo; **33** dokosola/Shutterstock.com; **34** Stockcreative/iStock/Getty Images; **35** ShutterWorx/E+/Getty Images; **37** Sermsak Rattanagowin/EyeEm/Getty Images; **38–39** (spread) George Steinmetz/Getty Image News/Getty Images; **40** George Pachantouris/Moment/Getty Images; **42** Stephane Granzotto/Nature Picture Library; **43** © Nora Shawki; **44** David Doubilet/National Geographic Image Collection; **46–47** (spread) Nick Fox/Shutterstock.com; **49** VCG/Visual China Group/Getty Images; **50** Islandstock/Alamy Stock Photo; **52** Derek Teo/Alamy Stock Photo; **53** Streetstyleshooters/German Select/Getty Images; **54–55** (spread) Luca Locatelli/National Geographic Image Collection; **56** (tl) Kaspars Grinvalds/Shutterstock.com, (tr) dowell/Moment/Getty Images, (cl) OneStockPhoto/Shutterstock.com, (cr) Ivan Kruk/Shutterstock.com; **57** DaniloAndjus/E+/Getty Images; **59** monkeybusinessimages/iStock/Getty Images; **60–61** (spread) Devasahayam Chandra Dhas/iStock Unreleased/Getty Images; **62** © Tyrone Turner; **64** Vladimir Zivojinovic/AFP/Getty Images; **66** TK Kurikawa/Shutterstock.com; **67** lazyllama/Shutterstock.com; **68–69** (spread) Lepretre Pierre/Moment/Getty Images; **70** estherpoon/iStock Editorial/Getty Images; **73** antorti/iStock/Getty Images; **74–75** (spread) © Michael Moran/OTTO; **77** © Nigel Dickinson Photography; **78** Jimmy Xiao/Moment/Getty Images; **81** V. Fournier/Jeune Afrique-REA/Redux; **82–83** (spread) Boston Globe/Getty Images; **84** Howard Kingsnorth/Stone/Getty Images; **85** Attila Cser/Reuters; **86** csp/Shutterstock.com; **87** Toby Canham/Getty Images Entertainment/Getty Images; **88** David Nunuk/AGE Fotostock; **90–91** (spread) Marcelo Chacón Aracena/500px Prime/Getty Images; **92** UPI/Alamy Stock Photo; **93** Kazuhiro Nogi/AFP/Getty Images; **94** kali9/E+/Getty Images; **96** Klaus Vedfelt/DigitalVision/Getty Images; **97** Preau Louis-Marie/Hemis.fr/Alamy Stock Photo; **98–99** (spread) Poras Chaudhary/Stone/Getty Images; **100** philippe giraud/Corbis Sport/Getty Images; **101** AGCuesta/Shutterstock.com; **102** (tr) Leszek Czerwonka/Alamy Stock Photo, (cr1) Purple Collar Pet Photography/Moment/Getty Images, (cr2) majeczka/Shutterstock.com; **103** Ze Martinusso/Moment/Getty Images; **104–105** (spread) RudyBalasko/iStock Editorial/Getty Images; **106** AA Film Archive/Alamy Stock Photo; **107** LucVi/Shutterstock.com; **108** studiocasper/E+/Getty Images; **111** BFA/Alamy Stock Photo; **112–113** (spread) John Lamparski/Getty Images Entertainment/Getty Images; **114** © Glenn Kasner; **115** Roberto Ricciuti/Getty Images Entertainment/Getty Images; **116** AscentXmedia/E+/Getty Images; **117** Jenny Adler/National Geographic Image Collection; **118–119** (spread) Carsten Peter/National Geographic Image Collection; **120** Tannis Toohey/Toronto Star/Getty Images; **121** (tl) Maika Elan/Bloomberg/Getty Images, (tc) Cavan Images/Cavan/Getty Images, (tr) Carlos Becerra/Getty Images News/Getty Images; **123** Loop Images Ltd/Alamy Stock Photo; **124** Thomas Barwick/Stone/Getty Images; **125** Courtesy of Tierney Thys; **126** Courtesy of Asher Jay; **127** Rebecca Drobis/National Geographic Image Collection; **128** Tutatama/Alamy Stock Photo; **131** © Corey Arnold; **132** Zuma Press, Inc./Alamy Stock Photo; **134–135** (spread) Covenant House International/Getty Images Entertainment/Getty Images; **136** Sven Torfinn/Panos Pictures/Redux; **137** © Nicky Loh; **139** Michael Dwyer/Alamy Stock Photo; **141** xavierarnau/E+/Getty Images; **143** Matej Leskovsek/Reuters; **145** Westend61/Getty Images; **147** Carolyn Drake/Magnum Photos New York; **148–149** (spread) Peter Hirth/laif/Redux; **150** filadendron/E+/Getty Images; **151** Museum of Science and Industry, Chicago/Archive Photos/Getty Images; **152** Peter Griffith/Stone/Getty Images; **153** Glasshouse Images/Alamy Stock Photo; **154** © Jenny Tough; **155** Maskot/Getty Images; **156–157** (spread) Westend61/Getty Images; **158** Jonas Hafner/EyeEm/Getty Images; **159** (tl) Wenn Rights Ltd/Alamy Stock Photo, (tr) Grzegorz Czapski/Alamy Stock Photo; **160** Burak Akbulut/Anadolu Agency/Getty Images; **161** © Dan Root Photography; **162–163** (spread) © Greg Goodman; **164** moodboard/Alamy Stock Photo; **165** Art Wager/E+/Getty Images; **166** Tuan Tran/Moment/Getty Images; **167** Edson Vandeira/National Geographic Image Collection/Getty Images; **168** DieterMeyrl/E+/Getty Images; **170–171** (spread) mihtiander/iStock/Getty Images Plus/Getty Images; **172** Courtesy of Andrés Ruzo; **174** Mike Ford/Alamy Stock Photo; **175** Beyondmylens Harsh/Photography/Moment/Getty Images; **176** Pikoso.kz/Shutterstock.com.